The Low Self-Esteem Club:

The Stories Behind Baseball's Most Unflattering Nicknames

By C. Terry Walters

Autographed baseballs from the author's collection:
Top: Walter "Boom Boom" Beck
Bottom: Hugh "Losing Pitcher" Mulcahy

Terremoto Grande Publishing LLC

Cover design by Lindsay Sowers

Library of Congress Control Number 2015919377

ISBN 978-0-9833285-3-7

Dedications

To the many colorful players who made the first 75 years of baseball memorable and helped to create America's first and lasting pastime.

To my grandson Noah who definitely would have earned a very stylish nickname.

Table of Contents

Preface

Why is the book titled *The Low Self-Esteem Club*?

The schoolyard has always been an incubator for cruel or demeaning nicknames. Fatty, Midget, Shorty, Sissy, and many worse names are thrown like daggers at classmates on the playground. One universal rule is that the recipient does not have to go home and begin answering to the vile names. So, then, how do we explain the long list of nicknames that baseball players have accepted into their lives?

Looking back through the archives to 1881 we find Fatty Briody. Is it possible that a player would walk into the ballpark for the first time and announce, "You can call me Fatty?" We also find Cuckoo, Creepy, Baldy, Leech, Greasy, Sap, Boob, seven Jumbos, and a plethora of feminine names.

Playground nicknames tend to separate individuals into two groups, the insiders and the outsiders. Nothing is more effective than branding someone with an insulting nickname. By virtue of one or more members of a peer group designating you as Fatty, you know where you stand; outside the circle. Inside the circle you will find no one with a body worthy of being classified as a "fatty". These names, then, are exclusionary. While the newly named individual is forced to accept the rejection, he is not required to adopt the name.

Adult nicknaming, as practiced by athletes, tends to be inclusionary, binding players into a unit with a specific purpose. Even though you look like a "fatty", you are one of us. As long as the name does not cause too much psychic pain, Fatty can answer to the name and feel like a part of the whole. He can also participate in the bonhomie of the dugout and the playing field. He can now freely address another of his teammates as Shorty or Baby Doll without fear of making an enemy.

But what of the player who does more than just assent to the name? Both Pat Paige and Walt French were called Piggy. They acquiesced to the use of an unflattering name in the dugout, but once they walked away from the game, they resumed being Pat and Walt. Frank Ward, however, became Piggy Ward in 1883 and will remain so for all of baseball eternity. Most people would recoil at the name. Perhaps Mr. Ward's table manners were disgusting to some teammates, but Piggy just did not care what they thought. Maybe he thought the name was funny. The passage of time has blown away any chance to crawl into Piggy's head and find the true reason.

In addition to peer acceptance as an explanation for assuming a new name, repudiating a family given name might also be an answer. Accepting the identity of a less than sterling nickname, can serve as a means of rejecting a given name or family name that has taken on an odious meaning to the owner. Morgan, O'Neill and Harre in *Nicknames – Their Origins and Social Consequences* describe the stigma of the name Horace after Walt Disney employed the name in an early Mickey Mouse cartoon. Horace Horsecollar was a hickish plough horse that helped Mickey through his adventures until losing his job to Goofy. A player might gladly jettison the identity of Horace the silly horse for a more colorful name, such as Stubby, Fuzzy, or Skeeter.

Family dynamics could have also entered into the equation. A personal rejection of one's family for various reasons might brighten the attractiveness of a nickname. A son abandoned by his father would take no pride in carrying the father's first name. A son trying to make his own way in the world may feel liberated by adopting a new name. Among the millions of boys with Junior attached to the back end of their name, there existed thousands who yearned for a distinctive name and an individual identity.

Finally, there were names that boys just grew up hating. A good example is the name Clarence. The archive of major leaguers reveals that 73 players had the first name Clarence. Fifty-two of these men elected to be known officially as someone other than Clarence. The calculator reports that 71% chose to give up the name on their birth certificate. The name Clarence has yielded one of the richest veins of entertaining and curious new nicknames, some deprecating and some not. Kid, Footsie, Cupid, Bubber, Cuddles, Ace, Pop-boy, Steamboat and Yam make up a partial list.

The *Low Self-Esteem Club* will explore this phenomenon of unflattering, insulting, insensitive, and occasionally laughable nicknames.

Introduction

More than all other nationalities, Americans have always enjoyed the game of renaming people, places and organizations that have had the good, or ill, fortune to step into the limelight. Over the years, we Americans have given nicknames to our heroes and our villains, our politicians, our towns and states, and notable events. Nicknames can glorify or they can mock. They can celebrate enviable traits or highlight unflattering characteristics, both physical and behavioral.

When a hero steps onto the American stage, we forge a connection by creating clever names, or by embracing the ingenious word play of others. When the First Regiment of the United States Cavalry and the Second Regiment of United States Volunteer Cavalry fought valiantly during the Spanish-American War in 1898, the American press borrowed a name from the old Pony Express days and dubbed them the Rough Riders. Colonel Theodore Roosevelt reported that the soldiers resisted the sobriquet initially, but capitulated after repeated usage by newspapers and finally the upper echelon of the military.

Roosevelt's name became synonymous with The Rough Riders, and he later acquired a few nicknames of his own, including the very masculine Bull Moose. Within a few years, his notoriety would help lead him into the White House.

During World War I, Americans thrilled to the exploits of Black Jack Pershing. As a young officer, John Pershing was credited with successfully training and marshalling the African-American soldiers under his command. The Black Jack nickname ensued.

Fast forward to the next war. In the European Theater, George Smith Patton, Jr. brought a much-needed discipline to his troops as well as a great ferocity toward the enemy. He became known as Old Blood and Guts. The Germans were so fearful of Patton's supposed invasion of France at Calais, that they wildly misallocated their troops into that area and were unable to stop the actual invasion on the beaches of Normandy.

Not all American icons have been good guys; and the purveyors of nicknames have not overlooked the villains.

In 1859, an unsettled youth from the slums of New York City traveled west to seek his fortune and fell into a life of crime. William Bonney's associates were enthralled by his youthful countenance and renamed him Billie the Kid. The nickname spilled into the newspapers and a legend was born. Billie the Kid was gunned down before reaching his 22nd birthday. Untold numbers of young Williams have inherited the name over the past century, not because they robbed banks or trains, but because those three words just capture the imagination.

During prohibition, George Kelly Barnes left his native Tennessee and headed to the Midwest with his wife Kathryn and found work as a bootlegger. He was arrested and imprisoned in Leavenworth, Kansas. After escaping, he promoted himself to bank robber and changed his named to George Kelly. His wife allegedly renamed him Machine Gun Kelly in honor of his favorite weapon, a Thompson sub-machine gun. He soon stepped up his game to kidnapping and was eventually convicted and sent to Alcatraz (nicknamed The Rock). Not only did Kelly never kill anybody, he reportedly never even fired his famous machine gun during a criminal enterprise.

Political nicknames can cut both ways. Ronald Reagan's admirers crowned him The Great Communicator. Senator Huey Long named himself The Kingfish while detractors named him the Dictator of Louisiana.

Richard Nixon was commonly referred to as Tricky Dick for his illegal or unethical shenanigans. Nixon, in fact, left us a true nickname legacy when he chose orchestrate the 1972 break in at the Watergate Hotel. From that moment on, any scandal in the United States has received a nickname ending with the suffix "-gate." A small sample includes Billygate, Monicagate, Nannygate, Nipplegate, Spygate, and Travelgate. [Billygate named for Jimmy Carter's brother, Billy Carter, Monicagate for the Bill Clinton's intern Monica Lewinsky, Nannygate for the two Clinton nominees who hired illegal immigrants for child care, Nipplegate for the "wardrobe malfunction" during Janet Jackson and Justin Timberlake's Super Bowl XXXVIII halftime performance, Spygate for the 2003 Valerie Plame CIA leak, and Travelgate for the alleged unethical practices of the White House Travel Office during the Clinton Administration].

From Beantown to Tinseltown, almost all American towns and cities acquired nicknames, frequently for the purpose of promoting the growth of tourism, business, or industry. Walla Walla, Washington, has been called The City So Nice They Named It Twice. Sometimes the nickname was not approved or appreciated by the local Chamber of Commerce. Sin City, La La Land, and Hangtown (Placerville, California) serve as fine examples of the cynicism and humor injected into the persona of a city.

Nowhere has the American penchant for nicknaming been more rampant than in sports. And no sport can approach baseball for the number of players and teams that acquired additional names, particularly during the 50-year period from 1875 until 1925. Baseball became the first truly national sport and appropriately was given the nickname America's Pastime. Kids played baseball after school much the same way they settle into a chair with the video game controllers today. So many fans attended professional baseball games that overflow crowds frequently crowded behind ropes in the outfield, sometimes a few feet away from the players.

By the latter part of the 19th century almost every town in America, small or large, had a local nine. Factories and mills recruited skillful local players to compete with teams from neighboring factories. Minor league professional teams sprouted up everywhere. Many team names evolved from prominent features of their uniform: names such as Blue Legs, Dark Blues, Red Stockings, Ruby Legs, Browns, Maroons, and Grays. Many other team names focused on some aspect of the community: names such as Haymakers, Oilers, Brewers, Sand Crabs, Miners, Fruitpickers and Coalheavers. With all the nickname sources available, some choices were quite quirky: oddities such as the Solons, Skeeters, Goobers, Omahogs, Bathers and Prohibitionists.

The American nickname machinery really started to hum when the baseball players began to acquire nicknames. The 1886 Cincinnati Red Stockings roster contains the following player names: Kid, Bid, Hick, Farmer, Leech, Lefty and two Pops. This trend grew to the point that a player without a nickname was the exception. During the 1950's the phenomenon began to slow. By the 1970's and 1980's, nicknames were still around, but mostly began to evolve into locker room inside jokes. Few players carried their nicknames away from the ballpark. Tony Perez of the Cincinnati Reds, for example, was known as Doggie, or Big Doggie to teammates and local fans, but not so much to the rest of the baseball world.

Much has been written about the disappearance of great nicknames in contemporary major league baseball. Many writers and speakers harken back to the days of The Sultan of Swat, The Yankee Clipper, The Big Train, etc. But many, if not most, of these celebrated nicknames were not really embraced by the players themselves. Many were concocted and assigned by the sportswriters of the time. Teammates, or even opponents created others. Ted Williams probably did not register at the team hotel as The Splendid Splinter. Mr. Aaron didn't walk into a room and introduce himself as Hammerin' Hank.

The real nicknames were those used by the players themselves; the names we look up in the record books. Mudcat Grant was Mudcat Grant. Lefty Grove will be forever remembered as Lefty Grove. Whitey Ford goes into the Hall of Fame as Whitey Ford. Some people know that Larry Berra became Yogi Berra. But most people probably don't.

In this context, a baseball nickname is the assumed name that a player used, or allowed to be used, in the box scores, lineup cards, and other official baseball record keeping. Kid Gleason was not William Gleason, or Bill Gleason. He was Kid Gleason. In the first fifty years of big league baseball, starting in the 1870s, nicknames were more the rule than the exception. The wide range of nicknames that players used is staggering. Many names were probably brought from home. The many young boys who grew up being called, Butch, or Buck, or Red, arrived at their first big league game with their name already settled.

But the young men who showed up without a nom de guerre were soon issued a new name to go along with their other standard equipment. If your given name or surname sounded German, you were Heinie, Dutch or Fritz. In some rare cases of total creative failure, the name Germany itself was assigned.

If your birthright was Native American, you probably became Chief for the rest of your public life. If you were red-haired, and didn't reach professional baseball with the name Red, you became a Red. If your origins were somewhat less than urban, you were Rube, Farmer or Hick.

If you came into the game with some medical knowledge, a medical family, or had a medical problem, you were most likely called Doc. If you pitched from the port side, the chances were good that you would become Lefty at some point. Even some position players became Lefty. Not all nicknames, however, put the player in a favorable light.

The main thrust of this book is to explore the uncomplimentary, and sometimes insulting, nicknames that players embraced or tolerated. Some element of their makeup allowed them to accept names such as Creepy, Dizzy, Fatty, Piggy and worse. Players with a strong sense of self-esteem resisted a permanent assignment of such unflattering nicknames. Those less secure in their sense of self-worth capitulated and carried their new identity to the end of their career and beyond; accepting a lifetime membership in the Low Self-Esteem Club.

The derivation of these nicknames will be broken down into these major categories:

1. Physical characteristics
2. Personality traits
3. Skill sets
4. Background (racial, ethnic, and geographical)
5. Word play
6. Miscellaneous and unknown

The second goal of this project is the resurrection of baseball players that are little known, have been long forgotten, or both. In fact, the only claim to fame of some of these players is the uniqueness (or just plain oddness) of the name they chose to be called, or allowed others to call them.

While few of the featured players were superstars of their era, many of them lived interesting lives during and after baseball. A large number of players mostly unknown by baseball enthusiasts today, still hold records that have yet to be eclipsed. Other players were involved in now forgotten odd and controversial incidents on and off the field.

More than 175 players have been profiled. All will have the same common trait; a less than complimentary nickname that they will carry with them for all of baseball eternity.

So let's celebrate these men who lived the dream of playing at the top of the baseball universe and did it with a sobriquet worthy of the great game of baseball.

Chapter 1 – Physical Characteristic Names - "You're Too Fat/Skinny/Tall/Short"

Chubby Dean

Alfred Lovell Dean carried about 180 pounds on his 5'11" frame, not your typical chubby physique. But Dean was chubby as a child in North Carolina and was so-named by his family. [1] He carried the name into adulthood. This family name must have been assigned so early in life that Dean accepted it before reaching an age where he would be self-conscious about it.

Dean was a first basemen for Connie Mack's A's beginning in 1936. He alternated as a starter with Lou Finney during his first two years. He made an occasional appearance on the mound, as well. In 1939, Mack put him in the bullpen and used him regularly. By 1940, he was in the starting rotation. Philadelphia released him in 1941 and the Cleveland Indians secured his services through 1943.

His career as a position player was respectable. He had a lifetime batting average of .274. Ironically, his best year was 1939 when he batted .351 while making the transition to pitching. His hitting skills far eclipsed his pitching. He retired with a 30-46 won-loss record.

Perhaps Connie Mack was impressed with Dean's lineage. His cousins Dizzy and Daffy Dean had the right stuff. Apparently, pitching skills did not seep into Chubby's end of the gene pool. The Dean family surely produced some good nicknames as well as fine athletes.

Dean entered the Army during World War II and served as director of athletics, first at Ft. Dix and later for the European Command in Germany. He died in 1970 in Riverside, New Jersey, at the relatively young age of 55 years. [2]

Jumbo Brown

Baseball-Reference.com lists seven major league players who went by the first name Jumbo. Another nine were commonly referenced as Jumbo but retained their given names. Five of the seven played in the 19th century. Walter George Brown was the last of the Jumbos but claims the crown as the *Jumbo King*. He weighed in at nearly 300

pounds and towered over his teammates and opponents with his 6'4"
height. To add more effect to his size, Jumbo Brown performed his job
functions from atop the pitching mound. Until 2005, he held the
unofficial record as baseball's top heavyweight until Walter Young
brought his 322 pounds onto the field for the Baltimore Orioles. Young
was a 6'5" first baseman, so Jumbo Brown remained the heaviest
pitcher in baseball.

Brown had a long career lasting from 1925 until 1941, pitching for the
Cubs, Indians, Yankees, Reds, and the Giants. Until the Giants
purchased him in 1937, he had been a reliever and starter. The Giants,
however, used him exclusively from the bullpen for the remaining five
years of his career, making him one of the early pioneers in the role that
would later become known as closer. Statisticians poring over old box
scores determined that Brown accounted for 29 saves during his tenure
with the Giants.

Brown passed away in 1966 at age 56 in Freeport (Long Island), New
York.

The name Jumbo has come to connote that something is large in the
extreme. Modern marketing has especially claimed this word to
describe package size. Zip-Loc Storage Bags for example, can be
purchased in the "Jumbo 2 Gallon Size". The Boeing 747 was
christened the jumbo jet.

The word *jumbo*, however, has not always been in our lexicon.
Americans can thank P. T. Barnum for this curious new word. In 1882,
he purchased a gigantic African elephant from the London Zoo for the
small fortune of $10,000. The name of his new pet was Jumbo, derived
from the Swahili word *jumbe*, meaning chief.

Barnum had long admired the creature which was there-to-fore
unavailable. Said Barnum after the purchase, "I had often looked
wistfully on Jumbo, but with no hope of ever getting possession of him,
as I knew him to be a great favorite of Queen Victoria, whose children
and grandchildren are among the tens of thousands of British juveniles
whom Jumbo carried on his back. I did not suppose he would ever be
sold." [3]

The whole of Britain was outraged by the sale. They assumed that the
Royal Zoological Society was finally tempted by the $10,000 offer.
What many did not know is that the six-ton Jumbo was becoming bored

in captivity and was "acting up" for his handlers. Once in America, the elephant became very even-tempered once again. [4]

America went berserk over Jumbo. *Jumbomania* broke out where wherever The Greatest Show On Earth raised its tent poles. We can easily explain why Jumbo Latham, Jumbo Davis, Jumbo McGinnis, Jumbo Schoeneck and Jumbo Harting all burst upon the scene in the mid-1880s. All tipped the scales near 200 pounds or more. These gentlemen may have fancied the name Jumbo as a way to celebrate their size and strength. Or maybe they were just greatly relieved not to carry the name Fatty or Tubby around from ballpark to ballpark.

Jumbo Elliott

One Jumbo remains. James Thomas Elliott was born in 1900 and began his big league career in 1923 with the St. Louis Browns. Elliott, a left-handed pitcher, could have joined the ranks as another in the long list of players named Lefty. But at 6'3" and 235 pounds Elliott was eligible to join the big man club. He could have been named Moose or Hunk or Mountain, but Jumbo Elliott had a nice ring to it.

Elliott is the most credentialed of all the Jumbos. While a lifetime record of 63-74 did not get him invited to Cooperstown, his 1931 season with the Phillies was outstanding. The Phillies had to be pleasantly surprised when one of their salary dumping trades actually turned out okay. Following the 1930 season, Philadelphia traded Lefty O'Doul and Fresco Thompson to the Brooklyn Robins for Elliott, Clise Dudley, Hal Lee and cash. [5] Elliott came within one win of being a 20-game winner for the sixth place Phillies. He led the league in victories and appearances. He even recorded five saves.

He closed out his career with the Boston Braves in 1934, retiring to Vigo County, Indiana, where he served as a deputy sheriff for many years. In 1968, he was involved in one the "biggest" elections in Vigo County history. Running for the position of sheriff, his opponent was former NBA center Clyde Lovellette.

While Elliott carried the name of a giant, Lovellette was one. Standing at 6'9" and weighing around 250 pounds, he was one of the few humans who dwarfed ol' Jumbo. Lovellette was also quite used to winning. He was an All-American basketball player at Kansas, winning the scoring title two times and being named College Player of the Year in 1952. His Kansas team won the national championship that year and he was tournament MVP. He also won an Olympic gold medal in 1952. His first pro team, the Minneapolis Lakers, won the NBA championship, as did the Celtics in 1963 and 1964. [6]

Lovellette had one other thing going for him, he was an Indiana boy. The election went to Lovellette even though he had never acquired a cool nickname. Had Elliott successfully gained the office, he would not have served a complete term. He died in January of 1970 in Terre Haute.

Tubby Spencer

The word tubby is generally defined as an adjective meaning short and fat, resembling a tub. The word became popular in English literature around 1873. [7] An individual so designated had the double whammy of being short and overweight. Edward Russell Spencer had the overweight part of the definition covered at 215 pounds, but stood 5' 11", quite tall by early 20th century standards.

R.C. Lane of Baseball Magazine described him as being "on the heavy side with very large shoulders." Judging by the normal standards of assigning nicknames, Spencer must have brought the name Tubby with him to the big leagues. Otherwise he would have assumed a name related to his most outstanding trait, his ability to consume great amounts of hard liquor in a short duration. Turning to R. C. Lane again, we learn that by age 18 he could imbibe a quart of whiskey and still take the field and play nine innings behind the plate. His career was described as a "ten year jag." [8]

Spencer, a catcher, debuted in 1905 with the St. Louis Browns where he played for four years, thereafter moving to the Red Sox and Phillies before dropping out of sight for five years. He drank and lived the life of a hobo until the Tigers signed him in 1916. [8] He rewarded them with a .370 season but soon reverted to earlier form and batted .230 his final two years. The Tigers released him in 1918. He later enjoyed five seasons in the Pacific Coast League before hanging up the mask and pads. His only claim to fame on the field was leading the American League in being hit by pitches in 1917.

There is one statistical anomaly in his record. During his career he successfully stole 13 bases. [9] Pitchers who assumed that a base runner named Tubby would not break for second base were in for an embarrassing surprise.

9

Tubby Spencer died in San Francisco in 1945 at the age of 61, outliving many teammates who were not self-confessed alcoholics.

Tub Welch

Twenty years before Tubby Spencer began to drink his way through the major leagues, James Thomas Welch (nee Walsh) played the 1890 season with the Toledo Maumees and then again in 1895 with the Louisville Colonels. Tub Welch, like Tubby Spencer, stood nearly six feet tall and weighed well over 200 pounds. He was born in St. Louis in 1866 and died in 1901. During his five-year big league hiatus, he played for a number of minor league teams including the Leavenworth Soldiers. He split his on-field duties between first base and catcher.

In other Tubby notes, two players were called Tubby by their teammates but did not embrace the name, Al Epperly (1938-1950) and Frank Reiber (1933-1936). Neither player seemed to be excessively short or fat.

In 1993, Greg Tubbs patrolled the outfield for the Cincinnati Reds. Had he lived and played in an earlier era, there is little doubt that his teammates would have dubbed him Tubby or some variation thereof.

Hippo Vaughn

James Leslie Vaughn was a Texas-size pitcher worthy of the Lone Star State's reputation for bigger-than-life everything. Standing on the raised mound, the 6' 4", 215-pound lefty must have intimidated many of the small-framed players of the dead ball era. Later in his career he was reported to have ballooned to almost 300 pounds. But Vaughn was not named because of his weight or likeness to a hippopotamus, but for the ungainly way he carried his frame when he ran. [10]

One might think that a name like Hippo could fall into the cruel category. There is evidence that Vaughn more than acquiesced to his nickname. In a call to the Chicago police in October of 1921, his wife reported that Vaughn had been missing for several days and his three-year-old son, Little Hippo, was crying for his daddy. Vaughn was not only content to be called Hippo; he passed on the nickname to his little boy. [11]

Vaughn debuted with the New York Highlanders (Yankees) in 1908 but could not stick with the team. After that false start, he was back with the Highlanders in 1910 and distinguished himself with a 13-11 record and a sparkling 1.83 ERA.

After a few uneventful seasons in New York and Washington, he was purchased by the Chicago Cubs in 1913. One year later his career took wings and Hippo was flying high. From 1915 through 1921 he averaged over 20 wins per season. In 1918, his league-leading 22 wins helped send the Cubs to the World Series against the Boston Red Sox. The Cubs, of course, lost to the Sox and a pitcher named Babe Ruth.

In 1917, pitching for the Cubs, Vaughn and Cincinnati's Fred Toney tangled in a pitching duel for all time. After nine innings, both pitchers had not yielded a hit. In the top of the 10th, Vaughn retired the first batter before Larry Kopf singled. After an error and a stolen base, Jim Thorpe walked to the plate. Thorpe dropped a swinging bunt down the third base line that Vaughn fielded. "I knew the minute it was hit that I couldn't get Thorpe at first, " reported Vaughn, "he was as fast as a race horse." Vaughn threw to the plate but failed to get Kopf. [12] Toney retired the Cubs in the last of the 10th and preserved his no-hitter. The game was known as a double no-hitter and was the defining moment of Vaughn's life.

Vaughn, himself, proclaimed the Toney matchup as the high point of his career. Even though 3,500 fans attended the game, Vaughn recalled over 10,000 people who later claimed they were there that day. Vaughn referred to the game-winning batter as Indian Jim Thorpe, a comment that underscores the racial and ethnic stereotyping of that era. [13] Only Thorpe's worldwide reputation spared him from becoming Chief Thorpe in the baseball world.

Vaughn's major league career ended in 1921 amidst a cloud of mystery and drama. On July 9, he took the mound in the Polo Grounds with a dismal 3-10 record. In the fourth inning he surrendered a grand slam homer to Giants catcher Frank Snyder. Insult then joined injury as pitcher Phil Douglas followed with his first career home run. Manager Johnny Evers then gave Vaughn the hook. Two days later, Vaughn was nowhere to be found and the Cubs announced that Vaughn would be suspended if and when he returned to the team. [14]

By early August, Vaughn was still AWOL and the Cubs reportedly suspended him for what the Chicago Tribune described as "failure to keep in fighting trim." Furthermore, Vaughn had allegedly signed a contract to play for the Beloit Fairies, a non-affiliated team owned by the Fairbanks Morse Engine Company that manufactured everything from typewriters to locomotives. A man named Hippo becoming a member of the Fairies does not present a pleasant visual image.

When Evers was suddenly fired as manager, his replacement, Bill Killefer, and Cubs President Bill Veeck, Sr. agreed to reinstate Vaughn if Commissioner Landis agreed. Landis, however, decided to suspend Vaughn for the rest of the season for signing the contract with Beloit. Vaughn never returned to the Cubs or the major leagues again. Various reports list different reasons for his departure. He was fed up with Evers. He had a sore arm. His weight had finally affected his performance. Vaughn kept the reason or reasons to himself. His new career in semi-pro ball lasted another 16 years when he finally hung up the cleats at age 49. [15]

Vaughn died in Chicago in 1966. At the time of his death, he still had bragging rights as the Cubs all-time leader in wins by a left-handed pitcher with 151 victories. Larry French was a distant second at 95. As of this writing, that distinction still belongs to the man called Hippo.

Tiny Bonham

Ernest Edward Bonham grew up strong and tough in Ione, California. Bonham described Ione as a gold mining "ghost town." As the 13th child in a family of 14, Bonham learned quickly that he had to work hard for a fair share of anything good that the world had to offer. While still a youth he labored on farms, docks and lumber camps. [16] As he matured he grew to 6'2" tall and carried 215 pounds. Built like a blacksmith, he attracted the ironic name of Tiny. While some newspaper writers attempted unsuccessfully to rename him Jumbo, no one dared to suggest the name Fatty or its like.

Opting for baseball over football, he joined the Yankees' minor league system in 1936 as a pitcher. By his fifth year in the minors, he was promoted from Kansas City to the Yankees in 1940. Joe McCarthy's pin stripers were struggling to repeat as American League champs and the pitching staff needed help. Bonham had consistently performed well during his stint in the minors, and his rookie big league year was no exception. Though his team could climb no higher than third place, Bonham started 12 contests, winning nine and losing only three. He threw 10 complete games. He finished his rookie season with an ERA of 1.90 and a remarkable 1.2 walks per nine innings. No Rookie of the Year Award existed in 1940, or Bonham might have claimed the honor.

After a moderately successful 1941 regular season, Bonham had to wait until Game Five of the World Series to see action. Game Four saw the infamous Mickey Owens passed ball that allowed the Yankees to steal the game and climb to a commanding 3-1 lead in the Series. The well-rested Bonham outdueled the Dodgers' Whit Wyatt and clinched the world championship with a four-hit 4-1 complete game victory. [17] Irving Vaughan of the Chicago Tribune described his performance; "The Dodgers attack was melted down to almost nothing by Ernie Bonham." [18] He was the first rookie pitcher in baseball history to win a World Series clinching game. As of 2007, only Whitey Ford and Jon Lester of the Red Sox managed to duplicate that feat.

Everything came together for Tiny Bonham in 1942. The Yankees repeated as American League champions and Bonham finished the year at 21-5, eclipsing the Yankees' star pitchers, Red Ruffing and Spud Chandler. He led the league in winning percentage (.808), complete games (22), WHIP (0.987), walks per nine innings (1.0), and strikeouts to walks ratio (2.96). He was named to the All-Star team and finished fifth in the MVP voting. [19] The only black mark on the 1942 season was the loss in the World Series to the St. Louis Cardinals in which Bonham started and lost Game Two. He also pitched three innings in relief in Game Four but did not figure in the decision. The Yankees lost that game 9-6.

The Yankees won the AL pennant again in 1943 and extracted revenge over the Cardinals in the World Series. Bonham crafted a 15-8 record and once again started Game Two of the Series but lost to the Cardinals 4-3. [20]

After a winning 12-9 season in 1944, he suffered through two losing seasons with the Yanks and was traded to the Pittsburgh Pirates for Cookie Cuccurullo in 1946. He rewarded the Pirates with an 11-8 record in 1947, but fell to 6-10 the following year. He decided to retire at the end of 1949 season and return to his native California. By September, he was ready to leave the game on a high note; he was 7-4 and had exceeded 100 victories in the major leagues.

After complaining of abdominal pain, he was admitted to Presbyterian Hospital in Pittsburgh, where he was diagnosed with appendicitis. During surgery, the surgeon discovered cancer. Within one week Tiny

Bonham would be dead at age 36. His wife Ruth would become the first widow to be awarded a death benefit under baseball's newly enacted player pension plan. [21]

Tiny Bonham, for all his strength and size, did not overpower batters. He won with pinpoint control and a pitch that most of his contemporaries could not master, the forkball. Large hands and/or very long fingers were a physical requirement to properly grip the ball. When thrown correctly, the ball would tumble or sink like a 12-6 o'clock curveball. Bullet Joe Bush has been credited as the originator of the forkball while pitching for the Red Sox following World War I.

More Guys Named Tiny

Oddly enough, there are no small players named Tiny in the major league archives. All of the remaining players who chose to be known as Tiny, were large men. The first was 6' 2" Dawson Francis Graham who had a one-year career with the Cincinnati Reds in 1914. Earnest Preston Osborne was a towering 6' 4" pitcher for the Chicago Cubs and Brooklyn Robins from 1922 to 1925. Osborne's claim to fame was a "save" credited to him in a 1922 game won by the Cubs 23-22 over the Phillies.

Finally, James Bailey Chaplin emerged in 1928 and played until 1936. He was a 6' 1" pitcher for the New York Giants and Boston Braves. Bonham was the last major league player to be listed as Tiny.

But where are the little shrimpy infielders that came along and had to endure life as Tiny? Well, most of them became Shorty, Stumpy or Stubby. Perhaps Eddie Gaedel, Bill Veeck's pint-sized pinch hitter, might have become the one-and-only truly *tiny* Tiny had he not been banned from professional baseball.

Shorty Fuller

Many men who are short of stature harbor feelings of insecurity as they negotiate their way through a world of taller peers. This insecurity may cause some individuals to shrink into the background of life, while motivating others to aggressively pursue fame and success. The latter response has been informally called a Napoleon Complex, Little Man Syndrome or a number of similar variations on that same theme. Nicknames referring to a person's short stature would be likely to create a pushback effect unless that name was lovingly assigned by a family and carried throughout a person's early life.

Not surprisingly, only five baseball players have adopted the name Shorty, and one of them was 6'4" tall. Furthermore, no player entering the big leagues after 1916 has held that name.

Another oddity is that only one player named Shorty appeared in more than 20 major league games. His actual name was William Benjamin Fuller. Fuller was a 5'6" shortstop who made the big leagues in 1888 with the Washington Nationals. Fuller appeared in the Old Judge Tobacco card series of 1887. His photo indicates that 5'6" was a generous assessment of his height.

Fuller shared the Nationals dugout with a young catcher named Cornelius McGillicuddy, who not only adopted the nickname of Connie, but also shortened his last name to Mack.

Following his rookie year, Fuller was sold to the St. Louis Browns for $800. [22] Would the price tag been higher if Fuller stood higher? In any event, the Browns got their money's worth, sending Fuller out to play over 400 games in four years.

In 1892, he moved on to the New York Giants where he played regularly until his final season in 1896. Fuller's prime accomplishment was his 60 stolen bases in 1890. Despite his proximity to the infield dirt, he twice committed over 90 errors in a season.

There is no anecdotal evidence to suggest that Fuller ever demonstrated the effects of a Napoleon Complex. But during Fuller's tenure in baseball, he competed against a 5'7" infielder who could be called the poster boy for Napoleon Complex. In fact, in addition to the nickname Mugsy, John McGraw was frequently called Little Napoleon (behind his back).

Shorty Des Jardien

The other players named Shorty were Maurice Leo Dee (5'6") who played in a single game for the St. Louis Browns in 1915, John Howe (height unknown) who played in 20 games for the 1890 and 1893 New York Giants, Chares William Gallagher (height unknown) who played in just two games for the Cleveland Blues in 1901, and finally Paul Raymond Des Jardien (6'4") who completed just one inning for the

Cleveland Indians in 1916. Des Jardien gave up two runs and will forevermore have a career ERA of 18.00. His minor league experience amounted to seven games, also in 1916. Was his nickname also a description of his athletic career, rather than his physical stature? No, read on.

Shorty Des Jardien attended the University of Chicago where he played football from 1912 to 1914. Playing center for the Maroons, he was named an All-American in 1913, when his team went undefeated and won the Big Ten Conference championship. [23] He was a four-sport letterman who pitched a no-hitter for his college team. He decided to try his luck at professional baseball but soon determined that his fortune would be easier made on the gridiron. He played professional football from 1916 through 1922 for the Cleveland Indians, Hammond Pros, Chicago Tigers of the inaugural NFL, and Minneapolis Marines. [24]

During that same stretch, Des Jardien also coached the Oberlin College football team (1916), played professional basketball for Pine Village (1916-1917), played on the US Army football team (1917) and was in charge of a German prisoner of war camp in Paris, France. [25]

James K. Skipper, in his seminal book on nicknames, reports that the name Shorty was just an opposite reaction to his body type. When or where the name originated is not indicated. [26] Logic would dictate that this ironic sobriquet would not have been appropriate until early adulthood when he began to tower over his peers. Des Jardien had enough confidence in his physique and athletic ability to share in the joke.

After his football and baseball exploits had ended, he moved to the Los Angeles area where he became an executive with a manufacturing firm.

Des Jardien died at the age of 62 in Monrovia, California, in 1956, eight months after being elected to the College Football Hall of Fame. [27]

Skeeter Newsome

The word skeeter has long been rural slang for the pesky mosquito. The nickname Skeeter was commonly assigned to adults and particularly children with a slight build. Lamar Ashby Newsome grew up in rural Alabama just across the Chattahoochee River from Columbus, Georgia.

Young Newsome had the short, thin body type that prompted his uncle to begin calling him Skeeter. [28]. Faced with the choice of being Lamar or Skeeter, he chose the insect name.

Despite his size, he was very athletic and settled into playing shortstop. While still in his teens, he landed a contract with Talladega in the Georgia-Alabama League in 1930.

Following a very good year with the 1934 Tulsa Oilers, Connie Mack brought him to Philadelphia to start the 1935 season as a back-up infielder. One season later he was the starting shortstop. He was released by the Athletics in 1939 and spent one year back in the minors before the Red Sox rescued him in 1941. With Boston manager Joe Cronin penciling in player Joe Cronin at shortstop, Newsome became a very valuable utility player and effective pinch hitter. The following year, Johnny Pesky became the Boston shortstop and Newsome was again relegated to the role of utility player. In 1942, Pesky enlisted in the war effort and the Skeeter finally joined Bobby Doerr in the middle of the infield.

Future Hall of Famer Doerr joined the Army in 1945 and Newsome moved from shortstop to second base. Following the return of Doerr and Pesky in 1946, he was deemed redundant and sold to the woeful Phillies where he was welcomed with the starting shortstop role at age 35. With the Phillies in a youth movement later to be called the Whiz Kids, Newsome knew that he was just keeping the seat warm for a youngster named Granny.

On September 28, 1947, the Skeeter was permanently swatted out of the major leagues. He played minor league ball for a few years before launching a successful career as a minor league manager.

Two interesting Skeeter stories have survived. In a 1945 game at Fenway Park, he stroked a single off the A's pitcher and decided to stretch it into a double. Outfielder Hal Peck's throw collided with a low-flying pigeon and the ball deflected right to the second baseman who tagged a surprised Newsome for the out. While Newsome dusted himself off and trotted to the dugout, the pigeon flew away a few feathers light. [29]

While still a member of the Philadelphia Athletics, Newsome took a close pitch with a 3-2 count and was called out on strikes. Like many other players, Newsome felt that the superstars of the game would get the benefit of the doubt on close pitches. He turned to umpire Bill McGowan and complained, "You wouldn't have called DiMaggio out on the that pitch."

"You're darn right I wouldn't," responded McGowan. "He would have hit it off that 457-foot sign in left-center field." [30] The Skeeter had been swatted again.

Newsome died in 1989 in Columbus, Georgia, on the opposite side of the Chattahoochee River from where he was born almost 79 years earlier.

A Swarm of Skeeters

The earliest Skeeter was Andrew Kemper Shelton born in 1888 in Huntington, West Virginia. This Skeeter landed in the Polo Grounds where the Yankees performed in 1915. Ten games later he was part of Yankee history as possibly the worst hitter to ever call himself a Yankee. In 43 plate appearances he successfully reached base three times, one single and two walks. Factoring in one sacrifice bunt, his career numbers display as 1-for- 40, or a batting average of .025.

James Laverne Webb was born in Meridian, Mississippi, in 1909. Another slightly built infielder, Skeeter Webb, forged a 12-year career with the Cardinals, Indians, White Sox, Tigers and A's. The high point of Webb's career was starting at shortstop for the Tigers' 1945 World Series championship team, playing in all seven games of the Series. Despite his low batting average, he was able to hang onto his starting job. His manager (and father-in-law) Steve O'Neill either liked Webb's fielding or was reluctant to demote his daughter's husband.

Frank John Scalzi was also a physical lightweight who had a very short career with the New York Giants. Unlike Skeeter Shelton, Skeeter Scalzi looked good in his brief appearance with Bill Terry's 1939 Giants. He batted .333 in 18 at bats. After losing his position in the majors, his minor league career lasted another 20 years. He appeared in one game with the Charleston ChaSox in 1959 before hanging up the cleats at the age of 46.

Everett Lee Kell was born in Swifton, Arkansas, in 1929. Skeeter Kell was another diminutive player that hailed from a rural area and rose to the major leagues for a brief tenure. His single year was different from most one-year players. He got into 75 games for the 1952 Philadelphia

Athletics. Unlike Skeeter Scalzi, he only played another two years in the minors before joining the Skeeter archives. Skeeter Kell also was the younger brother of Hall of Famer George Kell.

Finally, William Henry Barnes, a Skeeter who was an anomaly in several ways. He was not from a southern state or rural area. He was born in Cincinnati, Ohio. Additionally, Barnes entered the big leagues in 1983 when the hay-day of colorful nicknames was long past. In the corporate-image environment of 1983, a player adopting a name like Skeeter would be quite surprising. The truth is, Barnes never had a chance to pick his own name; his Mom declared him to be a Skeeter shortly after birth. When your mother lies in a hospital bed after surviving the pains of labor and childbirth, you are going to be a Skeeter if that is what she decides you will be.

Barnes enjoyed nine years with the Reds, Expos, Cardinals and Tigers. Maybe *enjoyed* is not the correct word. He was declared a free agent six times during his nine-year career. The uncertainty of seeking new employment almost every year must have been tough on him. In his final four years, he stuck with the Tigers and proved himself to be a valuable utility player, appearing at every position except pitcher and catcher.

The unofficial Skeeters include Carson Bigbee (1916-1926) and Lee Tate (1958-1959).

Two observations can be made about the Skeeters in baseball. None appear before 1915, suggesting that the word skeeter came into American slang around the turn of the 20th century.

Secondly, almost all Skeeters were born in rural areas, and almost all of them died within a few miles of their birthplace.

Bones Ely

Two players answered to the nickname Bones without assuming the name, Jim Blackburn (1948- 1951) and Dick Tomanek (1953-1959). William Frederick Ely, on the other hand, was satisfied to become Mr. Bones Ely, major league pitcher. At 6' 1" and 155 pounds, Ely gave the appearance of being very fragile when toeing the mound [31]. His skeletal carriage evoked the expression "just skin and bones" and led to his new moniker. Most photos of Ely show him with a healthy handlebar moustache, adding to the effect.

Like many 19th century players, Ely sprung from amateur or semi-pro leagues directly to the major league professional level. Joining the National League Buffalo Bisons in 1884, the versatile Ely attempted to find a place in the pitching rotation or the outfield. The Bisons allowed him one game at each position and bid him adieu.

He resurfaced with the American Association Louisville Colonels two years later and received a better audition, ten games in the outfield and six on the mound. He batted .156 and lost all four decisions as a hurler and found himself on the outside looking in for the second time.

Four years later, his minor league team, the Syracuse Stars were brought into the American Association and he was a big leaguer once again, this time as an outfielder. The third time was a charm and he got on track to a 14-year career that saw him come to the plate 500 plus times during eight seasons. By 1891, he played almost exclusively in the infield, ultimately settling at shortstop where he logged over 1,200 games at that position.

After Syracuse, he played for the Brooklyn Grooms, St. Louis Browns, Pittsburgh Pirates, Philadelphia A's, and Washington Senators. He was a member of Connie Mack's very first Athletics team in 1901.

He may have looked like a bag of bones, but he brought some muscle to the plate, as well. In 1894, he was tied for 11th in home runs only six behind leader Hugh Duffy. He batted .306 that same season.

Ely was born in Erie County, Pennsylvania, in 1863, shortly before the Battle of Gettysburg. He died in January of 1952. In a very wry twist of fate, the only player ever known professionally as Bones was cremated. His grave contains no bones, just ashes.

Ribs Raney

Frank Robert Donald Raniszewski had a long name and long body (6'4"). He cut his last name down to the bone, changing it to Raney. His nickname reduced his three given names to a mere four letters, Ribs. Had he arrived in professional baseball sans nickname, he might have become a "Skinny" or a "Skeeter," but he carried a perfectly descriptive name since his early teens. Said Raney, "When I was 14 years old, I was 6' 4" and weighed 150 pounds. We always played ball with our shirts off and all the kids could see my ribs." [32]

Raney was born in Detroit in 1923. At age 18 he joined the 1941 Paragould Browns of the Northeast Arkansas League. Paragould was a lowly Class D team, but it was affiliated with the St. Louis Browns. If he succeeded there, somebody on high might notice. His 6-10 record did not earn him a train ticket to St. Louis, but he was promoted to the Class C Huntington Jewels in 1942. For the Jewels, he turned in a gem of a season, winning 17 games against 7 losses and advanced to Class A Elmira the following year.

The 1943 season proved very eventful, he was bumped up to AA in mid-year, then bumped out of professional baseball by the war effort. After his discharge from the U.S. Navy he jumped back into action and labored in the minor leagues for another three seasons before signing a contract to play for the St. Louis Browns in 1949. During the 1949 and 1950 seasons, he was used sparingly by the Browns and bounced back and forth between St. Louis and Elmira/Baltimore.

The Browns declined to renew his contract for the 1951 season, effectively ending his major league career with a 1-3 record spread over two seasons and only four trips to the pitching mound.

He spent 1951 and 1952 in the minors and called it quits. His minor league stat line shows 10 seasons and a 78-92 won-loss mark.

He attended Western Michigan University in Kalamazoo, following in the footsteps of Stubby Overmire and preceding Jim Bouton.

Raney lived to the age of 80 before passing in Warren, Michigan, in 2003.

Skinny Graham

Kyle Graham is the first player to officially become known as Skinny. Graham is listed as playing at 6' 2" and 175 pounds, a fairly large physique for someone born in 1899. Since he did not become a large enough specimen to acquire one of baseball's "opposite" nicknames, he likely morphed into Skinny in his youth prior to bulking up in weight. The only explanation found for his nickname is Graham's height and weight statistics. [33]

Graham was another example of a player that acquired big-league-quality skills without playing in the minor leagues. The Boston Braves drafted him from Little Rock of the Southern Association in 1923, even though no records exist that he played that year. His first documented professional experience came in 1924 with the Boston Braves as a right-handed pitcher. He acquitted himself well but suffered an 0-4 record for the last-place Braves.

Graham spent three years with Boston and one season with the Detroit Tigers. His final won-loss record was 11-22. Five subsequent years of minor league play did not earn him a trip back to the major leagues.

He died in 1973 in Oak Grove, Alabama. Just like all of his Dixie cousins, the Skeeters, he was buried within a stone's throw of his birthplace.

Skinny Graham the Sequel

Arthur William Graham was born 10 years after (Kyle) Skinny Graham and entered the major leagues 10 years after Kyle, also in Boston (with the Red Sox). He stood only 5' 7" and weighed 162 pounds, easily qualifying him to be crowned with a small man's nickname.

Graham hailed from the Boston area and signed with the Reading Red Sox in 1934. He absolutely tore his way through the New York-Penn league batting .331 with 16 doubles, 15 triples and 18 home runs in 450 at bats. By September he had joined the real Red Sox and found himself standing on Fenway Park's outfield grass.

Graham returned to the Sox in 1935 but played in just eight games. Despite three hits in 10 at bats (all for extra bases), he spent the next seven years playing in the minors.

Graham's claim to fame occurred not within the confines of Fenway Park, but on the banks of the Charles River. With one mighty throw, Graham tossed George Washington and Walter Johnson into the dustbin of coin-throwing history. Washington allegedly tossed a dollar across the Rappahannock River in Virginia. On February 22, 1936, the town of Fredericksburg fashioned a celebration to honor George's 204th birthday. City officials invited Walter "Big Train" Johnson to try to repeat Washington's famous throw.

Johnson accepted the challenge, but had reservations. He could throw harder than anybody in baseball, but this would be a test of distance. A congressman from New York, Sol Bloom, doubted that Washington ever performed the apocryphal feat, so he offered a wage at 20-to-1 odds that Johnson would fail. The Free Lance-Star picked up the story and implored the citizens of Fredericksburg to pool their money and take the bet with the proviso that all winnings go toward purchasing Ferry Farm where Washington grew up to convert it into a museum. The good citizens of the region had raised nearly $5,000 to meet the wager.

More than 4,000 people lined the banks of the Rappahannock where Johnson would be allocated three tries. The crowd groaned when the first silver dollar splashed into the river. On toss number two, the silver dollar sailed over the water and bounced on the opposite shore. For good measure, Johnson let the third coin fly and it likewise cleared the river landing 286 feet from the launch point.

Let history record that Congressman Bloom reneged on the $100,000 payoff. Bloom claimed that Washington threw a piece of slate across a stream that was much narrower in the mid-1700s. [34] Had the winners been residents of New York, Bloom may have been *persuaded* to pay his debt.

Two days after the Rappahannock incident, Skinny Graham faced the Charles River and surveyed the far bank 300 feet away. Not once, twice or thrice, but four times Graham transported silver dollars across the Charles. [35]

Arthur Skinny Brown died in 1967 in Cambridge, Massachusetts, not far from the Charles River.

Skinny O'Neal

Oran Herbert O'Neal was ripe for a nickname his whole life. Born in Missouri in 1899, he grew up tall and, well, skinny. His MLB playing weight was only 160 pounds. The name Oran was an open invitation to seek another identity. Becoming Skinny O'Neal worked for him.

O'Neal dedicated 10 years of his life to the dream of playing major league baseball. His minor league career began in 1921 and transported him to three teams in three separate leagues in his first year alone. After spending one whole season in Bartlesville, Oklahoma, with the Grays of the Southwestern League, he began an odyssey that would make Ulysses look like a shut-in. In 1923, he pitched for four different teams in three different leagues. His last stop on the tour was Bloomington in the Three I League, a promotion to Class B. The following year he started the season back in the lower minors and climbed his way up to Double A with the Los Angeles Angels in the PCL. That 1924 Angel team was chocked full of future big league players. O'Neal would become one of those big leaguers as the 1925 season opened in Philadelphia.

He pitched in 11 games for the Phillies, including one start. Despite an ERA of 9.30, he managed to avoid losing any of the games in which he appeared. The Phillies exported him back to the minor leagues to play for the Beaumont Exporters. He spent the entire year in one place during the 1926 season, Springfield, Massachusetts, in the Eastern League. He successfully cobbled a 17-win summer, and the Phillies ponied up the cash to bring him to Philadelphia one more time to begin the 1927 season. He sipped from a bitter cup of coffee in Philly and was gone after two games and a 9.00 ERA. Sent packing, he landed back in the Eastern League with Bridgeport.

His big league career was over, but his wandering was not. In 1929, he sat in three more dugouts, two in the Texas League and one back in the Eastern League. He retired after the 1930 season. Including Philadelphia, he had plied his trade in 16 different cities in nine leagues. His minor league record was 92-107. His major league record was 0-0.

He may not have accumulated a lot of big league stories to tell his children and grandchildren, but he certainly could have taught them a lot of geography. In the back of his closet there must have been an old cardboard suitcase with travel stickers from all over the American landscape, from Los Angeles to Dallas to New England.

O'Neal passed away in Springfield, Missouri, in 1981, at the age of 82.

The Skinny Pretenders

Hal Brown (1951-1964), Charlie Kalbfus (1884), Carl McNabb (1945), and Wally Shaner (1923-1929) were called Skinny at one time or another in their careers, but none of them answered roll call when the name Skinny was announced.

Pee Wee's Clubhouse

The object of this project is to highlight the lesser lights of baseball that gladly agreed (or capitulated) to accept a new name. Harold Henry Reese meets one of these requirements but not the other. Baseball history is full of Pee Wee Reese information. He must be included here because his name is misleading, so a clarification is needed. Standing 5' 10" tall, he really was not a Pee Wee in size, not as a youth or as a man. His nickname came from his champion status as a shooter of marbles. [36] Had he favored a larger orb, he might have been renamed Bumbo, Bumboozer, or Bowler Reese. Instead, his identity was linked with the smaller variety of marbles known as peawees or peewees.

This writer was quite addicted to playing marbles as a boy. Had I been honored with a marble related nickname, Cats Eye might have been my new handle.

Two players in the modern era were informally called Pee Wee, Greg Briley (1988-1993) and Nate Oliver (1963-1969). Neither Briley nor Oliver was particularly small, but teammates chose to identify them in that manner. Oliver was said to have looked small compared to his Dodger teammates in his rookie year. [37]

Bitsy Mott

Elisha Matthew Mott was gravitationally challenged. Weighing in at 155 pounds at his heaviest, and standing just 5' 8" tall, he could have been named Skinny or Skeeter, but instead received the unique handle of Bitsy, as in *itsy-bitsy*, meaning very small, or tiny. Random House Dictionary states that itty-bitty and itsy-bitsy both evolved around 1890 as rhyming elements from the term *little bit*.

Until he reached high school, Mott was known as Junior. His classmates renamed him Bitsy and Bitsy he remained for the rest of his life.

Mott was an all-conference athlete in basketball, baseball, tennis and track. He turned down a football scholarship from Presbyterian College in Clinton, South Carolina. [38] Baseball was his first love. The slick-fielding shortstop signed with the Brooklyn Dodgers in 1939. After two years in the minors he was released and signed with the Cincinnati Reds. After the 1941 season, he was released again and joined a non-affiliated league in his native Florida.

A Phillies scout assigned to the Florida Orange Belt League was impressed with Mott's skills and inked him to a contract. Mott reported to the Utica Blue Sox of the Eastern League in 1944. Described as "peppery, " Mott was a fan favorite wherever he played. His sharp glove-work and a respectable batting average of .279 caught the attention of Phillies manager Fat Freddie Fitzsimmons. Mott was penciled in as the Phillies shortstop for the 1945 season.

Opportunity was definitely knocking on Mott's door, but so was the draft board. Late in 1944, World War II was still raging and Mott's services were needed. He preempted the draft by enlisting in the Navy. Just before his tour of duty began, a series of severe migraines derailed his military career and he was discharged. He rejoined the Philadelphia Phillies and made his major league debut on April 17, 1945.

He was leading a charmed life. Whenever a bad break would knock him down, a lucky break would appear and reset the game. He could have been in combat somewhere in the Pacific; instead he was leadoff man and starting shortstop for the Phillies. Jimmie Foxx, Vince DiMaggio and Granny Hamner shared the same dugout. But 69 games into the season, bad luck entered his life again. Freddie Fitzsimmons was fired after compiling a horrid 18-51 record.

A utility player named Ben Chapman was elevated to the manager's chair. Mott's fan club lost one very important member. By season end, the Phillies had done no better under Chapman, finishing an astounding 52 games behind the Chicago Cubs. The Philadelphia media raved about the double-play combination of Mott, Freddy Daniels and Turkey Tyson. [38a] But the bottom line showed that Mott had committed 27 errors and batted only .221. Skeeter Newsome would become the Phillies shortstop in 1946.

Mott's mojo disappeared for the next 12 years as he tried in vain to reclaim his big league credentials. Unlike the itsy-bitsy spider that had been washed down to the bottom of the waterspout, Bitsy could not find a way to climb back. He played for nine different teams in six leagues. The end of the rainbow was the Tampa Tarpons in 1957. He was back in the Phillies system again, but the pot held no gold, just a pink slip. Three games in a Tarpon uniform and his baseball days were over.

After a long trial separation, Mott and Lady Luck reunited in 1956. Mott's older sister married a guy named Tom Parker who liked to refer to himself as the Tampa dogcatcher. The self-deprecating brother-in-law was actually the head of the Humane Society in Tampa. Parker did have one affectation, however, he liked to be called Colonel Tom Parker. [39]

Colonel Parker had another job. He managed a young singer by the name of Elvis Presley. Parker offered Mott a job as a security guard for his young singer. Mott later described himself as "head of security" for Elvis.

The washed up ballplayer was soon hanging out at Graceland and nabbing small roles in Elvis Presley movies. In *G.I. Blues* he appeared as a drill sergeant chewing out a cinematic version of Elvis. [40] Thousands of photos of Elvis feature Mott standing somewhere near the star.

Mott had one more opportunity to reinvent himself. Following the Elvis years, he morphed into Bobo the Hobo and became a popular party clown in the Brandon, Florida, neighborhoods.

Mott's wife, Charlotte did not discover that Mott's real name was Elisha until after they were married. She collected a scrapbook of articles about her husband while he was on the road with Parker and Presley. When he retired from the road, he edited Charlotte's scrapbook. Each time he saw the name Elisha, he crossed it out. "He hated that name," she said. [41]

Bitsy Mott, not Elisha Mott, died at age 82 in 2001.

One additional note about Colonel Tom Parker; he not only made himself into a Colonel, he made himself a Parker, as well. He was born in the Netherlands as Andre van Kuijk. He fell through the cracks of the naturalization process and never became a U.S. citizen. [42]

Stubby Overmire

Standing 5' 7" tall and weighing 175 pounds, pitcher Frank W. Overmire did not look like most members of the pitching fraternity. With his squat physical appearance, he soon found himself answering to the name Stubby.

In 1939, Overmire matriculated at Western State Teachers College in his native Michigan. If he entered college with the thought of becoming a teacher, he graduated in 1941 with a new plan to become a professional baseball player. Shortly after completing his education, he signed with the Detroit Tigers and was assigned to Class C Muskegon in the Michigan League. After only two seasons in the minors, he was promoted to the Detroit Tigers to begin the 1943 season. Like many other moderately talented athletes, young and old, he benefitted from the absence of top-flight players during World War II.

He made the most of his opportunity by securing a spot in the back end of the Tigers rotation behind Hal Newhouser and Dizzy Trout. While his best year was 1947 when he finished 11-5 for Detroit, the highlight of his career was pitching in the 1945 World Series against the Cubs. He was the losing pitcher in Game Three despite allowing just two runs in six innings. The Cubs' Claude Passeau tossed a one-hit shutout that day. Detroit eventually claimed the Series in seven games.

After the 1949 season he was released by the Tigers and signed by the Browns. In 1951, he was traded to the Yankees who used him sparingly and cut him at the end of the season. He returned to the Browns for one final season. He left baseball with a 58-67 record during his 10 seasons. His lifetime ERA was 3.96.

Overmire dropped to the minor leagues for two years before accepting a player-manager gig with the Southern Association's Little Rock Travelers in 1954. That position launched him into a minor league managing career that lasted over 20 years. He also served as pitching coach for the Tigers from 1963 to 1966.

Overmire suffered a severe stroke on New Year's Eve 1976 and died the following March after resting in a coma for over two months. He was only 57 years of age.

Stubby Magner

Edmund Burke Magner was not just the first to be called Stub or Stubby, he was the most deserving of the name. Stubby Magner was born in 1888 in Kalamazoo, Michigan. When he reached his full height as a young adult, he stood only 5' 3' and tipped the scale at 135 pounds.

After graduating from Cornell University, he played shortstop for the Wilkes-Barre Barons in 1911. That same summer, he was signed by the New York Highlanders two years before they were renamed the Yankees. No fielding records exist for the Barons, but Stubby must have looked good defensively because he batted only .196.

In 13 games for the soon-to-be Yankees, he hit .212 playing both short and second base. In 1912, he returned to Cornell to join the alumni in the annual contest with the Cornell varsity baseball team. According to the Cornell Alumni News, Magner captained the team and went 2- for-4 as the leadoff batter for the alums. [43]

No further records exist for Magner's baseball career. Bearing in mind that baseball players were not highly valued in early American society, the Magner family no doubt exerted some pressure for Edmund to make something respectable of himself. This would be especially true of a chap who graduated with honors from an Ivy League school. Magner was a member of the Quill and Scroll Society, a secret organization similar to the Yale Skull and Bones Society. Magner received a law degree from Cornell in 1913. [44] He served in the U.S. Navy as a Lieutenant during World War I.

Does Magner have a baseball claim to fame? Taking Eddie Gaedel out of the equation, Magner shares the distinction of being the shortest player in MLB history. One of the other members of the all-shortest team is Yo-Yo Davalillo who will be profiled in a later chapter.

One of the things that makes baseball great is that the sport never let's its players completely fade away. As an example, in a tongue-in-cheek article lampooning Bob Costas, Mike Freeman proclaims "I'm the Einstein of sports, the Martin Luther King of broadcasters, the Mozart of Mayhem, the tiny tenderoni who can recite the batting average of Stubby Magner while deep in R.E.M. sleep." [45] Stubby Magner metaphorically arose from the grave to help cast a few humorous stones at Bob Costas.

Magner died in 1956 in Chillicothe, Ohio, and was buried in the Dayton National Cemetery (Section 10, Row 12, Grave 48).

Stub Smith

James Abner Smith is the first known ballplayer to answer to the name Stub or Stubby. He was born in 1873 in Elmwood, Illinois. Stub Smith grew to the height of 5' 6" and weighed in at 145 pounds. He had a brief career in which he appeared in three games as a shortstop for the Boston Beaneaters. He batted .100 collecting a single in 10 trips to the plate.

One can only imagine how much fun it was on a Beaneaters' road trip listening to the rival fans and players expound on the bodily functions of anyone who proudly called himself a Beaneater.

Smith labored for seven years in the minor leagues, all of them coming after his less-than-stellar experience with Boston.

For almost a century, Smith was lost to the baseball world, except for his brief statistical profile. In 2006, a SABR researcher picked up a trail and with the help of fellow members gleaned some post baseball information on our first Stub. He moved from the minor leagues to the *miner leagues* after moving to western Pennsylvania and going to work in a coal mine in West Deer Township around 1920. By 1930 he was living in Fall River, Massachusetts, his wife Helen's home state. [46]

Shortly before his death at age 73, he listed his occupation as a ballplayer. His obituary stated that he played "a few years with the Boston Braves." [47] These facts can only be interpreted as possessing great pride in being part of the eternal baseball fraternity. Despite the fact that his last professional game occurred 41 years in the past, Smith would forever consider himself a ballplayer. The over-statement of his tenure with the Boston club could be due to confusion by the family. The reference to the Boston Braves may indicate that the Smith family did not want their beloved Stub to be associated with a group of men who fancied themselves Beaneaters.

Stubby Clapp

Richard Keith Clapp is a rare specimen. Very few ballplayers in the final decades of the 20th century allowed their official name to carry an unflattering connotation. Even better, Clapp was on the roster of the 2001 St. Louis Cardinals, pushing him into the 21st century.

Richie Clapp has been known as Stubby since childhood.

Clapp, born in Windsor, Ontario in 1973, is listed at 5' 8" and 175 pounds during his single MLB year. He played shortstop and second base for the Texas Tech Red Raiders before the Cardinals drafted him the 36th round of the 1996 amateur draft.

Clapp managed only a .200 average with the Cardinals and was returned to the Memphis Redbirds from whence he came. His final year in baseball was 2006, more than a century after the original Stub surfaced in Boston. There may never be another Stubby in a major league dugout.

Had he not arrived with the ready-made name of Stubby, his teammates could have had some fun with the last name Clapp.

Clapp's claim to fame did not occur in the major or minor leagues, but in the 1996 Summer Olympics. The scrappy Canadian team made it into the semifinals but ran into the confident American team. In the 11th inning, a guy named Stubby came to the plate with the bases loaded and singled in the winning run. One day later, Stubby Clapp bowed and received his bronze medal. By the time he participated in the 2004 games in Athens, he was a national hero. When he would come to the plate. Canadians would stand and scream, "Stubby! Stubby!"

Stub Brown

Richard P. Brown arose from the streets of Baltimore and brought his hulking 6' 2", 225-pound frame directly onto the mound for the National League Baltimore Orioles in 1893. The burly lefthander was anything but a stub of a man and subsequently picked up a name that was the opposite of his physique.

Not much is known about Stub Brown before or after his baseball career, but his rookie year was spent with the likes of John McGraw, Uncle Robbie Robertson, and Hughie Jennings. A further look at the roster of the '93 Orioles team reveals Crazy Schmit, Boileryard Clarke, Sadie McMahon and the wonderfully named Piggy Ward.

With the addition of Wee Willie Keeler and Dan Brouthers in 1894, the Orioles surged into first place in the National League. Brown played a larger part in his sophomore year going 4-0 in nine games, six of them as a starter. He was released from the Orioles that same year and found refuge with the Lynchburg Hill Climbers in the Virginia League. After disappearing from the face of the earth in 1895, he showed up again on the roster of the Hill Climbers in 1896.

31

He ascended to the major leagues once more in 1897 with the Cincinnati Reds. Manager Buck Ewing needed only two games to realize he had stubbed his toe in bringing Stub Brown to the Reds. After his release he bounced around until 1897 when departed from affiliated baseball.

For the remainder of his long life, he could claim bragging rights to a winning record (4-1) and regale friends and family with the memories of sharing the field or the dugout with a slew of Hall of Famers including the aforementioned McGraw, Robertson, Keeler, Brouthers, Ewing; plus Joe Kelley, and Bid McPhee. Brown died and was buried in Baltimore in 1948 at the age of 77.

Some additional notes on the Baltimore Orioles of Brown's era: Many fans remember that the American League franchise called the Orioles moved to New York in 1903 and became the New York Highlanders and eventually the Yankees. The 1899 Orioles manager, John McGraw, reconstituted the Orioles and guided them into the new American League in 1901. McGraw was hired by the New York Giants in 1902 and consequently never had any affiliation with the Yankees except to face them in the World Series in 1921, 1922 and 1923.

Hunkey Hines

At 5' 7" and 165 pounds, Henry Fred Hines very well could have been called Stub or Stubby. Instead, he became one of the only two players designated as a hunk of a man. In the modern vernacular, it would be quite flattering to be called Hunk or Hunkey. Around 1895, however, it was definitely meant in a pejorative manner.

Hines played for the Brooklyn Grooms in 1895 at age 27. He played in only two games but managed to walk to the batter's box ten times where he singled twice and walked twice for a lifetime .250 average and one RBI.

Hines was born (1867) and died (no date available) in Rockford, Illinois.

Hunky Shaw

Is it possible that Royal N. Shaw was named in honor of the great Hunkey Hines? No, probably not, so the name must have come from his stubby build. His career consisted of just one game and one plate appearance in 1908 with the Pittsburgh Pirates. Sadly, he blew his chance to go down in history with a 1.000 batting average. Talk about all or nothing, his line reads .000 instead.

Shaw was born (1884) and died (1964) in Yakima, Washington.

Baldy Louden

Seven players had the informal nickname of Baldy and wisely chose not to go down in history as "follicly challenged." William P. Louden, however, did not mind the perpetual reference to his premature loss of hair, and therefore retains the honor of being the only major league player with the name Baldy.

Louden was an infielder born in Pittsburgh in 1883. His professional career began in 1906 at the age of 22 with the Greenville Hunters in the Texas League. In 1907, he moved to the Dallas Giants and performed well enough to attract the notice of the New York Highlanders. He got the call to New York in September of 1907 and made his debut on September 18. After 11 plate appearances he managed only one hit and two walks. Back to the minors he went.

Louden struggled for three years in the Eastern League playing for Montreal, then Newark. Finally, in 1911, everything clicked and the Detroit Tigers selected him in the Rule V Draft.

As the 1912 season got underway, Louden was starting at second or third base and sharing the dugout with Ty Cobb. He lost the starting job to Ossie Vitt in 1913 but still played in over 70 games for the Tigers. Louden's salary for the 1913 season was $2,700.

The Carolina League formed in 1912 as a minor league, and changed its name to the Federal league in 1913. They unilaterally declared themselves to be a "major league" in 1914 and set out to raid the National and American leagues for top-draw talent. Offering bigger paychecks, they almost stole Walter Johnson from the Senators and did manage to grab other big leaguers such as Bill McKechnie and Hal Chase.

Louden succumbed to an offer for higher pay and jumped to the Buffalo Buffeds to begin the 1914 season. He enjoyed his best season as a professional batting .314. The team changed its name to the Blues in 1915. Louden again had a decent year for Buffalo but found himself unemployed when the Federal League imploded.

The stranded players from the newly defunct Federal League were sold to the highest bidders from the National and American leagues and most found new homes. Some notables who were blacklisted included Joe Tinker, and Mordecai Brown. [48]

Louden was purchased by the Cincinnati Reds where he ended his career after the 1916 season. He was one of seven men who played shortstop that year. He became the odd-man-out when he could not raise his average above the low .200 level.

He died in 1935 in Piedmont, West Virginia, and buried just across the Maryland border in Westernport.

Pug Bennett

Justin Titus Bennett was not named for a "pug-ugly" countenance. In fact, the 1906 St. Louis team photo shows a dark-haired, handsome man. Bennett was handed his nickname for the expression on his face. Teammates felt that he looked pugnacious, an impression that probably helped him avoid some confrontations, but may have caused others. According to baseball historian Tom Shea, Bennett was a misunderstood man. While he may have displayed a truculent appearance, he was not that way by personality. [49]

Bennett was born in 1874 in Ponca, Nebraska. At that time, Nebraska had only been a state for seven years, the 37th in order of statehood. Baseball had found its way to every remote corner of the country. In 1897, Bennett attended Blackburn College in Carlinville, Illinois, near St. Louis.

In 1900, he signed to play with his first professional team, the venerable Toledo Mud Hens of the Interstate League, primarily as a third baseman. He then bounced around the Southern Association for five more seasons with four different teams before moving to the PCL and signing with the Seattle Siwashes. He batted .303 for Seattle and caught the eye of the St. Louis Cardinals who selected him in the Rule V Draft.

He made his big league debut at age 32 with the 1906 Cardinals. He did not set the National League on fire with his play, but he held down the second base job and recorded 595 at bats, leading the league. He batted an acceptable .262 and stole 20 bases for the Cards.

The second base position was his to lose in 1907, and sadly, he hit only .227 and lost his job. The Cardinals sold him back to Seattle. He spent the next 10 years in the Northwestern League where he thrived as a good-hitting second baseman. He retired after the 1917 season.

Pug Cavet

Tillar H. Cavet peered into the mirror enough to know that his most prominent facial feature was his "pug nose." He was probably not shocked when the nickname Pug was assigned to him. Whether or not he understood that the name would define him for the rest of his life is unknown.

At first glance, Cavet did not appear to have a substantial baseball career. After a "cup of coffee" with the Detroit Tigers in 1911, the lefthander pitched for the Tigers two more seasons, 1914 and 1915. His won-loss record was an unremarkable 11-9 with the Ty Cobb-led Tigers.

Beneath the surface, however, one can find a prodigious minor league career that spanned 22 seasons and netted him almost 300 victories. Born in 1889, the tall, thin Texan wasted no time in launching his professional career. At the age of 18, he signed with the Dallas Giants in 1908. The Class C Texas League team was near his hometown of McGregor; a comfort to a teenager away from home for the first time. He played very little for Dallas and did not earn a spot on the 1909 Giants. Instead, he found work in Oklahoma pitching for the Muskogee Navigators in the Western Association. He turned in a credible job and his 13-16 record propelled him to a Class B team in Rock Island of the Three I League.

At Rock Island, he won 18 games and earned a shot with the Detroit Tigers. On April 25, 1911, future Hall of Famer Hughie Jennings sent Cavet to the mound to make his major league debut. The four-inning stint was certainly not horrible (two earned runs in a no-decision), but not good enough to prompt Jennings to keep the rookie on the roster for the rest of the season. The disappointment of falling off the Tigers roster was softened by the news that he would become a member of the Class AA Minneapolis Millers.

Over the next two seasons he won a combined 28 games but did not get the call to rejoin the Tigers. In 1913, he exploded with 23 wins for the Southern Association Mobile Sea Gulls. Jennings welcomed him back to Detroit with a spot in the bullpen the 1914 Tigers.

On May 25, he was given a starting assignment against Washington. Cavet and the Tigers were clobbered 10-1. Unlike 1911, Jennings did not give up on Cavet and gave him the ball again. Once again he lost, this time 5-4 to Connie Mack's A's. He failed to win his third, fourth, fifth and sixth start. Finally, on August 2, he defeated the Yankees 4-3. By the season's end, he climbed back to a 7-7 record. He had appeared in 31 games, 14 as a starter, and pitched 151.1 innings; not a bad year for a rookie.

When the 1915 season began, Jennings still did not entrust Cavet with a spot in the starting rotation. Harry Covelski, Hooks Dauss and Jean Dubuc earned the lion's share of the starts. Cavet, Bernie Boland and Bill Steen had to platoon as the fourth starter. The Tigers were in a heated pennant race with the Red Sox and White Sox so Jennings went with the players he trusted. By season's end, Detroit finished in second place to Boston, and Cavet had lost his seat on the bench. His 4-2 record did not save him. He would spend the next 15 years trying to get back to the big leagues.

Following his dismissal from the Tigers, Cavet migrated west to the Pacific Coast League where he joined the San Francisco Seals. After 18 uninspired outings, he returned to the Mobile team in 1916 and experienced the worst season of his life, a 14-23. In 1917, he bounced to the Nashville Volunteers and a newfound success that sustained him over the next decade and a half.

By the time he retired at age 40, his minor league career took him to 16 different teams in 10 different leagues. His longest tenure was at Indianapolis from 1918 to 1923. During that period, he claimed 90 victories with and for the Indians. His final career won-loss record was 291-243 in the minor leagues, good enough for hall of fame consideration if compiled in one league.

While never a proficient batter (.239 lifetime) he set a record in Mobile in 1916 for batting safely in 13 straight games with 20 hits in 42 at bats. [50]

Cavet's major league career was not without its highpoints. His ERA in 1914 was 2.44 with a WHIP of 1.143. He was among the league leaders in games finished, a precursor to the closer position. He outdueled Boston's Dutch Leonard for his only shutout 3-0 on August 28, 1914. He was on the mound for the Tigers the day Nap Lajoie stroked his 3,000th hit. He won that contest 2-1.

He died in San Luis Obispo, California, in 1966 at the age of 76.

Cupid Childs

Clarence Lemuel Childs was born near Baltimore in 1867. Like many Clarences before and after, Childs was willing to grasp onto any nickname that would replace his given name. How the name Cupid landed on Childs is a matter of some controversy.

Joseph McBride suggests that Childs' nickname was a sarcastic opposite referral to his bad temper. [51] James K. Skipper suggests that he may have had angelic facial features.

Bill James opines that Childs was called Cupid from childhood, which only touches on the source and not the derivation. James does note, "He was also called 'The Little Fat Man,' as he had a Kirby Puckett-type body." [52]

The largest "body" of evidence points to his physical build. Whether named by his family early in life, or by teammates later, his body reminded people of the famous chubby little cherub. Another nickname given him was "Dumpling."

The following story reveals more insight into his appearance. In 1888, he sought a tryout with a semi-pro team in Kalamazoo, Michigan. The manager thought it a joke, telling Childs that he was more suited to be a fat man in the sideshow. When Childs persisted, he was told to go practice with the regulars. Upon discovering that no uniform would fit the short wide body, someone provided a pair of divided skirts that were cut off at the knees. When he finally took the field, his "uniform" cracked up the other players to the point that practice halted. Once play resumed, his infield play made everyone's eyes pop. Kalamazoo signed him on the spot "to a good salary" and he became a league sensation. [53]

The Grand Rapids Democrat went on to say, "Childs is the most curiously built man in the baseball business; he is about as wide as he is long…" In further support of the body-type explanation for the nickname, the newspaper concludes, "Besides being one of the greatest ballplayers in the business, he is said to be one of the best humored, not a single instance of his ever losing his temper in a game being on record."

Childs grew up on his father's small farm with 10 siblings. Somehow he found time to learn baseball on the sandlots of Baltimore. He became a skilled middle infielder and by age 16 was playing professional ball in the North Carolina State league for $4 a week plus room and board.

In 1885, he was back in Baltimore working for a can factory and playing in the top amateur league in the area. A year later he was playing in the Virginia State League, then jumped to the Pennsylvania State League that same summer. He bounced around Pennsylvania with Shamokin, Johnstown and Allentown.

The National League came calling in early 1888 and he signed with the Philadelphia Quakers. He played just two games, batting four times with no success. He was released by Philadelphia due to lack of experience. [54]

He ventured west to Michigan and secured a contract with Kalamazoo for the rest of the 1888 season. One year later, he was back in the big leagues with the Syracuse Stars of the American Association. The Stars provided the stage for Childs to showcase his offensive and defensive skills. At age 22 he batted .345, scoring 109 runs and driving in 89.

In 1891, Childs signed with his hometown team, the Baltimore Orioles for $2,300. Cupid's life was becoming as sweet as his name. Unfortunately, the American Association withdrew from the national agreement, the early version of the current players' union contract. Childs did not wait around for the fallout; he jumped to the Cleveland Spiders of the National league, contending that his contract had been voided. The Baltimore club took him to court for breach of contract but lost.

Offensively, his 1891 season was unremarkable, but he was carving a reputation as one of baseball's best second baseman. The Spiders, managed by Robert Leadley, were a mediocre team living in the middle of the pack. At the midpoint in the season, Patsy Tebeau was named player/manager and the team began to take on a new shape.

Richard Scheinin in his book *Field of Screams* contends that Tebeau was cheated out of his rightful place in baseball history. Tebeau was a brawler and a cutthroat who would lead his team into whatever lowdown tactics were needed to win a baseball game. Unfortunately for Tebeau, John McGraw was performing the same act with the Baltimore Orioles and later the New York Giants. McGraw led his team to National League pennants while Tebeau could not get higher than second place. McGraw's stature grew over the next few decades while Tebeau retired to his saloon in St. Louis. McGraw fought his way into the Hall of Fame. Tebeau took his own life at the age of 53. [55]

Childs flourished under Tebeau's violent regime. In 1892, he led the league with 136 runs scored and an on base percentage of .443. His Cleveland tenure lasted from 1891 until 1898, batting over .300 during five of his eight seasons.

In 1899 he was sold to the St. Louis Perfectos (who changed their name to the Cardinals in 1900). St. Louis decided that the club did not need Childs. He moved on to the Chicago Orphans where he played two more decent but not spectacular campaigns. The 1901 season was his last. He was out of the league at age 34.

Despite the name "Cupid" he quickly adapted to the rough-play and carousing of Tebeau's Spiders. Luke Salisbury describes an incident in a Cleveland saloon whereby Childs poured out a beer in a manner that allowed it run down the fingers and arms of an amply endowed womanfriend of Patsy Tebeau. Teammate Jimmy McAleer "followed the rivulet with his tongue." The stream of beer ended before reaching "the ruffled portion of her anatomy where nature had been so generous." [56]

Further evidence that Childs did not earn his nickname with cherubic deeds: he was part of a "cheating" scandal uncovered in 1888. While coaching third base for the Phillies, Childs stood with his foot in a puddle of water when he could have easily moved to a drier spot. Arlie Latham, often referred to as "the freshest man on earth," noticed this odd circumstance and told teammate Tommy Corcoran. After Philly hitters ripped a couple of hard hit balls, Lathan accused Childs of stealing signs. Childs left the muddied spot and resumed his normal habit of hopping up and down along the base line, making Latham even more suspicious.

Between innings Tommy Corcoran ran out to the wet spot and dug up a wooden block with a buzzer attached. He began pulling until a wire was discovered lying just under the turf. As Corcoran continued pulling, the wire led hundreds of feet to the clubhouse porch where a man later identified as Morgan Murphy sat with binoculars on his lap. Presented with the evidence, Murphy stood up and marched to a spot on the Philadelphia bench. Thus was it explained why the Phillies had become such a terror batting in their home park. [57]

A natural athlete, he could throw equally well with both arms. He was described as "on base machine." During the 1893-1894 seasons he drew 227 walks and struck out a ridiculously low 23 times. Yet, Childs has been overlooked for the Hall of Fame. Jimmy Keenan of SABR makes the case for Childs: "Child's lifetime major league on-base percentage of .417 is higher than every second baseman in the Hall of Fame except Rogers Hornsby and Eddie Collins. His .306 lifetime batting average is higher than nine of the second basemen who have already been inducted into the Hall. It seems that for now, Cupid's arrow has missed its mark in Cooperstown." [58]

Childs died at the very young age of 45 in Baltimore. Loudon Park Cemetery where he was interred lists him as Clarence Algernon "Cupid" Childs. Other references list his middle name as Algernon, as well. He may have lived as Lemuel, but he apparently died as Algernon. Cupid was a tricky little cherub.

Above: left – Tiny Bonham   right – Cupid Childs
Below: left – Bitsy Mott   right – Jumbo Elliot

Chapter Two – Personality Traits: "You're Weird But You're One of Us"

Cuckoo Christensen

In a more modern vernacular, Walter Neils Christensen was a character, a class clown. Many jokers and pranksters have enlivened the dugout and the team bus with their antics, but the man called Cuckoo Christy was special. When the average player crosses the white lines, the high jinks end and serious baseball takes over. With Christensen, the comedy act rarely ended. The fans loved the sideshow that Christensen provided. In one stunt, he would take his outfield position with a newspaper and casually appear to peruse the day's news. Carefully placed holes in the prop allowed him to keep an eye on the action at the plate. [1]

His signature act was a perfectly timed somersault while a high fly ball was beginning its descent. The acrobatic feat would position him under the ball and the catch would be made. Yes, the trick did backfire on him once in a while. In 1929, he was playing with the Mission Reds in the PCL. The Reds held a one-run lead in the ninth inning with two runners on base. In a stunningly ill-timed decision, he launched into his trademark flip and proceeded to drop the ball. After the shock of watching the tying and winning runs cross the plate, Manager Red Killefer took flight and chased his Cuckoo all the way past centerfield and into the locker room.

While playing with the minor league Milwaukee Brewers during the 1930's, the House of David team came to town to oppose the Milwaukee Red Sox of the State League. Despite the appearance of long-retired Pete Alexander with the House of David team, Christensen stole the show without ever entering the playing field. Alexander refused to grow the long beard or hair dictated by the Benton Harbor (Michigan) cult. Christensen coached third base for the MilSox wearing long fake whiskers. [2]

Christensen's vaudevillian performances were not confined to the baseball park. In 1931, he appeared on the stage of the Tosa Theater in Milwaukee where he impersonated Al Jolson in blackface. He sang Jolson's trademark song "Mammy" to help raise funds for the Wauwatosa Community Relief Fund. [3]

Christensen acquired a family-based nickname before his crazy persona endowed him with a new moniker. Playing in St. Paul, Minnesota, he was known as Seacap because his mother often sent him to grade school in a sailor suit. [4] His physique might have also qualified him to be a Skinny, Stubby or Shorty. He stood only 5' 6" and pushed the dial on the scale barely past 150 pounds.

Christensen spent four years playing for the St. Paul Saints where he batted .306 and earned a shot with the Cincinnati Reds in 1926. His rookie year exploded like a bottle rocket. He played in 93 games and hit .350 for the year. He led his league in OBP with .426. His teammate, Bubbles Hargrave, edged him out for the batting title. A note for trivia lovers: Hargrave was the first catcher to win a batting title.

Like all bottle rockets, Christensen's career quickly plummeted. In 1927, he hit just .254 and the Cuckoo was forced to fly out of the nest. From then on, all of his somersaults would land in minor league outfields. The Reds' quick decision to drop Christensen may have been fueled by a bad decision the front office made. After their rookie's sizzling freshman year, they traded outfielder and future Hall of Famer Edd Roush to the Giants for High Pockets Kelly.

His hitting stroke returned in the minors during the final eight years of his playing career. He left baseball with a .309 minor league batting average to go along with his .315 major league record.

Christensen spent his remaining active years as an umpire at the college and semi-pro level, occasionally appearing in the PCL as a substitute. He died in Menlo Park, California, in 1984 at the age of 85.

Bug Holliday

When America's favorite "cwazy wabbit" debuted in 1940, he was named Bugs Bunny. The character was new, but the nickname was not. The first two decades of the twentieth century produced a slew of Bugs. The name was derived from the word "buggy" meaning crazy, insane or peculiar. James Wear Holliday was the doyen of the buggy club. He was born in 1867 in St. Louis and reached the majors in 1885, more than 50 years ahead of Bugs Bunny.

James K. Skipper attributes the name to his small size, but a newspaper article announcing his death revealed a different source. The Pittsburgh

Press reported, "He got the nickname of 'Bug' through his funny antics in the coaches box, on the bases and in the field, always trumping up stunts to amuse the fans. Bug was one of the greatest diamond clowns the game ever saw." [5]

Coming to prominence shortly after the death of the infamous Doc Holiday, gambler and gunman of western fame, it is surprising that no one saddled him with the nickname Doc.

Holliday's debut with the National League's Chicago White Stockings was quite crazy and peculiar, as well. The White Stockings, who would later become the Cubs, were locked in a duel with the St. Louis Brown Stockings of the American Association. This showdown between the two leagues was a precursor to the modern World Series. The White Stockings found themselves one outfielder short for the fourth game of the match.

Young Bug Holliday was plucked from the obscurity of a St. Louis sand lot and thrust into the spotlight. The 18-year-old found himself in the company of baseball icons such as Cap Anson, King Kelly and Billy Sunday. He failed to hit safely in four trips to the plate. He would never get another shot at post-season play. He was, however, the first player to ever make his debut in a post-season game. The feat was not duplicated until Mark Kiger appeared as a defensive replacement in the 2006 American League Championship for the Oakland Athletics. Though Kiger saw action in two games. Unlike Holliday, he never managed to make a plate appearance.

Holliday's one-game stint with the White Stockings did not lead to a contract with the Chicago club, or even their St. Louis rivals. He did receive an offer to play for the St. Joseph Reds in the Western League. His launching pad to the big leagues was Des Moines, Iowa. While playing for the Des Moines Prohibitionists, he earned a shot at the American Association Cincinnati Red Stockings in 1889. He soon established himself as one of the team's star players, batting .321 and leading the league with 19 home runs.

One year later the American Association folded and the Cincinnati club joined the National League as the Cincinnati Reds. Holliday played out his career in Cincinnati retiring in 1898 with a lifetime .312 batting average.

A sharp drop in production in 1895 coincides with a near-death experience following as ruptured appendix in 1895. [6] He was unable to play a regular role with the Reds afterward. Had he continued on the same pathway as his first six years, he may today be remembered as one of the premier stars of the 19th century.

Holliday was involved in a controversial no-hitter on September 18, 1897. The Bug had apparently ruined Cy Young's bid for a no-hitter by stroking two ground-ball singles during the game. In the eighth inning both hits were changed to errors by the third baseman, Bobby Wallace. Cy Young was credited with a no-hitter. [7]

Quoting the Pittsburgh Press, "Bug played ball in Cincinnati for 10 years without losing his popularity with the fans, who would rather see him walk to the plate in a pinch or chase a fly than any other many stars who have played with the Red Stockings." [8]

After baseball, he remained in Cincinnati and covered horse racing for a local newspaper, also serving as starter at the Latonia Race Track across the border in Kentucky. Holliday died in 1910 shortly after his 43rd birthday from gangrene of the foot and leg. [9]

He was the only player named Holliday until Matt Holliday joined the Colorado Rockies in 2004.

Bugs Raymond

Arthur Lawrence Raymond was not the first or last Bugs to enter the game, but he may have most deserved the name. Raymond was an unabashed alcoholic, claiming he would drink anything that flowed from a bottle. The most prevalent explanation for his name was his behavior when drinking. Despite the fact that he won over 70% of his decisions in the minors, he was released from most of the clubs who were tempted to tame him. Two other facets of his personality acerbated his addiction to alcohol; he was stubborn and possessed a quick temper. If he wanted to stay out late and bust curfew, he was going to do just that. [10]

He won 19 games with the Waterloo Microbes in 1904 and earned a chance to play with the Detroit Tigers toward the last few weeks of the season. In five games, including two starts, he acquitted himself well with a 3.07 ERA and one complete game (a losing effort).

The Tigers evidently studied the risk-reward equation and decided that the risk outweighed the reward. He was back in the minor leagues in 1905. The Class A Atlanta Crackers gave him a contract but released him after a 10-6 season due to his drinking. Broke and unemployed, he accepted a position as a bartender in Atlanta while he worked on a new pitch, a spitball. [11]

He talked his way into a job with the Savannah Indians in the Sally League by boasting that he could lead them into a championship if they would only give him a chance. He won 18 games and Savannah won the pennant. Savannah showed their appreciation by offering him a chance to seek employment elsewhere.

Elsewhere turned out to be Jackson, Mississippi, for a short duration, then back to the Sally League where the Charleston Sea Gulls took a chance on him. Raymond fully exploited this opportunity by posting a 35-11 record in just a partial season. The St. Louis Cardinals came calling and Raymond found himself in a big league dugout once again for the conclusion of his magical 1907 season. He posted a 1.67 ERA for the last place Cardinals in the month of September. At last, a team actually wanted him to stay and begin another campaign with them. He would pitch for the 1908 Cardinals.

Once again, he pitched well for the dismal '08 Cardinals but suffered in the loss column. He led the National League in losses with a 15-25 record. The Cardinal front office was ambivalent about their buggy pitcher. Bigger paychecks and a bigger city brought out the personal demons. He was uncontrollable off the field and sometimes brilliant on the field. And the St. Louis fans loved him for his uninhibited in-game behavior. Whenever he would manage a base hit, he would arrive at the destination and circle the base in a celebratory jig. [12]

In December of 1908, Raymond was a principal in a blockbuster three-team trade. The Cardinals sent Raymond and Red Murray to the New York Giants for Roger Bresnahan, who was to become the St. Louis manager. The Cincinnati Reds sent catcher Admiral Schlei to the Giants and received Ed Karger and Art Fromme in return. [13]

Giants' manager John McGraw felt he had the right stuff to control Raymond. McGraw would fine him over and over again until he had no money to buy booze. What McGraw failed to understand, was that a dedicated alcoholic could always find a way to wet his whistle. One day Raymond disappeared after McGraw suspended him and was found the following morning behind a New York tavern dispensing drinks in his Giants uniform. McGraw and Raymond once engaged each other in fisticuffs in a railroad sleeping car. [14]

McGraw extracted one good season from Raymond before his lifestyle eroded his abilities. In his first season in New York he won 18 games while compiling a 2.47 ERA. The following year was arguably his worst at any level. His ERA ballooned to 3.81 as he lost 11 games against only four victories. In 1911, McGraw's Giants won the National League pennant before losing to Connie Mack's A's. Raymond was no longer part of the starting rotation. McGraw had Christy Mathewson, Rube Marquard, Hooks Wiltse and Red Ames taking the mound on a regular basis. Raymond was a spot starter and reliever. McGraw no longer had to tolerate Raymond's aberrant behavior. He was released in June and missed his only opportunity to appear in a World Series.

By 1912, he was living in Chicago. His potential had been greatly dissipated by alcohol, but he still could have helped a big league team, when sober. The rest of the league measured McGraw's lack of success in harnessing Raymond's talent, and collectively chose not to take on the challenge. He played briefly on a local team before succumbing completely to the lure of the bottle.

On September 7, 1912, Raymond was found dead in a Chicago hotel room. A coroner's inquest concluded that death was due to heart disease aggravated by excessive heat. Authorities were persuaded to investigate the death and they learned that Raymond had a fractured skull and succumbed to a fatal cerebral hemorrhage. A Chicagoan named Frank Cigrans came forward and admitted that he was involved in a fight with Raymond at a ball game a few days before his death. Cigrans confessed that he had beaten Raymond about the head. Shortly after that revelation, more witnesses stepped up to the plate and reported that Raymond was involved in a brawl with several men who smashed him in the head with a baseball bat. When McGraw learned of his former player's death, his comment was decidedly uncharitable. Mugsy responded, "that man took seven years off my life." [15]

If talent could be dispensed to anyone who desired it, the line of applicants would be almost endless. Raymond had that talent in abundance but valued it far less than a shot of whiskey or a mug of beer. Taking the field in a perpetual hangover, he still had enough ability to consistently perform at the big league level. By age 30, most of his peers were reaching the apex of their careers. At the age of 30, Bugs lay dead in a Chicago hotel with a fractured skull.

Other Twentieth Century Bugs

Jacob Reisigl was the next member to join the club, apparently in a secret ceremony. Skipper's search for the origin of Bugs' nickname led him to Reisigl's family. Their response can be paraphrased as, "Bugs who? Everybody called him Jack."

Reisigl, a right-handed pitcher, spent one year in the big leagues with the 1911 Cleveland Naps. His rookie year was disappointing, resulting in 13 innings and an 0-1 record with a 6.23 ERA. His eight seasons in the minors proved to be more rewarding as he fashioned two 20-win years and compiled a 102-93 record, mostly in the Connecticut State League and the PCL.

Reisigl died in 1957 in his native state of Missouri.

The last of the Bugs to crawl out of the woodwork was Joseph Harley Bennett. Bennett tried to deny his "bugginess" by using his given name during his rookie year with the St. Louis Browns in 1918. He had a brief stay with the Browns and dropped back into the minors until the White Sox gave him a look-see in 1921. The Sox looked and they saw that Bennett was not what they needed. He spent the last part of the 1921 season with St. Louis and ended his career without experiencing the joy of winning a game. His major league record was 0-5.

Crazy Schmit

Frederick M. Schmit was called Germany by some teammates. It was not uncommon for a player with a German name to end up with the nickname Heinie, Fritz, Dutch or Germany. Other teammates went right to the core of his personality and named him Crazy. Even the look on his face resembled a person with mayhem on his mind. When the dust cleared, he became known officially as Crazy Schmit even though he appeared to be sensitive to the nickname. In a letter to the Sporting News in 1900, he signed his name Frederick Schmit after this request, "I hope you will not add any nicknames to my name." [16]

Born in Chicago in 1866, Schmit does not show up on the rosters of professional baseball until the age of 24. There were doubtless many industrial and regional teams around the area where he could have sharpened his skills as a pitcher and outfielder.

In 1890, he signed with the Pittsburgh Alleghenys as a pitcher. His 1-10 won-loss record and 5.83 ERA were not good enough to secure a spot on the 1891 roster, despite the fact that Pittsburgh ranked with the worst teams in baseball history with only 23 wins against 113 losses.

In 1892, he returned to the major leagues with the National League Baltimore Orioles, another dreadful team. He pitched in seven games and played in the outfield one time. His record of 1-4 was not impressive, but his ERA was 3.24 and earned a spot on the 1893 Oriole roster. He pitched poorly to begin the 1893 season and was sold to the New York Giants. The Giants released him after four games and a 7.40 ERA.

Schmit played semi-professional and minor league ball for the next five years. His career as a major leaguer appeared to be over. In 1899, another horrific team needed his assistance. The Cleveland Spiders lost player/manager Patsy Tebeau and others to the newly formed Players League. To add insult to injury, Tebeau moved only across town to the Cleveland Infants. The reconstituted Spiders spun their wheels on the way to a 20-134 slate and finished in twelfth and last place. Schmit fully participated in the debacle with a 2-17 season.

Ironically, Schmit was not bowed by his performance. He described his season like this: "I pitched some 14 exceptional good games for Cleveland last summer. I am like a gnarled oak and am getting better every year." [17] Compared to his pitching partners, 2-17 probably did not look terribly bad to him. Jim Hughey was 4-30, Charley Knepper 4-22, Frank Bates 1-18 and Henry Collflower 1-11. Cleveland released Schmit at the end of the season.

He was unable to secure a steady job in 1901, but contacted John McGraw and signed on with the new American league Orioles for 1902. McGraw jettisoned him in June despite a 1.99 ERA. His big league career was over, and he logged one of the worst lifetime winning percentages of all time, .163 (7-36). Schmit was renowned for his bad memory. He was a serious student of the game, charting tendencies of the league's hitters. The only problem was that he could not recall his notes when he actually took the mound and faced a particular batter. His solution was a small notebook that he would secrete in his back pocket. One story reports that he had to face Cap

Anson in a game during the 1894 season. Pulling out his cheat-sheet, he reviewed the notes and said out loud, "Base on balls." True to his research, he walked Anson and dealt with the next batter. [18]

Schmit may be responsible for one of baseball's most enduring changes to the physical layout of the field. In 1900, the formerly square (positioned like a diamond) home base was changed to a five-sided shape, with the point of the 45-degree angle facing the catcher. Schmit claimed that it was he who suggested the new configuration to James Hart, chairman of the Rules committee, in 1888.

The 1900 Spalding Guide explained the reason for the change, "The change is undoubtedly an advantage alike to the pitcher and umpire, as it enables the pitcher to see the width of the base he has to throw the ball over better than before, and the umpire can judge balls and strikes with less difficulty." [19]

Schmit died in 1940 in his hometown of Chicago. No one has ever provided proof that he was, or was not, responsible for the pentagon with two parallel sides that has remained home plate to this day.

Putsy Caballero

Ralph Joseph Caballero was too young to fully grasp the significance of the nickname his grammar school classmates gave him as a boy. Derived from the Yiddish word putz, the least offensive definition describes a person who behaves in an idle manner; to putter around. The most common connotation depicts a fool or an idiot. Finally, the word is also a vulgar synonym for penis.

Caballero, a Cajun from New Orleans, realized early that everyone in his circle would get a handle. "Everybody down here has a nickname. Like I have a brother named Monroe and they call him Money. I've got a brother named Raymond and they call him Rainbow, you know? It's something that sticks with you. Putsy, that's what they call me. Only two people in New Orleans know my first name is Ralph." [20]

Hand Caballero a baseball or photo and ask him to sign, and you may get a bonus inscription: "16 years old 1944 – Youngest Major League 3B ever." Therein lies his claim to fame. In June of 1944, Caballero finished high school and three months later found himself kicking the infield dirt in New York's Polo Grounds. The war-depleted Phillies had signed the teenager on September 9th and five days later sent him onto the field in the midst of a 12-1 blowout at the hands of the Giants. He appeared in three more games and failed to reach first base.

The following year he was sent to Utica to play for the Blue Sox in the Eastern League. Blue Sox manager Eddie Sawyer oversaw a roster of future major leaguers, several of whom he would later manage in Philadelphia, including Richie Ashburn and Granny Hamner. Caballero's successful first year earned him a late season call-up to the Phillies where he was used primarily as a defensive replacement. In his solitary plate appearance, he grounded out but drove in his first run. He labored in the Phillies minor league system during the next two years. In 1947, he took advantage of another cameo appearance in Philadelphia by stroking his first big league hit. After three short visits to the major leagues, he was batting .083 but was finally managed to get "off the schneid."

In 1948 he made it to Philadelphia as the regular third baseman, one of the Whiz Kids, as the Phils were soon nicknamed. By 1949, Willie "Puddin' Head" Jones had claimed third base and Putsy became a valuable utility player, filling in at all infield positions except first base. He remained with the Phillies through 1952. During the Whiz Kid's pennant year in 1950, he saw action in three World Series games against the Yankees but batted only once, failing to get a hit.

After failing to make the Phillies roster in 1953, he played three more years in their farm system before hanging up the cleats and returning to his native Louisiana. He got into the pest control business and eventually owned his own company in Metairie.

During his playing days, Caballero collected memorabilia and autographs from his contemporaries and past stars including Babe Ruth. In retirement, he not only had tangible evidence of his major league career, he had thousands of dollars of collectible items in his Lake View, Louisiana home. Then came August 29, 2005. When Katrina had finished with the Gulf Coast, Caballero had almost nothing but his memories. His son was the first to enter the flooded home and recovered only a photo of the Whiz Kids and his father's Phillies uniform. The former Phillie relied on aid from the Red Cross and food stamps to survive. [21]

With the support of his seven children Caballero is putting his life back together and still possesses a ready smile and instant recall of his playing days.

Creepy Crespi

Most people would wonder why Frank Angelo Joseph Crespi tolerated the name Creepy Crespi. One source stated that Crespi looked like a Hollywood gangster. But Crespi told James Skipper that the name had been applied to him because of the low-to-the-ground style he used defensively as a second baseman. He seemed to be "creeping up" on the ground balls while running full speed. The name seemed like an apt description and Crespi must have considered it a fair deal.

He was born in St. Louis in 1918. Fresh out of high school, Crespi signed with Shelby in the North Carolina State League. Defensively, he was still green, but his bat earned him a promotion to Springfield in the Western Association. From 1938 through 1940 he bounced back and forth from the minors to the St. Louis Cardinals where he only dipped his beak into the good life of the major leagues. He saw action in only 25 games during the 1938–1940 seasons.

In November of 1940, the Cardinals sold regular second baseman Joe Orengo to the Giants. Crespi started the 1941 season at second base and finished the season with 145 games under his belt. The Cardinals were on the rise in the National League under manager Billy Southworth, climbing to second place. In addition to Marty Marion, Johnny Mize, Enos Slaughter and Terry Moore, they had a rookie on the bench named Stan Musial. Musial only got to the plate 49 times, but he hit .429.

One year later, the Cardinals' talent led them to the pennant and a World Series victory over the New York Yankees. Crespi did not have a stellar year at the plate, batting .243, but committed just 16 errors during the season. His double play partner, Marty Marion, called him "by far the best second baseman I ever teamed up with." [22]

In 1943, the wartime draft finally called his name. As sole support of his mother, Crespi had a way out of the service. He opted not to file for an exemption saying, "I don't think I'm too good to fight for the things I've always enjoyed."

Crespi never reached the battlefield with the Army, but he still managed to get injured. First, he broke his leg turning a double play in an Army base game. After the leg healed he was assigned to training with tanks and was involved in a tank accident and broke his leg again.

While still in the hospital, he engaged another patient in a wheelchair race and re-broke the leg after crashing into a wall. One last bit of bad luck visited him when a nurse over applied boric acid to his leg resulting in serious burns and permanent limp. [22a] Crespi would never creep along a big league infield again.

Baseball not only lost a defensive talent, but also a swift and courageous base runner as well. During winter of 1939, Crespi became part of Cuban baseball mythology. He was playing for Habana in the Cuban League. During a game at spacious La Tropical Field, he was on second base when Bobby "El Tarzan" Estalella hit a ball 475 feet that was caught at the wall. Crespi tagged and scored from second. [23] Cuban legend, of course, glorifies Estalella for the long ball, but Crespi's speed and daring should probably count for 50% of the credit, if not more.

With the advent of the player pension plan, Crespi tried to creep back into the league as a coach and complete the necessary years of service to qualify for a retirement check. The man who was willing to fight for his country could find no takers. He signed on with McDonnell-Douglas and worked as a budget analyst for the giant aerospace corporation. During the early 1970s, he retired and soon discovered that a paperwork glitch had occurred 30 years back. According to major league records, Creepy Crespi had never retired from baseball; he was just on the disabled list. The pension he had been unable to secure had grown into a handsome payout.

Crespi crept out of this world in 1990 after suffering a heart attack near St. Louis, his birthplace.

Boob Fowler

Joseph Chester Fowler may be the prime candidate for poster boy of the Low Self-Esteem Club. A *boob* is defined as a stupid or foolish person. Going through life as Boob could signify a deeply held feeling of unworthiness.

Many references refer to him as Boob "Gink" Fowler. Did his teammates feel that the name Boob Fowler was not sufficiently strange or insulting? The meaning of the word gink is a person regarded as foolish or odd. Usage examples show *gink* to be comparable to the word *jerk*. Was poor Joseph Fowler so weird that he needed a redundant set of pejorative nicknames?

An obscure publication refers to a "pugilist" named Gink Fowler who defeated a foe named McGirk in a 1920 boxing match in Pittsburgh. This would not be the first example of a baseball player assigned a nickname because of some resemblance or connection to another person known to that particular social group. [24]

Peeking into the Fowler family genealogy, one finds a list of prominent Fowlers born after 1900. Henry Fowler was Secretary of the Treasury. William Fowler was an astrophysicist. Thomas Fowler was a World War II hero. The list is a long and impressive one except for a single strange fact; Boob Fowler's name sits atop the list. [25] The Fowler clan is most proud of their family Boob.

One could turn the argument on its head and theorize that Boob Fowler had enough selfconfidence and self-esteem that he could wear the name as a badge.

Another answer might be that the name was given as a tribute to a popular Rube Goldberg comic strip called Boob McNutt. Fowler would have been a young man when the McNutt strip reached it pinnacle in the early 1920s. Nicknames derived from the comics were not unusual during the first half of the twentieth century. McNutt is described as a "clumsy, buffoonish fellow who was quite friendly and attempted to be helpful in his incompetent way." [26] To heighten the drama and comedy, Goldberg constantly assigned very important tasks to McNutt, which he invariably botched in a devastating manner. To be associated with a Rube Goldberg character would not be a horrible fate.

Fowler was born in Waco, Texas, in 1900. He attended Texas Christian University in 1920 and soon became the sixth TCU player to reach the big leagues. Pete Donohue, who preceded Fowler by two years, eventually claimed 134 wins primarily pitching for the Reds. When the Reds were scouting Donohue at TCU, they stumbled upon Chester Fowler playing shortstop. [27]

After just one year with Newark in the International League, Fowler made the 1923 Cincinnati roster as a backup shortstop. His sophomore year would be his most productive as he played in 59 games and batted .333.

During the 1925 season he split his time between Cincinnati and the Minneapolis Millers in the American Association. He only saw action in six games for the Reds. Even though he stroked two hits in five at bats, Cincinnati cut him loose. He spent 1926 back in Minneapolis before the Boston Red Sox gave him a shot to back up Fred Haney at third base. After only two games, Red Sox manager Lee Fohl had seen enough. Fowler produced more errors than hits and his major league career had come to an end. His final batting average was .326.

Fowler continued to play in the minor leagues through 1933. By age 32 he had sunk down to the Class C Henderson Oilers in the Dixie League.

Fowler died in 1988 in Dallas, Texas, at the age of 87. He may have been a Boob, but he lived and died as a .300 hitter.

Bobo Newsom

Lewis Norman Newsom, born in Hartsville, South Carolina, in 1907, was one of the true characters in baseball history. The word "bobo" is Spanish for "fool." Newsom, however, was not so-named because of his flakey demeanor. In fact, he gave himself the name Bobo. The fact that the name corresponded to the Spanish meaning was a coincidence, but not all together off base. He was frequently called "the Dizzy Dean of the American League." [28]

Newsom was nicknamed Buck by his family but could not pronounce the word. It came out of his mouth sounding like "Bo." He had a habit of speaking about himself in the third person, so he initially called himself Bo, and then soon expanded it to Bobo. Like Babe Ruth, Newsom had trouble remembering his teammates' names, especially since he bounced from team to team more than anyone of his era. To make his life easier, he began to call everyone Bobo.

Newsom was a very accomplished right-handed pitcher, but labored for many second rate teams. He was a 20-game winner for the St. Louis Browns in 1938. The following May he was 3-1 when he was traded to the Detroit Tigers. He added 17 more wins to secure his second consecutive 20-game season. On the flip side of the coin, he suffered through three seasons in which he lost 20 games. When his 20-year career came to an end, he had accumulated 211 wins, but lost 222 times. Only two pitchers in baseball history can claim 200 wins or more and still sport a losing record. Newsom and Jack Powell (245-254 from 1897 through 1912) share that distinction.

To say that he played for eight different major leagues teams does not paint a detailed picture of his nomadic ways. He played for the Washington Senators five separate times, the St. Louis Browns three times, and A's and Dodgers twice each. Newsom spent seven years in which he changed teams during the season. His braggadocio and flakiness just wore on owners and managers. Apparently, Senators' owner Clark Griffith brought him back multiple times because Newsom was his favorite bridge partner.

Newsom's bragging was most often backed up by his performance. At the start of the 1938 season, Browns' owner Don Barnes offered to buy Newsom a new suit if he won on opening day. After nailing down the win, he was handed a wad of money by Barnes and told to go buy a suit. Newsom returned the money and said, "Bobo bought the suit before the game. The bill for it is on your desk." [29]

While playing for the Red Sox, Newsom moved some rabbits into his hotel room for companionship. He absentmindedly left them alone during a road trip. They ate their way through the hotel furnishings and manager Joe Cronin was stuck with a bill for the damage. Cronin shipped him off to the Browns shortly thereafter.

Newsom was a very tough competitor. He had to be. He was accident prone and injured many times, frequently by line drives. He was named the Opening Day pitcher for the Senators in 1936. President Franklin Roosevelt was in attendance. An errant throw from the Washington third baseman struck Newsom in the face. As he lay on the ground he emphatically refused suggestions that he leave the game. "Listen, he said, "when the President of the United States comes to see ol' Bobo pitch, ol' Bobo ain't gonna let him down."

Ol' Bobo proceeded to complete his four-hit shutout, after which he was treated for a broken jaw. Manager Bucky Harris reported that Newsom's injury caused him to only talk half as much as normal, which was twice as much as anybody wanted to hear. [30]

Bobo Osborne

Larry Sidney Osborne has the distinction of being one of the latter-day players to acquire a nickname that stayed with him throughout his career. While playing in the minor leagues, Osborne had the good fortune to be mentored by his manager, Charlie Metro. A few of the veteran players on the team named him "Charlie's little bobo." [31] The name stuck. Perhaps Osborne was unaware of the negative connotation of the word bobo. Another factor in his decision to maintain the name Bobo, was the fact that he grew up in the household where a parent had been given an unflattering nickname.

Osborne was born in Chattahoochee, Georgia, in 1935. The Osbornes were a baseball family. His father, Earnest "Tiny" Osborne (see Chapter 1), spent four years in the National League pitching for the Cubs and Dodgers in the early 1920s. Three of his brothers played professionally but never ascended to the major leagues. [32]

Osborne, joined the Detroit Tigers in 1957 as a first baseman and part-time outfielder. He played sparingly in his first two seasons. In 1959, he played in 86 games but could not reach the Mendoza line. Detroit sent him to the minors to learn a new position, third base. He returned to the Tigers for the 1961 and 1962 seasons. In 1963, Detroit traded him to the Washington Senators for Wayne Comer. Although he became a regular with the Senators, appearing in 125 games in 1963, Washington demoted him to the Toronto Maple Leafs in the International League, managed by Sparky Anderson. He never climbed back to the big leagues.

Bobo Osborne spent the rest of his life in baseball, reaching the position of senior scouting consultant with the San Francisco Giants, which he held until his death at the age of 75 in Woodstock, Georgia. His obituary referred to him as Bobo, not Larry.

Daff Gammons

John Ashley Gammons reportedly earned his nickname from his eccentric behavior off the field. [33] The old English word *daff* identified a person as a fool. If Daff Gammons was a flake, he was a flake with Ivy League credentials and a sterling resume during and after college. He attended not one, but two Ivy League schools, Brown and Harvard.

At Brown he played both football and baseball. On the baseball field, he held down an outfield position during Brown's national championship season of 1896. On the gridiron he carried the football for three years as a starting halfback. After graduation, he played professional football for four years, in the Pittsburgh area. In his final year as a football player, he helped launch the Pittsburgh Stars in the

57

nascent NFL. One of his teammates was another baseballer named Christy Mathewson.

In 1901, he signed with the Boston Beaneaters in the National League. After one desultory season on the diamond, he quit to begin his career as an insurance agent.

He returned to Brown to coach the football team in 1902 and again in 1908 through 1909. From 1902 to 1920, when he was not holding down the head-coaching job, he was an assistant coach.

Gammons married in 1910 at the age of 34 in Andover, Maine. His marriage license stated his occupation as an insurance agent. [34]

In 1915, he purchased the Providence team in the International League from Red Sox owner John Lannin. He later accepted a position with the Bureau of Mines in Washington, after the outbreak of World War I.

Gammons died in 1963 at the age of 87. He is buried in New Bedford, Massachusetts, near his birthplace.

Showboat Fisher

George Aloys Fisher would not have appreciated being called a "hot dog." In fact, no player of record ever was given that as a nickname. A show-off is frequently called a hotdog or hotdogger, a negative term implying that the team's best interests have been subjugated to the individual's need for attention. Showboat, on the other hand, suited George Fisher just fine. The definition of showboat, as it applies to a person, is virtually the same as the meaning of hotdog. The term came from the paddle-wheel steamers that served as floating theaters in the mid-to-late 19th century. [35]

Fisher spent five years in the minors where he reportedly picked up the reputation as a show-off. This fact seems somewhat odd for a player born (1899) and raised in Iowa. The stereotypical Iowan is reserved and quiet. An additional factor in his new moniker may have been the popularity of the Broadway musical "Showboat" ay that time. [36]

His usual position on the field was the outfield, but in 1920 he took the mound 17 times for the two minor league teams. Teammates who lost opportunities to get in the game might have claimed a good case for calling him a show-off, particularly because he won more games than he lost with a 6-3 record. He also batted .370 that year.

Fisher climbed the minor league ladder and debuted with the Washington Senators in 1923. With Goose Goslin, Nemo Leibold and Sam Rice all hitting .300 plus, Fisher had few opportunities to showboat in the Senators outfield. He spent most of that season with New Haven in the Eastern League, where he continued to shine at the plate.

Ditto for 1924, he produced a great year with Minneapolis and earned a 15 game call-up to the Senators where he batted only .220. The Senators were not impressed and Fisher sunk back into the minors where he sparkled for five years but could not claw his way back to the major leagues.

Finally, in 1929, the St. Louis Cardinals noticed his 36 home runs and .336 batting average with the Buffalo Bisons and signed him for the upcoming 1930 season.

On opening day against the Cubs, Fisher, still a rookie, stroked four hits. The next day he duplicated that feat and drove in four runs.

Fisher's first full season with the Cardinals had all the earmarks of a budding big league career. He ambled to the plate 286 times and batted .374 with 61 RBIs with an astounding OPS of 1.019. Only Shoeless Joe Jackson batted higher as a rookie (with a minimum of 150 at bats). [37]

He once hit safely 10 consecutive at bats. [38] His pennant-winning Cardinals faced the Philadelphia Athletics in the World Series. Fisher batted twice and stroked a double in a losing cause.

When all of his 1930 accomplishments were evaluated, Fisher was rewarded with a demotion to the Rochester Red Wings for the 1931 season. Despite another stellar year, the Cardinals kept him on the farm thereby paraphrasing an old saying, "Nobody likes a Showboat."

A closer look at the 1930 season reveals that Fisher jumped out to an average well over .400 in the early part of the season. With two other hot rookies, George Watkins and Gus Mancuso, pushing for playing time, Fisher became relegated to pinch-hitting duties. [39]

On June 30, 1932, the Browns obtained him from the Cardinals in a trade and put him back in the outfield at Sportsman's Park, playing in a different uniform. By his time his skills had abandoned him and he struggled in vain to reach the .200 mark. After only 18 games for the Browns, his major league career ended. He had been released.

Despite the nightmare that was 1932, his lifetime major league batting average of .335 put him into baseball's high-rent district. He lived a long time in that neighborhood, not passing away until 1994 at the age of 95.

Buttercup Dickerson

Lewis Pessano Dickerson was born in Tyaskin, Maryland, before the outbreak of the War Between the States. Making his debut in 1878 with the Cincinnati Reds, he is credited as the first Italian-American baseball player. Had his surname been more ethnic in nature, his nickname might not have been so...floral. Playing well before the dawn of political correctness, his nickname might have been Dago or Wop. Standing just 5' 6" tall and weighing 140 pounds, he could have also been dubbed Skinny or Skeeter.

Buttercup at first blush seems to fit into the feminine category of names given to players who did not join in the off-field pursuits of drinking, smoking, cursing and womanizing. Dickerson, however, has been identified as part of the hardest drinking team of all time, the 1883 Pittsburgh Alleghenys. [40]

So, whence the name Buttercup? James K. Skipper's research reports a very simple explanation; this hard-drinking Italian-American simply loved flowers.

Dickerson earned a spot in the Reds outfield at age 19. The 1879 season was his best. He led the National League with 14 triples.

He played a total of seven seasons for such professional teams as the Troy Trojans, Worcester Rubylegs, Pittsburgh Alleghenys, St. Louis Maroons, Baltimore Orioles, Louisville Eclipse and the Buffalo Bisons.

During his many stops, he never played in more than 81 games in a season. His roster spot on the 1885 Bisons ended abruptly after just five games owing to a microscopic batting average of .048

He found employment in 1886 with the Chattanooga Lookouts in the Southern Association. His .279 batting average in 50 games was a big improvement, but he was unable to hold the roster spot and his professional baseball career was at an end.

Dickerson died in Baltimore, Maryland, in 1920. Fifty-seven years later he was enshrined in the National Italian American Sports Hall of Fame. The NIASHF identifies him as "Lewis Pessano, better known as Buttercup Dickerson." [41] Another resource claims that Dickerson's real name was Louis Pasano. [42] He would not have been the first player to change his name to mask his ethnicity (see Ping Bodie).

However he began life, as a Pessano or a Dickerson, he will always be our little Buttercup.

Lady Baldwin

Pre-Civil-War baseball, as played by the Knickerbocker Base Ball Club and the Excelsior Club of Brooklyn, was a "gentleman's game." But it was inevitable that the common man would find pleasure in the sport. The gamblers, carousers, mercenaries and toughs would soon follow. A keg of beer would often sit next to third base as a reward for any player who had the skill or good fortune to advance that far around the base paths. [43] A good father would absolutely forbid his daughter to associate with such ruffians.

When a gentleman throwback would join a new team and decline to participate in the pleasures of drinking, gambling, smoking, brawling and womanizing, he ran the risk of acquiring a derisive nickname. These names were very frequently feminine in nature, so as to imply a lack of masculinity on the part of the newcomer. When a feminine name did not seem to fit the personality, religious names such as Preacher were assigned.

Charles B. Baldwin was one such gentleman player, and an early adopter of the feminine nickname. Born in Oramel, New York, in 1859, he grew to a height of 5' 11" and sported a very unlady-like handlebar moustache. He obviously had a positive self-image and was able to accept the nickname with equanimity.

Baldwin first hit the radar screen in 1884 pitching for the Milwaukee Brewers of the Union League. The following year he joined the Detroit Wolverines of the National League and complied an 11-9 record while splitting the season between there and Milwaukee, then downgraded to minor league status.

In 1886, Baldwin claimed his place in baseball history by posting a 42-13 record as Detroit jumped from sixth to second place. He completed all but one of the 56 games he started. His pitching teammate, Pretzels Getzien, was nearly as impressive with a 30-11 mark.

Baldwin's 42-win season is still tops in the National League and will probably never be eclipsed. Matt Kilroy of the Baltimore Orioles of the American Association holds the top honors with 46 wins in 1887. Lefty Grove's 31-win season in 1931 is tops in the American League.

Baldwin did not repeat his great success in 1887, but he did complete all 24 starts and ended the season 13-10. Detroit won the National League pennant and Baldwin had a second chance to make something special of the 1887 season.

He faced the American Association champion St. Louis Browns five times in the pre-modern World Series. Baldwin defeated the Browns four times to help the Wolverines clinch the title 10-5 in games. His ERA was 1.50 and his WHIP was 0.905. If an MVP award had been given in that era, Baldwin would have been a strong candidate.

Baldwin played two more MLB seasons, 1888 with the Detroit and 1890 split between the Buffalo Bisons in the Players League and the Brooklyn Bridegrooms in the National League. He won only a total of six games over that period.

He hung on for two more seasons in the minor leagues with the Binghamton Bingos in 1892 and the Grand Rapid Rippers in 1894.

After baseball, he was a farmer and later a real estate agent. He died in 1937 in Hastings, Michigan, a month shy of his 88th birthday. [44]

She Donahue

A nickname cannot get any more feminine than the one assigned to Charles Michael Donahue. Donahue was born in Oswego, New York, in 1877. He (She) first shows up in the baseball archives playing for the Spokane Blue Stockings in the Pacific Northwest League in 1901 at the age of 24. After two more years in the minors, he earned a shot at playing second base and shortstop for the 1904 St. Louis Cardinals. He logged only four games for the Red Birds and was shipped to the Philadelphia Phillies in midseason.

The Phillies employed him regularly as an infield utility player, using him at every base, but primarily at shortstop and third base. He batted only .215 and fielded at a .828 clip. As the 1904 season ended, so did his major league career. He spent the next four years in the minors before hanging up the cleats.

Other than basic statistics, the baseball history books have little to say about Donahue, except to include him in a hypothetical lineup of players with feminine names:

First base – Mary Calhoun
Second Base – Sadie Houck
Third base – She Donahue
Outfield – Gail Henley
Outfield – Baby Doll Jacobson
Outfield – Estel Crabtree
Catcher – Bubbles Hargrave
Pitcher – Lil Stoner
[45]

Baseball's penchant for renaming players with female names is quite curious in light of the fact that true females had been effectively banned from the game until 1952 when Ford Frick made it official after the Harrisburg Senators signed a young stenographer named Eleanor Engle.

Donahue was the only player in major league history who could have a "he said, she said" conversation all by himself.

She passed away in the Bronx in 1947 and was interred in his hometown of Oswego.

Sadie Houck

Sargent Perry Houck was born with a very masculine first name and easily could have been called "Sarge" but somehow was endowed with a double-feminine name. The name Sadie is a diminutive of Sarah, a Hebrew name, and means "lady" or "princess" depending on which translation you favor.

No definitive explanation (or guess) for his nickname has ever been proffered. Perhaps he had a girlish or baby face. Like many straight-laced players, the name might have been a tease for his rejection of the wild side of life. An incident in 1882 dispels that explanation, however. Houck and teammate Mike Dorgan were suspended for the remainder of the 1882 season for "dissipation." That word was euphemistic for excessive "drinking and whoring." [46]

The name may also have been a reference to a local or regional celebrity named Sadie.

Houck was born in 1856 and made his big league debut in 1879 with the Boston Red Caps of the National League. He played in almost every game of the Red Caps' 84-game schedule, seeing action in both the infield and outfield.

Houck was never a star player, but his versatility always served him well. He played eight big league seasons, all told, putting in time with the Providence Grays (NL), Detroit Wolverines (NL), Philadelphia Athletes (AA), Baltimore Orioles (AA), Washington Nationals (NL), and New York Metropolitans (AA).

Bill James named Houck and Joe Farrell as the worst double play combination of all time for their performance with the 1886 Baltimore Orioles. [47] The two players combined committed 93 errors that year.

Houck also has the distinction of being blacklisted by the owner who designed the infamous reserve clause. Arthur H. Soden owned the Boston Red Caps and was understandably loved by his fellow owners and despised by the players. According to Ty Cobb, in 1879, Houck refused to doff his cap to Soden and was blacklisted for his heretical behavior. [48] He was reinstated a short time later and signed by Providence.

Houck is tied for second with dozens of other players for most triples in a game. On August 27, 1884, he tripled three times playing for the Athletics. George Streif, also of the Athletics, broke the record one year later. Bill Joyce of the New York Giants duplicated the feat in 1897. [49]

Houck left this world in 1919. He was buried in Washington, DC, not far from where he was born 63 years earlier.

Tillie Shafer

Arthur Joseph Shafer followed John McGraw into the Giants locker room to meet his new teammates, the 1909 New York Giants. Following McGraw's introduction, outfielder Cy Seymour stepped up and kissed Shafer on both cheeks and asked, "Tillie, how are you?" [50]

Whatever connection was made in Seymour's brain between Shafer and the feminine name Tillie has never been determined. Shafer's background can be considered as a probable reason. He was the son of a very wealthy family. No doubt, the other Giants already had the scoop on their new infielder. As he stood next to John McGraw, the tall, thin 20-year-old would have presented a stark contrast to Mugsy McGraw.

Shafer instantly hated the nickname but felt powerless to resist his first hazing in professional baseball. Unfortunately for Shafer, the name stuck. Had the rookie made a better effort to fit in with the rough-and-tumble Giants, he may have been able to slip out from under the nickname. After many home games, a chauffer-driven automobile awaited him. [51]

His aversion to practice and hard work did not help him to become one of the boys. He pushed back against the tough discipline of a McGraw managed team. Still, McGraw appreciated Shafer's abilities and tried to keep him focused and on the team. McGraw threatened to fine any player who insulted Shafer. Still, the playboy wanted to play, and not necessarily baseball. He loved to travel and spend his family's money. [52]

By 1913, he had become a valued member of the Giants, seeing action in almost every game. He logged 79 games at third base, but frequently filled in at second base, shortstop and the outfield. He batted a very respectable .287 for the season. McGraw saw him as his regular third baseman for the upcoming 1914 season. Shafer's father had other plans. Pater bought his son a chain of clothing stores throughout the west coast and told him he wanted him to end his "dusty, muscular chores." The right bait had been used and Tillie Shafer disappeared into the baseball archives. Arthur Shafer was reborn and eventually became a very successful real estate broker in Los Angeles. Golf became his athletic outlet as he made a name for himself locally as a very good amateur player. [53]

Shafer's distaste for his name sheds some light on the predicament of players who were not comfortable with a pejorative nickname but did not yet possess the gravitas to fight back.

In 1914, the Federal League undertook a recruitment drive to fill the rosters of the six-teams. Tillie Shafer was invited to join the party. Shafer replied that he was "done with baseball." [54]

Convinced that Shafer still possessed some love for the game, McGraw tried to lure the infielder back to the Giants in 1916. [55] The desire to avoid the nickname Tillie, undoubtedly played some part in the decision to turn down the offer.

Most modern publications call him Tillie. All period articles refer to his name as Tilly.

Shafer died in 1962 at the age of 72 in Los Angeles, California. The Los Angeles Times obituary hailed him as the first native Angeleno to become a big league ballplayer.

Dizzy Nutter

Everett Clarence Nutter was born in Roseville, Ohio, in 1893. He played in the minor leagues from 1914 through 1919 before getting his shot with the Boston Braves. Playing centerfield, he failed to impress the big league club and was back in the Eastern League the following year, rejoining the 1920 New Haven club managed by future Hall of Fame pitcher Chief Bender. Nutter played one more season for New Haven in 1922.

Nutter left a very small footprint in the annals of major league baseball, his nickname being the most notable. During his six seasons in the Eastern League, however, he established himself as one of the memorable players in that circuit. In 1949, the Bridgeport Herald looked back at the past stars of that league and included Nutter with the likes of Jim Thorpe, Lou Gehrig and Leo Durocher. The Herald adds to the lore of Dizzy's name by recalling his penchant for circus catches: "Who, having once seen him, could ever forget Nutter, the eccentric New Haven outfielder who delighted in making easy catches look hard by taking fly balls behind his back, nabbing the ball in time after letting it bounce off his glove, or hesitating for a while before making a mad dash to complete what should have been a simple play?" [56]

The Hartford Courant in 1925 called Nutter the most eccentric ballplayer to ever play in the Eastern League. Curiously, the writer refers to him as Everett and not Dizzy. [56a] The same publication referred to him as "the New Haven comedian." [57]

Nutter returned to his hometown of Roseville and opened a barbershop that he operated into the 1950s. He died in 1958 and was buried in Rosedale.

Dizzy Sutherland

Howard Alvin Sutherland appears to be another of the hundreds of players who made a cameo appearance in the majors then faded quickly into obscurity. Even worse, Sutherland's one shot in the big leagues was an unqualified disaster. The lefthander recorded just three outs starting for the 1949 Washington Senators, but not until he had allowed five runs on two hits and six walks. He was saddled with the loss and carried an ERA of 45.00 and WHIP of 8.00 to his grave. The real story of Dizzy Sutherland, however, took place before his professional baseball career ever began.

Born in Washington DC, in 1922, he took a job as a cab driver shortly after high school. In 1943, Sutherland joined the Army and was selected to become a member of the airborne corps. Later that same year, he was part of an airborne insertion at Salerno, Italy. By some tragic miscalculation, his battalion was dropped behind German lines. Sutherland was wounded three times before his capture by Nazi troops. He was transported into Germany and installed at a Prisoner of War camp, where he remained until American forces liberated the camp in 1945.

He returned stateside 100 pounds lighter than when he was captured. As he regained his strength, weight and vitality, he went back to driving cabs in D.C. during the week and playing semi-pro ball on the weekends. In 1949, a scout for the Washington Senators liked what he saw and signed Sutherland to a minor league contract. At this point in his life, he was still known as Howard. [58]

The Senators shipped him to their Class B affiliate in Charlotte, North Carolina. The 27-year-old turned his first professional baseball job into gold. By late September, he was the ace of the Hornets' staff, boasting an 18-10 record, eight wins better than his closest teammate. He won his last eight decisions after losing four straight and sinking to 10-10. [59]

Despite the physical and mental scars of his time in Italy and Germany, Sutherland entertained his fellow Hornets with crazy antics both on and off the field. For this he was bestowed with the nickname Dizzy. [60]

The last-place Senators rewarded their rookie pitcher with a shot in the majors. They purchased his contract from Charlotte on September 29, 1949. [61] He took the mound at Griffith Stadium against the St. Louis Browns. By the time the Brownies had battered six Washington pitchers for 15 runs, Sutherland was the losing pitcher. [62] His major league career was over statistically, if not formally. After returning to the Hornets in 1950, he was called back to Washington in September but did not see any action.

He performed well in Charlotte during the 1950 and 1951 seasons, winning 31 games against 23 losses. After a hiatus in 1952, Sutherland signed with the Richmond Colts in 1953 but did not take the mound. He ended his minor league career with a 49-33 record.

Sutherland died in Washington, his hometown, in 1979 at the age of 57. He did not become a baseball star, but he died a real hero. For his bravery in Italy, he received a Purple Heart for his sacrifice. He was one of 22 baseball players/umpires who were POWs. Ironically, the Germans, who were not a baseball-playing people, allowed the American prisoners to play baseball using equipment supplied by the American Red Cross. On the other hand, the Japanese, who were crazy about baseball, used prisoners as slave labor, killing many in the process. [64]

Flea Clifton

Herman Earl Clifton was not skinny or short. Sportswriters sometimes called him "diminutive" although he stood 5' 10' tall and weighed around 165 pounds. In no way did his body size remind anyone of a tiny insect. There is no evidence that he pierced the skin of those around him and sucked their blood. So how did he get stuck with the name Flea, an insect considered vermin by most clean people? Clifton picked up his name as a result of his personality. James Skipper claimed that dealing with Herman Clifton was like suffering bites from a hostile gang of sand fleas. The Detroit Tigers Encyclopedia contends that Clifton's picked up the nickname from his manager while playing for Beaumont (TX). [63]

Bites from a sand flea cause painful welts and rashes that can last for days. In addition to nettlesome itching, fevers are not uncommon. A sand flea is not a flea at all. In fact, it is not even an insect. The small shrimp-like creature, also known as a sand fly, beach flea, no-see-um, or biting midge, is a crustacean. They are known to hop as high as two feet into the air, putting them in range of the torso of anyone lounging on the beach.

What element of Clifton's personality permitted him to assent to such a name? Clifton had a very tough childhood. A less-than-elegant new name would have paled in comparison to the traumas of his early life.

Clifton was born in Cincinnati, Ohio, in 1909. At the age of eight, he lost his father to World War I. While still in his mid-teens, his mother was murdered, strangled by an acquaintance using Clifton's tie. His stepfather then rejected him and ordered him out the house. He was homeless for the next year of his life.

The early version of Flea Clifton was a relentless spitfire. He tried to model his playing style after his hero, Ty Cobb. "I'd get a base hit or walk and I'd give the pitcher hell on the way to first base. I'd steal second and then I'd give the catcher hell for having a goddam pretzel arm. And I couldn't understand why these old pitchers who had real good control kept hitting me in the ribs. I was hit by a pitch 19 times in the first half of my first year at Raleigh."

One day, Clifton sat on the bench with a teammate named Bill Lewis and wondered out loud why no one else was getting plunked so often. Lewis was incredulous that Clifton was so clueless.

Said Lewis, "Repeat after me: 'I give the pitcher hell, I give the catcher hell, I give the infielders hell, I give the outfielders hell.' You're giving everybody hell, so their control's not so good when you come to the plate." [65]

That was day Flea Clifton learned to keep his mouth shut on the baseball diamond.

In 1930, at age 20, Clifton secured a position with the Raleigh Capitals in the Piedmont League. A 19-year-old first baseman from New York

City was likewise in his first year of professional ball. By mid-season, Hank Greenberg was promoted to Hartford in the Eastern League, then on to Detroit for a one-game taste of the big time. Though Clifton stayed behind in Raleigh, a life long friendship had begun.

He spent one more year in Raleigh before ascending to Class A Beaumont in the Texas League, where he met up with his former teammate Hank Greenberg. The 1932 Beaumont Exporters' roster was chocked full of future major leaguers such as Schoolboy Rowe, Rip Sewell, Skeeter Newsome, Luke Hamlin and Greenberg. The Tigers were amassing a young core of players that would soon assault the American League.

Greenberg was promoted to the Tigers in 1933, Clifton one year later. The 1934 Tigers won the American League pennant. Clifton played sparingly and only got to the plate 17 times with just one base hit to show for his effort. Manager Mickey Cochrane did not use him in the World Series. The Tigers lost the Series to the St. Louis Cardinals in seven games.

The 1935 season was a huge improvement for the Flea. He played in 43 games and batted .255. His friend Hank bashed 36 homers and drove in an astounding 170 runs. The Tigers were again the AL champs.

Clifton was a just reserve infielder on the pennant-winning 1935 Tigers. Just sitting on the bench during the first two games of the World Series against the Chicago Cubs was a thrill most ballplayers would never experience. During Game Two, Greenberg broke his wrist. Third baseman Marv Owen moved across the diamond to anchor first base. Suddenly, Flea Clifton was the starting third basemen for the remainder of the Series.

A nice Cinderella story was shaping up for Clifton, but unfortunately he went to the plate 18 times and never managed a single base hit. Despite his lack of offensive participation, he held down third base and the Tigers defeated the Cubs in six games. When the season was over, he was lauded as a hero by his teammates for his defensive contributions. [66]

The 1936 and 1937 seasons were much like his rookie year of 1934. He saw little action from inside the white lines. The Tigers finished second both years and Clifton did not get another chance to hit safely in a World Series.

The Tigers sold his contract to Toronto in 1938. The Maple Leafs were affiliated with the Philadelphia A's who two years later sent him to the Cleveland Indians organization. Clifton then bounced around like a ping ball for three more years before calling it quits in 1943. Following his demotion from the Tigers he labored for seven different teams over a six-year period.

During his final year with the Minneapolis Millers, he was still garnering praise for his fielding skills. Said former teammate Earl Caldwell, "He'll make a lot of hitters moan by cutting off sure hits." The Milwaukee Journal described his glove work as "scintillating." [67]

After baseball, Clifton returned to Cincinnati with his wife and launched a long career in the insurance field.

Shortly before his death, Clifton was interviewed for a documentary titled *The Life and Times of Hank Greenberg*. The film was released in 1998. He never had the chance to view the film about his old friend. Clifton died in 1997 at the age of 89 in his hometown of Cincinnati. He never learned that the film would earn multiple awards in 2000 and finally a Peabody Award in 2001. He never had the chance to watch Flea Clifton, the once homeless, throwaway teenager appear on the silver screen.

Above: left – Cuckoo Christenson   right – Creepy Crespi
Below: left – Bug Holiday   right – Buttercup Dickerson

Chapter Three – Skill Sets (Or Lack Thereof)

Bunny Brief

His name at birth was Anthony John Grzeszkowski. The decision to change his name is not difficult to understand. The story behind his decision to choose Brief may be apocryphal, but funny. As told to Warren Brown of Baseball Digest: "I wasn't in baseball very long before someone objected to having to spell (Grzeszkowski). I asked him if he had any suggestions. He said he hadn't, but almost anything would do as long as I made it brief. So I made it Brief." [1]

The Bunny part of his name has been attributed to his speed as a runner.

Brief is a classic example of a baseball player who excelled at the highest level in the minor leagues but could not come close to duplicating the results in the majors. He is ranked in the top 10 minor league players of all time, with seven home run crowns and four RBI titles to his name. He blasted 42 home runs playing for the Kansas City Blues in 1921. [2]

Brief blasted 37 home runs for the Milwaukee Brewers in 1925. He felt that a raise in salary would be forthcoming. When his new contract called for the same compensation as the previous year, he met with Brewers owner Otto Borchert. Brief reminded Borchert of his home run production and made his plea, "That should be worth something, you know."

"Yeah," answered Borchert, "but look at all the balls you lost." [3] Baseball Digest reports that Brief hit 47 home runs for Milwaukee. That is incorrect. His highest home run total with the Brewers was 37.

Snake Henry

In some circles, Frederick Marshall Henry might have felt that his nickname provided him with a benefit. A snake has a reputation as a dangerous creature. The nickname would have lent him an added degree of manliness, or edginess.

In other circles, identifying yourself as Snake would not be so good. At the Thanksgiving dinner table, his mother most likely would not say, "Snake, honey, please pass the turkey to your father."

The church bulletin would not list Snake Henry as someone helping with the offering that day. If he applied for a loan, identifying himself as Snake would cause the bankers some trepidation. Going through life as Snake Henry had its pros and cons, and that is why he is included in this section.

At first blush, the name might suggest a certain flexibility of morals or ethics. But Henry was not a "snake in the grass." The moniker was derived from the way he handled throws to the first base bag. The lanky left-handed first-sacker was an early proponent of the stretch position that allowed the baseball to reach his glove a few milliseconds sooner.

Henry was born in 1895 in Waynesville, North Carolina. He attended Atlantic Christian College (now known as Barton College) in nearby Wilson for four years and starred on their baseball team.

After three years in the low minors, he inked a deal with the Chicago White Sox. After playing with teams such as the Petersburg Goobers, he now had an opportunity to move up to Class A baseball in the Western League beginning in 1917.

Playing for the dual-city franchise of St. Joseph/Hutchinson, he acquitted himself very well and was ticketed for the Windy City for the 1918 season. World War I brought those plans to an abrupt halt. He joined the U.S. Army and moved up the ranks just as quickly as he did in baseball. When the war ended, Sergeant Snake Henry returned to baseball, but his one-year layoff prompted the Sox to send him down to the minors for the 1919 season. [4]

Instead of becoming a member of the 1919 Black Sox, he stayed at a safe distance from the scandal, playing in Terre Haute of the Triple-I League and Milwaukee in the American Association. Had he made the 1919 Chicago team, he might have traveled in Chick Gandil's crowd and got sucked into that maelstrom of corruption and treachery.

After Gandil was banned from baseball, Henry could have taken his spot at first base for the 1920 season. Instead, he was sold to the Columbus Senators in the American Association where he turned in a good, but not great year. He was sold again, this time to San Antonio in the Texas League, a step down from the Senators.

While the long and winding road seemed to be leading him farther away from the big leagues, he was sold one more time to the New Orleans Pelicans in the Southern Association. The Pelicans roster consisted mostly of former and future major leaguers. Before the 1922 season was over, he finally got the call. He would play first base for the Boston Braves.

He appeared in just 18 games in the fall of 1922 and failed to lift his batting average over the .200 level. He stayed on the Boston roster for the 1923 season but had a miserable spring where he hit .111. The Braves punched his ticket back to New Orleans, and his major league career ended.

After arriving back in New Orleans, he began to hit the ball again. In 1925, he was team MVP. In 1926, he blasted 100 extra base hits and batted .369. In 1928, he was the Western League MVP. [5]

Before he called it quits in 1939, he forged a successful minor league career that saw him become a frequent all-star. He amassed 3,384 career minor league hits, fifth all-time, including 200 triples, ranking him second all-time.

The Snake was not totally fangless. The only incident that matches his nickname with his disposition was a riotous reaction to an umpire's call in 1939. Henry was managing the Kinston Eagles in the Class D Coastal Plain League. Henry literally attacked the umpire with a knee to the groin. A near riot among the fans ensued and Henry was suspended for a year

Henry died in 1987 in his native North Carolina. The Snake was 92 years old.

Snake Wiltse

Lewis DeWitt Wiltse was the first major leaguer to answer to the name Snake. He was born in 1871 in Bouckville, New York.

One of seven boys, Lewis and his brother George learned the pitching trade by throwing baseballs against the family's barn door. Impressed by Wiltse's curveball, someone in the family gave Lewis the name

Snake. George would later become Hooks Wiltse and star alongside Christy Mathewson for John McGraw's Giants. Hooks will receive his due in a later chapter. Their father moved the family to Syracuse and entered the carpet business, effective ending the barn door training. [6]

Wiltse does not show up on any professional team until the age of 28. Nor do any colleges appear in his biography, suggesting that he labored for local or regional teams until signing with the venerable Toledo Mud Hens in 1900. The mystery was solved in a book about the Bouckville Summits baseball team. The Summits, dubbed the "Pride of Cidertown," featured brothers Lewis, George and Arthur Wiltse. [7]

Snake Wiltse was an accomplished pitcher who could competently handle first base and the outfield. He did not hurt his cause at the plate, either.

In 1901, he signed with the Pittsburgh Pirates. The Pirates were disappointed with his 1-4 record and released him. His batting average of .158 did little to save his job.

Within a month he was on the Philadelphia Athletics roster. Under Connie Mack's wings, he flourished. He became Mack's workhorse, averaging eight innings each time out. He won 13 games losing only five times. At the plate, he batted .373. [8]

Halfway through the 1902 season, Mr. Mack got rid of the Snake, selling him to the Baltimore Orioles. The Mack Men went on to win the AL pennant without the Snake. His record was 8-8 with the A's and 7-11 with the O's. He led the league in surrendering runs.

He went along for the ride when the Baltimore franchise moved to New York in 1903, but struggled with the Highlanders and was released that same year.

He returned to Baltimore the next season and played for the Eastern League team that claimed the abandoned Orioles nickname. His first two years back in Baltimore were terrific as he went 19-12 then 20-8. Following the 1904 season, the Eastern League found the antidote to Snake's venom and ended his effectiveness as a topnotch pitcher. His final fling in professional baseball was in 1910 with the Syracuse Stars of the New York State League.

Wiltse's claim to fame occurred at the plate, not on the mound. On August 10, 1901, he smacked two doubles and two triples against the Senators and became the only rookie pitcher in baseball history to record four extra-base hits in one contest. [9]

In fairness to history, Wiltse also holds the record for most earned runs surrendered in a season (172 in 1902).

Wiltse died in 1928 in Harrisburg, Pennsylvania at the age of 56.

Snake Deal

John Wesley Deal was born in Lancaster, Pennsylvania, in 1879, and attended Villanova University where he played baseball and basketball. His style of play on the hardwood led to his nickname Snake. He entered professional baseball with his name already in place.

Deal was playing first base for the Lancaster Red Roses in 1906 when he was "discovered" by the Cincinnati Reds. Manager Ned Hanlon was told that Deal would be a shining light for the second division Reds. But Hanlon soon learned that Snake was not "the real deal."

Said Hanlon, "They said he could field, he could hit, he could slide, he could run, he could do everything." The Pittsburgh Press pulled no punches by reporting that Deal's batting efforts "look like a joke." They twisted the knife even more by stating that Hanlon has discovered "large holes in his fielding." Paraphrasing Hanlon, the newspaper reported, "He may be traded, or he may be sold, but he has to go." [10]

The offensive stats support Hanlon's appraisal. Deal batted only .208 playing a position where better results are expected. He committed just 10 errors in over 600 chances for a fielding percentage of .985. Considering the rudimentary glove Deal would have used, his manager was a bit harsh in his judgment.

Most likely, a certain Cincinnati scout also left the organization following the 1906 season.

He was, indeed, sold as the Pittsburgh Press predicted. He was back with Lancaster in 1907 and remained in the minor leagues until 1916.

Deal died in 1944 in Harrisburg, Pennsylvania. There were three "Snakes" in major league baseball, and two of them died in Harrisburg; just a coincidence, no doubt.

Baby Doll Jacobson

Unlike dozens of players who were chided and nicknamed for their gentile lifestyles, William Chester Jacobson acquired his moniker after smashing a powerful home run during a minor league game in 1912. The massively built slugger was in his fourth year in the minor leagues playing outfield for the Mobile Sea Gulls in the Southern Association. While circling the bases, the hometown band began playing "Oh, You Beautiful Doll."

The next day, the local newspaper, the Mobile Register, displayed a photo of Jacobson with the caption "That Baby Doll." From that day onward, teammates, sportswriters and fans would know him as Baby Doll Jacobson. [11]

The old-timers from Mobile have a "part two" that story. Eyewitnesses claim that the ball hit by Jacobson cleared the entire ballpark and landed in a fright car bound for New Orleans. If the tale is true, Jacobson hit the longest home run in baseball history. [12]

Shortly after graduating from Genesco High School (Illinois), the husky farm boy began his professional career with the Rock Island Islanders in the Class B Three-I League in 1909. Switching back and forth from behind the plate to the outfield, he had a poor first year and was demoted in 1910 to the Battle Creek Crickets, a Class D team. By the end of that season he was back in Rock Island.

He had a very good 1911 season in Rock Island and earned a spot on the Class A Mobile roster in 1912. In 1914, he joined the Chattanooga Lookouts and enjoyed his finest season to date, walloping 15 homeruns and batting .319. The Detroit Tigers signed him to play outfield and first base on their 1915 team. His days as a catcher were behind him.

In August of his rookie year, the Tigers shipped him and $15,000 in cash to the St. Louis Browns for a starting pitcher named Big Bill James. The Baby Doll batted only .209 for the Browns and was demoted to the Little Rock Travelers in 1916.

Back in St. Louis in 1917, Jacobson again found his batting stroke and claimed a starting position in the outfield. Events out of his control would decide where he would spend 1918. World War I had been raging in Europe since 1914. After German advances in 1917, the Allied troops began making headway and pushing the German armies out of occupied lands. Jacobson joined the war effort and spent the 1918 season in a U.S. Navy uniform. The Navy had a good use for Jacobson's skills; they named him manager of the Norfolk Sailors in the Navy's baseball league. [13]

He returned to the Browns in 1919 and began a run of nine successive and successful years in the majors. From 1920 through 1924 the St. Louis Browns could claim one of the premier outfields with Jacobson, Ken Williams and Johnny Tobin.

The Browns traded their Baby Doll to the Philadelphia A's in 1926 for Bing Miller. That same day Connie Mack traded him to the Boston Red Sox. In 1927, he was sold to the Cleveland Indians who released him a month later. Connie Mack plucked him off the waiver wire and put him back into an A's uniform for the last two months of the 1927 season, his last in the big leagues.

At age 37 he was back in Chattanooga in the Southern Association. He hung up the spikes in 1929 after sliding back to Class B in the Three-I League.

His lifetime major league batting average was an impressive .311. During the 1924 and 1925 seasons, he smacked a total 34 homeruns. His top RBI year was 1920 when he chased in 122 runs on 216 base hits.

During his years in the major leagues, he was considered the league's biggest player, physically. Still, he was more than adequate in the field, at one time holding 13 fielding marks. In 1924, he recorded 484 putouts, a record he maintained for the next 24 years. [14]

Jacobson's behavior did not fit his nickname. The Browns of his era were a tough bunch that loved to brawl, and Baby Doll was no exception. They would slide with spikes up, or bad-mouth opponents mercilessly, hoping to instigate a fight. [15]

Jacobson hailed from Cable, Illinois, coming into this world in 1890. He departed this life from much the same point 86 years later in 1977.

Boom Boom Beck

Walter William Beck was a journeyman pitcher whose major league career spanned 22 years, although he only logged 12 MLB seasons. The gap years were spent bouncing back and forth from the minors to the majors and back again. Born in Decatur, Illinois, in 1904, Beck went straight from semi-pro ball to the St. Louis Browns in 1924. He pitched one scoreless inning at age 19 and did not step onto a major league field again for three years.

Back with the Browns again in 1927, he pitched in three games and achieved a flawless 1-0 record. During those four years, he saw action with Marlin/Palestine (Texas, not the Holy Land), Bloomington, Tulsa and Milwaukee.

He spent much of the 1928 season with the Browns but saw limited action, playing in just 16 games. He was back to the minors again in 1929 through 1932. His career finally gained traction with the Memphis Chickasaws where he claimed a combined 62 wins in three years, 27 of them in 1932.

His 1932 performance earned him a shot with the Brooklyn Dodgers for the 1933 season. He started a league-high 35 games and joined the sorry list of pitchers who lost 20 games in a season. Beck, however, pitched pretty well for manager Max Carey's sixth-place Bums, finishing with a 3.54 ERA.

After an unspectacular 1934 season in Brooklyn, he descended once more into the minors until surfacing with the Phillies in 1939. He served with the Army during World War II. His longest big league tenure was in Philadelphia where he labored for five years with one of baseball's worst teams.

He ricocheted from Detroit to Cincinnati to Pittsburgh during 1944 and 1945 and sank back to the lower leagues until he retired in 1950.

Sometimes called Elmer the Great by his teammates, a reference to a Ring Lardner character, the right-hander officially went by the name Walter until 1934 when a temper tantrum changed his name forever.

Beck was on the mound for the Brooklyn Dodgers against the Phillies in the Baker Bowl, a small facility squeezed into a North Philadelphia neighborhood. Sometimes referred to as the Cigar Box or the Band Box, the right field wall was only 280 feet from home plate and centerfield 300 field deep. Guarding the field was a 60-foot high wall, creating a target similar to Fenway's Green Monster, which is only 37 feet tall by comparison. After years of outfielder complaints about the rough masonry surface, a layer of tin was applied to the edifice. Players no longer had their skin sandpapered from their bodies when colliding with the wall. Baseballs made a distinctive banging noise when smashed against the metal sheeting.

On that day, Phillies batsmen were pummeling Beck until Dodger manager Casey Stengel had seen, and heard enough. Right fielder Hack Wilson felt the same way. Nursing a hangover, Wilson was forced to negotiate a retrieval of several Beck misadventures. As Stengel approached the mound and reached for the baseball, a frustrated Beck turned and fired the ball toward the infamous tin wall. Wilson, his back turned to the plate to converse with fans, heard the familiar banging noise above him and reacted. He quickly tracked down the ball and fired a perfect strike to second base as the fans went berserk with laughter.

When the inning ended, a woozy and embarrassed Wilson returned to the dugout and began screaming at Beck. "All day long all I heard was boom, boom, boom, against the fence. When I heard the last boom, I was sure it was another hitter!" [16]

According to James K. Skipper, it was sportswriter Edward T. Murphy who made the connection and affixed the new name Boom Boom to Mr. Beck.

During the rest of 1934, Beck's last year in Brooklyn, fans made a ritual out of Beck's insertion into a ballgame. Author Rudy Marzano describes his first visit to Ebbet's field as a seven-year old. Dodger pitcher Ray Benge was being removed from the game in favor of a relief pitcher. As the new pitcher began his trek to the mound, the fans chanted "boom, boom, boom" in cadence with his footsteps. Marzano's older brother explained that the fans "kid" Beck by screaming, "boom" when he walks, when his pitches hit the bat, and when the ball hits the wall. [17]

Like many players before him, Beck did not fight the name and decided to enjoy the crowd's game. He decided it was a gesture of acceptance and appreciation, rather than a form of derision. He even made "Boom Boom" a part of his autograph (see the photo on the back cover).

Beck died in Champaign, Illinois, in 1987 at the age of 82 and was laid to rest near his birthplace in Decatur.

Footsie Blair

At first blush, Clarence Vick Blair's large feet earned him a spot in the chapter dedicated to nicknames derived from body characteristics. Blair, however, shared this physical trait with many of his contemporaries. What inspired his teammates to name him Footsie was not the size, but the speed those large feet generated. His 6' 1" frame was anchored by a large foundation that should have prevented him from quickly and fluidly moving around the base paths and covering large patches of the infield.

Blair was born in 1900 in Enterprise, a small town in the "nowhere" section of eastern Oklahoma. He did not get his first professional contract until age 23 with the 1924 Texarkana Twins in the lowly Eastern Texas League. Playing mostly at second base, he rose through the minors until 1928 when he hit .294 for the Little Rock Travelers in the Class A Southern Association. The Chicago Cubs liked what they saw and in 1929 he joined the mighty Chicago team in time for their ascent to the National League pennant.

Blair spent just three years in the major leagues, all with the Cubs. His claim to fame is the role he played with the 1930 Cubs team. With their great star Rogers Hornsby out with a serious injury, the Cubs moved Blair from third base to second to cover Hornsby's spot. Although Blair hit at a respectable .273 clip as a second-year player, he fell 100 points behind Hornsby's expected output. The Cubs came within two runs of being one of the few teams in history to score 1,000 runs in a season, but were unable to overtake the Cardinals for the pennant.

In 1931, Hornsby returned to the lineup, forcing Blair back into a utility role. He hit .258, which paled in comparison to the five regulars to hit .300 or better. The following year, playermanager Hornsby cut back his playing role and took over the infield utility role, making Blair expendable.

Blair returned to the minor leagues and played until he reached the age of 40. Ironically, his last season, 1941, was his best in terms of average, hitting .344 with the Jackson Senators of the Southeastern League. Although he claimed only three years in the majors, he could regale his minor league teammates with tales of playing side-by-side with Hack Wilson, Kiki Cuyler, Gabby Hartnett, Woody English, High Pockets Kelly and, of course, the fabulous Rajah.

Blair could also brag about his one appearance in the World Series when manager Joe McCarthy sent him, a mere rookie, to the plate as a pinch hitter in the ninth inning of Game One with the Cubs trailing 3-0 to the Philadelphia A's. The fact that pitcher Howard Ehmke induced him to ground into a fielder's choice was irrelevant. Unlike the vast majority of baseball players, he had the thrill of standing on first base in a World Series contest. The next batter struck out to end the game, but he had a memory with a lifetime guarantee.

This lifetime ended in Texarkana, Texas, in 1982, the site of his first professional season. He was just two weeks shy of his 82nd birthday.

Spook Jacobs

Forrest Vandergrift Jacobs was born in Cheswold, Delaware, in 1925. He played for his high school team in Pennsville, New Jersey, and signed with the Dodgers in 1946. He labored in the minors for a long time, but he possessed a knack that made him the envy of his teammates. When the ball left his bat, it seemed to know exactly where and how far it needed to travel to fall safely between the fielders. During his second season in the minors, a Johnstown (PA) sports writer commented how "spooky" he was. "Spooky" morphed into Spook and a nickname was born.

Jacobs only enjoyed one full year and two partial years in the major leagues. The full year, his rookie season, was spent with the Philadelphia A's during their last season in Philadelphia. True to his name, he slapped four singles in his debut to become the first player in history to go four-for-four in his first game. Willie McCovey and Delino DeShields later joined that exclusive club. Jacobs reminisced, "Four straight hits, I was a rookie on opening day...I was on Cloud Nine." [18]

He split the 1955 campaign between the Kansas City A's and the Columbus Jets. His final year, 1956, was even crazier. The A's bounced him between Columbus and Kansas City, and then traded him to Pittsburgh. With the Pirates he divided his season between Hollywood in the PCL and Pittsburgh.

The one spot in a major league ballpark that his batted balls never visited was over the fence for a home run. Despite a lifetime .247 batting average, his good eye at the plate enabled him to amass a very decent .329 on base percentage.

His MLB All-star and Hall of Fame credentials may be light, but he was once a star in Cuba. He won the Cuban Winter League batting title in 1955-1956 batting .321. In January of 2009, he was named to the Cuban Baseball Hall of Fame along with Negro League icons James "Cool Papa" Bell and Josh Gibson. Said his son Bobby, "He was a hero in Cuba. They loved him. They absolutely loved him." [19]

Former Cuban major leaguer Tony Taylor said of Jacobs, "I remember watching him (in Cuba) and I used to say, 'someday I wish I could play baseball like that man.' When I signed into professional baseball…I got traded to the same team where he played second base, and I got to practice with him to learn how to play second base." [20]

Another Cuban star, Minnie Minoso, concurred, 'I remember him very well because I used to hate the way he hit us! He used to be a crazy hitter in Cuba."

He also won the batting championship in the Panamanian Winter League in 1950-1951 with a record .359 average.

He was inducted into the Delaware Sport Museum Hall if Fame in 1991 and the Bridgeton, New Jersey Hall of Fame in 2009. Spook joined the spirit world in 2011 in Milford, Delaware, a mere 20 miles from his birthplace.

Boots Poffenberger

Cletus Elwood Poffenberger was born in 1915 with a name that just begged for a humorous nickname. His teammates made sure that he got one. A self-professed country boy, he could have become known as Hick or Rube, but a special defensive flaw would come to define him. Boots Poffenberger was a right-handed pitcher of considerable talent. But once the ball was hit in his general direction, he wanted nothing to do with it. When he had no choice, he would frequently "boot" the ball, hence the nickname. His first year in the minors with the 1935 Fieldale

Towlers produced a 16-win season. He might have logged more wins, if not for his 11 errors.

He spent his sophomore season with the Charleston Senators and won another 16 games. The Tigers promoted him to their Class A1 affiliate in Beaumont, Texas, to begin the 1937 season. His short wind-up produced a natural sinkerball that he was learning to use effectively. He broke from the gate with a 9-1 record and 2.50 ERA.

Meanwhile, in the Motor City, Schoolboy Rowe injured his arm and looked like he may be on the shelf for an extended period. The Tigers needed a pitcher to replace the 19-game winner. The call went out to Beaumont to send Poffenberger ASAP. The Tigers waited for word that their new rookie pitcher had arrived at the train station. They waited, and they waited some more. No Poffenberger. The average player on the brink of reaching the big leagues would have been on the earliest and fastest train to Detroit, but not Boots. He claimed that he really liked the nightlife in Beaumont and he was in no hurry to leave Texas. Detroit management had observed the first hint that Poffenberger was not a normal ballplayer.

After running out of excuses, Poffenberger trained to Michigan and made his debut on May 21, 1937. He opposed and defeated Lefty Grove in his first contest. He completed the season with Detroit and contributed 10 wins (10-5) to the Tigers' second place showing in the American League.

Poffenberger began to display the behaviors that would land him on the list of all-time baseball "characters." He spent most of his spare time in bars and frequently was a no-show on game-days.

The following spring, he was offered a raise from $355 to $500. He felt that his rookie season entitled him to more money, so he held out and stayed home when the team reported to spring training. [21] Said Poffenberger, "If I can win 10 games in the major leagues while staying out at night, imagine how many games I could win throughout a whole season in perfect condition." [22] This boast would prove to be purely hypothetical, since Boots sunk deeper and deeper into his pursuit of drunken revelry.

Wisely recognizing the Tigers' intransigence, he gave in and joined the team. Manager Mickey Cochrane had reserved a spot for Poffenberger on his "bad side." Boots never managed to give up his reservation in Black Mike's doghouse.

One day, Cochrane attempted to dress down his delinquent pitcher in front of the whole team by loudly and repeatedly demanding to know where Poffenberger spent the previous day. Finally, Boots, looked at Cochrane and responded, "I refuse to reveal my identity." The locker room erupted with laughter and Cochrane was further incensed. [23]

Poffenberger misjudged the effect that drinking and carousing would have on his performance. As the 1938 season wore on, he lost his role as a starter and then lost his roster spot altogether with a 6-7 record and 4.82 ERA. He was demoted to the Toledo Mud Hens in the American Association. Perhaps the nightlife in Toledo was limited, or he decided to concentrate on pitching, but for some reason he pitched well and finished the year at 8-3.

The Tigers invited him to spring training in 1939. He wore out his welcome almost immediately when he "smart-mouthed" Tigers general manager Jack Zeller. Before he could ever take the mound in a game, he was shipped to Brooklyn for $25,000.

When he arrived in Brooklyn, manager Leo Durocher took an instant dislike to him. Poffenberger now had a new doghouse to live in. Durocher's doghouse, however, did not allow long-term residents. After only three games, the trap door sprung open, and Poffenberger was given a train ticket to Montreal and the minor leagues. He never reported to Montreal, heading home to Williamsport, Maryland, instead.

After a year of local baseball, he returned to the Dodgers organization with the Nashville Volunteers in the Southern Association. By the end of the 1940 season, he had compiled an amazing 26-9 record. The closest rival won just 18 games. He returned to Nashville in 1941 but could not duplicate his success from the previous year. Following a year in the PCL, he enlisted in the U.S. Marines and was shipped to the Pacific theater.

In one of baseball's richest ironies, Poffenberger, a very handsome man, was chosen as the model for the U. S. Marines recruitment posters. One of baseball's wildest free spirits became the symbol of tough, disciplined fighting men defending the world from fascism.

After the war, he returned to baseball for two seasons but could not climb back to the major leagues.

Like many of the outsized personalities in sports, Poffenberger was credited with quotes and feats that never happened. The "Breakfast of Champions" tale is one such humorous bit of folklore. As the story goes, he was being interviewed on a Detroit radio show that was sponsored by a cereal company. The interviewer asked him to name his favorite breakfast after prompting him to name the sponsor's fare. Poffenberger, not one to be manipulated, replied, "Ham, eggs and two bottles of beer." The author of that alleged quip denies that it ever took place.

One famous story that unfortunately is true is the conflict with an umpire that resulted in Poffenberger firing the baseball point blank into the ump's chest. Playing for Nashville in 1941, Boots was not scheduled to pitch and threw himself a party with the main guest being a bottle of gin. When George Jeffcoat, the starting Nashville pitcher, developed a blister on his finger, Poffenberger was summoned to the mound. From the minute he stepped on the field he displayed a loud belligerence to the umpires and opposing players alike.

After only a few calls by home plate umpire, Dutch Hoffman, Poffenberger approached the plate and threw the ball at point blank range. Hoffman cushioned the impact with his chest protector and removed his assailant from the game. He received a 90-day suspension, which effectively shut him down for the season.

Poffenberger died at the age of 84 in 1999 and was buried near of the upper reaches of the Potomac River in his hometown of Williamsport, Maryland.

Turkey Gross

Ewell Gross was not a prototypical shortstop. His 6' 0" height was unusual for a middle infielder of his era, and he ran with a slow and awkward gait. Teammates thought he ran like a turkey and appropriately renamed him Turkey Gross. [24]

Although he spent most of his adult life as a baseball player, he only enjoyed one season in the big leagues. Born in Mesquite, Texas, in 1896, he secured his first professional job at the age of 19 in his home state playing for the Paris Red Snappers of the Western League. He was the everyday shortstop for the Red Snappers for two years (1915-1916) before the war effort snapped him up.

When he returned to civilian life in 1920 he signed with the San Antonio Bears for whom he played over the next five years. On December 4, 1924, he received some shocking but happy news, the Bears had just traded him to the Boston Red Sox for Danny Clark, a third baseman. [25]

Opening Day, 1925, was a red-letter day for Gross. He started the game at shortstop and reached base twice, a triple and a walk, scoring two runs in a 9-8 loss to Philadelphia. The following day he went hitless in four tries. He started the first six games for the Red Sox, but had only three hits. The following day he sat on the bench. On April 28 he made his ninth and last appearance in a major league game, failing to hit safely in two at bats. [26] His "lifetime" batting average was just .094. He was sold to the Dallas Steers in the Texas League and remained in the minors until his retirement in 1928.

Gross died in Dallas in 1936 and was buried in Mesquite. He was only 39 years old.

Ice Box Chamberlain

Elton P. Chamberlain was a 19th century pitcher who accumulated 157 wins in just 10 seasons in the major leagues. He was renown for his coolness under pressure, if he felt any pressure at all. On October 3, 1888, the right-hander cruised to a huge lead pitching for the St. Louis Browns in the American Association against the Kansas City Cowboys. Exhibiting the ultimate in self-confidence, he took the mound in the eighth inning and began to pitch left-handed, a feat he had performed four years earlier in the minor leagues. Chamberlain iced the Cowboys, blanking them the last two innings. For this kind of cold-blooded efficiency, his teammates named him Ice Box. [27]

Chamberlain was born in Buffalo, New York, an icebox of a city perched on the shores of Lake Erie. After a short apprenticeship in the minor leagues, he signed with the Louisville Colonels in 1886. He was sold to the St. Louis Browns late in the 1888 season and helped them clinch the American Association pennant. Chamberlain took the mound almost every other day down the stretch, finishing with an 11-2 record in just over one month on the Browns' roster. In the pre-modern World

Series against the New York Giants, he started five games, winning two and losing three. The Giants claimed the title six games to four.

The following year he reached the pinnacle of his career, going 32-15 for the Browns. Midway through the 1890 season he was sold to the Columbus Solons. Six months later he was sold again, this time to the Philadelphia Athletics. He posted a 22-23 record for the second division A's.

This Ice Box was well used, going to the Cincinnati Reds in 1892. His three-year tenure with the Reds resulted in a 45-44 record. He finished his career with a brief stint in Cleveland, pitching in just two games for the Spiders in 1896.

During his days with the Browns, a St. Louis construction company built a string of new railroad stations and named several after his favorite hometown players. Chamberlain and Doc Bushong were among the honorees. [28]

Chamberlain died in 1929 in Baltimore, Maryland, at the age of 61.

Buckshot May

William Herbert May was born just weeks before the turn of the century in Bakersfield, California. May could have explained his nickname by claiming to be a crack marksman with a shotgun. The name Buckshot certainly projected a masculine aura. Unfortunately, the truth lent a completely different connotation to his name. May was a reputed to be a left-handed pitcher who sprayed fastballs to all corners of the batter's box. The short duration of his major league career was said to stand in testimony of his lack of control. He pitched a total of one inning for the 1924 Pittsburgh Pirates. [29]

May's minor league record would tend to contradict such a harsh assessment of his abilities. Over 13 seasons in the lower realms of professional baseball, he pitched 2,692 innings, allowing only 867 walks, a pace of 2.9 per nine innings. He posted 176 wins against 138 losses, not the kind of record expected of a pitcher who could not find the plate.

His professional debut took place in 1922 with the Seattle Indians of the Pacific Coast League. The Indians' roster was chock full of future major leaguers, so the 22-years-old pitcher saw little action. In four appearances, he logged only eight innings, allowing two runs. His sophomore campaign in 1923 netted him an 18-15 record with the Omaha Buffaloes of the Western League. After winning 15 more games in 1924 with Oklahoma City, his contract was purchased by the Pittsburgh Pirates.

After his small sip of coffee with the Pirates, he was returned to Oklahoma City where he continued to dominate Western League batters. He notched 65 wins over the next three seasons with Oklahoma and San Francisco. He concluded his career in 1935 without ever receiving another shot at the big leagues. Perhaps he was a victim of his unfortunate nickname. A major league owner, hearing of a 26-game winner named Lefty, for example, might have been more inclined to bring him into the fold.

His playing days over, he returned to the Bakersfield area where he lived a long life, passing away in 1984 at the age of 84.

Above: left – Baby Doll Jacobson   right – Bunny Brief
Below: left – Ice Box Chamberlain   right – Boots Poffenberger

Chapter Four – Background: Racial, Ethnic and Geographical

Players with a rural background, whether they talked, looked, or acted the part, frequently found themselves renamed Rube, Hick, etc. These rustic nicknames were very condescending, as if the rest of the team consisted of sophisticates and urbanites. Worse was the fate of anyone whose facial features were Asian. They might become Jap or Chink. But the most egregious name may have been reserved for the dark-skinned. Three players elected to be identified as Nig for the rest of their lives.

Another nickname, politically incorrect by modern standards, was universally applied to the hearing impaired. Although the name Dummy did not reflect racial/ethnic background or appearance, it is included in this chapter because of the sheer boorishness and insensitivity of those who assigned it to someone less fortunate.

Rube Waddell

Rube Waddell does not meet the profile of lesser-known players, but his impact on baseball demands some attention. In addition to his fame and accomplishments on the field, he had a broad-reaching effect on the culture of the game. Thirty baseball players have gone down in history with the name Rube. Three of them were born with the name Rueben, a name commonly shortened to Rube (Rube Fischer, Rube Melton and Rube Oldring). The majority of those remaining owe their adopted name to George Edward Waddell, the original Rube. Most Rubes, like Waddell, hailed from rural or small town America. A few picked up the name because they had something in common with Rube Waddell; they pitched like him or had a brush with him at some point.

The word "rube" is defined as an unsophisticated person from a rural area, a hick. The term originated toward the end of the 19th century, the same time as the young Waddell was beginning to ply his trade as a left-handed pitcher. The name Rueben was viewed as a country name. The pejorative nickname was shortened to Rube. A simple boy from the back woods trying to make his way in "the big city" was frequently branded as Farmer, Hick or the name of the small town he called home. Waddell was the unfortunate recipient of the new insult gaining traction in metropolitan areas, Rube.

Waddell was born in Bradford, Pennsylvania in 1876. Bradford, near the New York state border, boasts of its proximity to Allegheny National Forest. An oil boom occurred a few years after Waddell's birth, and the population began a surge that peaked in 1940 at 18,000 people, but the area was still isolated and decidedly rural in nature. The 2000 Census counted 9,000 remaining residents.

Waddell arrived in Louisville, Kentucky, in 1897 as a 20-year old with scant experience. He pitched for local baseball teams throughout northern and western Pennsylvania until a scout from the Louisville Colonels ventured north to check him out. Louisville offered him the princely sum of $500 to join the Colonels for the last two weeks of the season. He started two games but did not really distinguish himself. Nor did he extinguish the Colonels' interest in his skills.

Louisville manager Fred Clarke packed him off to the Detroit Tigers of the Western League with the intention of getting him back, if warranted. His performance for Detroit was just average, but Louisville pulled him back to the National League for the 1899 season. After a promising rookie season (7-2 with a 3.08 ERA), he was sent to Pittsburgh along with Fred Clarke and 10 other players, including Honus Wagner. The National League was contracting to eight teams and Louisville lost the game of musical chairs.

As the century turned over, so did Waddell's career. Despite a lackluster won-loss record of 8-13, he led the league in ERA, WHIP and strikeouts per nine innings. During the 1901 season, the Pirates sold him to the Chicago Orphans. Waddell then jumped to Los Angeles in the California League, and then back to the Philadelphia Athletics in the one-year-old American League.

Waddell suddenly blossomed into the premier strike out artist of his time. In an era dominated by slap-hitters, his fastball/curveball arsenal redefined the model of the big league pitcher. He led the American League in "Ks" for next six years, exceeding 300 for two consecutive years, 302 in 1903 and 349 in 1904. No American League lefthander in the modern era has yet eclipsed his 349 strikeouts in a season. He won 27 games in 1905, his finest season. He also led the league in games, ERA and, of course, strikeouts. Connie Mack declared that Waddell had "the best combination of speed and curves of any pitcher who played the game."

Mack sold him to the St. Louis Browns in 1908. He played out the remaining three years of his big league career with the Browns. He spent 1910 through 1913 in the minor leagues, an uncommon occurrence among players with Hall of Fame credentials. He spent 1913, his final year as a player, at Class C Fargo-Moorhead in the Northern League. His 3-9 record convinced employer and employee that the end had arrived.

Reason dictates that the name Rube did not originate with the players and fans of rural Pennsylvania, most of them candidates for "rube" status themselves. One might think the name was affixed during his brief stay with Louisville in 1897, or possibly in Detroit the following year. But that would be wrong. In 1896, he traveled to Franklin, Pennsylvania, to try out for the local team. One of the players, upon seeing the hayseed from an even smaller town, called out "Hey, Rube." The name would last. [1]

Had his teammates not been so hasty in sticking a name on him, he most likely would have been branded with a sobriquet worthy of his extremely eccentric nature. He has been described as a real-life Peter Pan, a nut job, flaky, irresponsible, alcoholic, wild, crazy and childish.

Waddell was aptly-described by Joe MacKay: "He had no concept of responsibility and, feeling that life was one constant good time, sought out excitement with a childlike glee, chasing fire engines, marching in a parade twirling a baton, or wrestling an alligator when he was scheduled for pitching assignments. Inside that masculine body (he was big for his day), which stood at 6' 1½' and weighed around 200 pounds, was the spirit of an impish child." [2]

The reason for his sale from Pittsburgh to Chicago, then Philadelphia to St. Louis, was directly related to his unpredictable antics. He once excused himself from the mound to chase a fire truck that had raced past the ballpark.

On the Beer Drinkers and Hell Raisers section of the Deadball Era web site, Waddell is profiled: "Rube…had three passions in his life: baseball, fishing and following fire engines! Not the most cerebral ballplayer of all-time, he was an easy going, slow witted sort who loved to have a good time."

Waddell fittingly died on April Fool's Day in 1914. He was just 37-years-old. Sadly, many faster and bigger fire trucks would be missed.

In 1946, the Old Timers Committee elected him to the Hall of Fame. Were he alive, he might have run off to a fishing hole the day of the induction.

Rube Ward

John Andrew Ward was the first member of the Rube Class of 1902. He was the first player after Waddell to become known as Rube. He debuted in April of 1902 as an outfielder for the Brooklyn Superbas. He gained his nickname from his rural upbringing in the heart of central Ohio. He appeared in just 13 games for the Superbas and acquitted himself well with a .290 batting average. Sadly, the Brooklyn club chose to release him in August of 1902. Three years of minor league play and his professional playing days were over.

He died in 1945 in Akron, Ohio.

Rube Kisinger

By September of 1902, the baseball world had a new star pitcher, Rube Waddell. By the end of that month the game had two more players named Rube. Charles Samuel Kisinger made his debut with the Detroit Tigers on September 10. Like Waddell, he was from the "sticks." And like Waddell, he was a pitcher, albeit a right-hander, so teammates and scribes had two reasons to name him Rube. He was born in 1876 in Adrian, Michigan, once called "the fence capital of the world."

Tigers' manager Frank Dwyer named the 25-year-old as a starter five times in the waning days of the season. Kisinger completed all five games for a 2-3 record and a respectable ERA of 3.12. His rookie performance was good enough for a spot on the 1903 roster and the last spot in the four-man rotation. His 1903 record was 7-9 with a 2.96 ERA, which placed him last among the four starters. In October, the Tigers included him in a five-player trade with the Buffalo Bisons of the Class A Eastern League (later absorbed into the International League).

Unlike many players demoted out of the major leagues, Kisinger flourished and carved out a very successful career as a minor league pitcher. He won 24 games in 1904, 20 games in 1905 and 23 in 1906, all with Buffalo. During his seventh year in Buffalo he was traded to the Jersey City Skeeters and continued to amass victories in the soon-to-be International League.

Beginning in 1912, he moved to the Southern Association and continued to pitch at a high level for Memphis, New Orleans, Atlanta and Nashville until his 39-year-old arm could no longer do the job on a regular basis.

Looking back on his minor league career, he could boast of 205 wins against only 160 losses. Sporadic record keeping prevents a career ERA calculation, but we can report a WHIP of 1.095 over the span of 15 years and 3,282 innings. A nickname that originally taunted him for his background, could easily link him to the celebrated career of Rube Waddell.

Kisinger died in 1941 in Huron, Ohio, as an obscure former baseball player.

In 2008, the International League was raised from the dead and reorganized as a Triple A league. The following year, the IL named 14 players to its 2009 Hall of Fame class. Joining such stars as Red Schoendienst, Harry the Hat Walker and Stump Merrill, is Rube Kisinger. Long relegated to the dustbin of baseball history, the "hick" from Michigan lives again.

Rube Vickers

At the dawning of the twentieth century only one player in the major or minor leagues was nicknamed Rube. As the term "rube" grew in popularity, and the exploits of Rube Waddell spread across the nation, this moniker began to metastasize throughout American culture, not just the baseball world. The term was already popular in the peculiar world of traveling carnival workers. Whenever a "carnie" detected trouble from a local, the rallying cry "Hey, Rube" would send out an alarm to co-workers to come join the fray. But now the term became an easy handle to stick on an unsophisticated baseball player. The name could also used as a flattering reference to the skills of Rube Waddell, or even mockingly to tease a pitcher of modest skills and high ambitions.

Harry Porter Vickers joined the Cincinnati Reds just 11 days after Rube Kisinger's debut in Detroit. St. Marys was (and still is) as small town in southwestern Ontario, Canada. The area was rich in limestone, which was used to construct many of the town's buildings, leading to the nickname "The Stone Town." Vickers had a double whammy working against him. He came from a small town in a rural area in another country with its own accent and vocabulary.

He joined the Class B Terre Haute Hottentots in 1902 as a 24-year-old pitcher. Over 321 innings later, he had a 19-17 record and a call-up to the Cincinnati Reds. Perhaps he had nothing left in his right arm, because he did poorly in his three starts and finished the 1902 season 0-3 with an ERA of 6.00.

Vickers lost his gig with the Reds and signed with the Holyoke Paperweights in 1903. He torched the Connecticut League with a 22-10 record, even batting .295 to help his own cause. Once again he earned a late-season shot in the big leagues with Brooklyn. The team was called the Superbas, but Vickers was anything but superb. In four games he surrendered 23 runs for 10.93 ERA average and an 0-1 record. As the 1903 season ended, he was still searching for his first major league victory.

Holyoke welcomed him back in 1904 and he rewarded them with 28 wins over a season and a half. With Seattle in the PCL he won 39 games in 1906. To his great disappointment, no big league invitation resulted from his incredible season.

He returned to the east in 1907 to play in Williamsport, Pennsylvania. Once again he excelled while posting a 25-9 record, leading the league in wins. Connie Mack gave him a chance to make the Philadelphia A's squad, and this time Vickers made it work, winning two late season games. Coincidentally, Rube Waddell was also on the roster that year. For the first time in his career, Vickers was asked to start the new season in the major leagues. Unfortunately for A's fans, Vickers was the only Rube left on the roster, Waddell was sold to St. Louis.

In 1908, he became the workhorse of the Philadelphia staff, throwing 317 innings. Teammates Eddie Plank, Chief Bender and Jack Coombs all pitched many fewer innings. Vickers' 18 wins (18-19) led the team, as did his 156 strikeouts and six shutouts. He allowed no homeruns during the season, obviously leading the league in that category. For the first time in career, he could feel that he was living up to the Rube Waddell connotation of his name, and not a reference to the hick from Canada.

For the second time in his life, he followed a 300 plus inning season with a poor showing in 1909. Coincidence or not, he again could not duplicate his success from the previous year. He could only win two games for the Mack Men and on October 9, 1909, he pitched his last big league game.

He joined Jack Dunn's Eastern League Baltimore Orioles in 1910, once more tossing over 300 innings and winning 25 games. Ditto in 1911, this time claiming 32 wins. In 1913, at age 35, the gas gauge was approaching empty. He pitched just one inning in which he was touched for four runs. Jack Dunn had a replacement in the wings; a young pitcher named Ruth would join the Orioles in 1914 and change baseball history.

One last try with Jersey City in 1914 would prove what everyone else knew, this Rube was done as a pitcher.

Rube Vickers still holds the Pacific Coast league mark for strikeouts (409 in 1906) and innings pitched (526 also in 1906). One must bear in mind that the PCL played a 200 game season in that era. [3] Vickers also played in the California Winter League that year with Santa Barbara. [4] The wear and tear on his pitching arm undoubtedly compromised his ability to pitch effectively during various junctures in his career.

Vickers only possesses one record in the major leagues, a mark that he would not include on his resume'. In 1902, while playing in his rookie season with Cincinnati, he was instructed by manager Joe Kelley to get behind the plate and catch. This was the final game of the season and the weather in Pittsburgh was dreadful, cold and drizzly. The field was a mud track. The Pirates owner, Barney Dreyfuss, refused to cancel the meaningless game. His club was just one victory away from the National League record of 103 victories. Kelley was so incensed that he told his players to turn the game into a farce. Outfielders were sent to the mound to pitch. Many of the Reds lit cigars and blew smoke into the Pirates' faces. During the process of playing the clown, Vickers allowed six passed balls, a single game record that exists to this day. [4a]

Oh yes, the Pirates got their win, 11-2, but the fans were so incensed that Dreyfuss had to refund everyone's money.

Vickers lived to be 80 years old, dying in 1958 in Belleville, Michigan. Vickers would have been proud to learn that the Canadian Baseball Hall of Fame was moved to his hometown of St. Marys in 1994. On the other hand, he may have been disappointed that a search for his name among the inductees would come up empty.

Rube Vinson

Earnest Augustus Vinson was born in Dover, Delaware, in 1879, not too far from Philadelphia and Baltimore. Despite its proximity to two metropolitan areas, Dover was decidedly rural and contributed to Vinson's new nickname.

Vinson first played professionally with the Providence Grays of the Eastern League in 1904. His .360 batting average earned him a shot with the Cleveland Naps in September of that same year. He appeared in 15 games in the outfield and hit .306. Manager Nap Lajoie invited him back for the 1905 season. The good times in Cleveland soon ended. He failed to raise his 1905 average up to the .200 level and he was shipped off to the Chicago White Sox. He hit just .250 for the Sox and lost his roster spot. He found employment in the Three-I League but could not duplicate his earlier success and retired following the 1910 season with Danville in the Virginia League.

Vinson appears in the baseball history books due to a quaint and obsolete rule called the "courtesy runner." Under this rule, which existed until 1950, a player unable to perform the duties as a base runner could be replaced by a teammate on the base paths for the duration of the inning or until he crossed home plate. The temporarily disabled player could reenter the game defensively for the next half inning. In 1906, Vinson's White Sox teammate, Frank Hemphill had been plunked in the head while batting and wobbled away from the plate. Nap Lajoie, manager of the Cleveland team gave his blessing to a substitute runner, Rube Vinson. The story had a happy ending when Hemphill later took his place in left field. [5]

Knowing what we know today about concussions, maybe the ending was not so happy. Hemphill then played sparingly for a short period of time and was sold to Altoona in the Tri-State League.

Vinson lived a long life, but still checked out prematurely. At age 72, he was cleaning the upstairs windows in his home in Chester,

Pennsylvania. He fell to the ground and died three days later from his injuries.

Rube Kroh

Floyd Myron Kroh left his hometown of Friendship, New York, at age 19 and began his pitching career in Albany with the Senators of the New York State League. He set the league record for 15 strikeouts in a single game. [6] After 30 games he was sold to the Boston Americans (also known as the Pilgrims and renamed the Red Sox two years later).

The great Rube Waddell had just completed the best year of his career in 1905 and was the talk of the baseball world. Kroh shared two traits with Waddell, he was a competent left-handed pitcher and he hailed from a rural area. He was quite amazed and perplexed by the big city and its unfamiliar ways. Rube was his new name.

Joining the Boston club late in September, he was only able to log one game before the season ended. He took full advantage of his brief opportunity by pitching a complete game, two-hit shutout. He would start the 1907 season as a member of the big league team.

He saw limited action for Boston in 1907 (seven games) and was sold to the Johnstown Johnnies in the Tri-State League to begin the 1908 season. His success with Johnstown led to his purchase by the potent Chicago Cubs. He spent three years with Chicago but could not crack the starting rotation led by Mordecai Brown and Ed Reulbach. He saw action in just 27 games in three seasons and compiled a 12-5 won-loss record.

He spent all of 1911 and most of 1912 in the minor leagues with the Louisville Colonels of the American Association before the Boston Braves bought out his contract and called him back to Beantown. After three games with the Braves in 1912, his major league career was over. He spent the next four years working in the minor leagues before entering the military to play his part in World War I.

Kroh spent two years in France as a master sergeant before a war wound sent him stateside to recover. He attempted a comeback in the minors in 1920 through 1922 but was handicapped by an injury that prevented him from performing at a pre-war level. [7]

Kroh will forever have a prominent niche in baseball lore for his role in the famous play known as "Merkle's Boner." Kroh was a little-used pitcher for the 1908 Chicago Cubs team that was fighting the New York Giants and Pittsburgh Pirates for the National League pennant. On September 23, the Cubs and Giants squared off in New York with both clubs in a dead heat. The Giants came to bat in the bottom in the ninth with the score tied at one run each.

Fred Merkle, at age 19, the youngest player in the National League, was given his first big league start due to the fact that regular first baseman, Fred Tenney, woke up with a sore back. Merkle came to the plate in the ninth with Moose McCormick on first base and one out. Cubs' starter Jack Pfiester was still on the mound. Merkel singled down the right field line moving McCormick to third base. Al Bridwell, the Giants shortstop, walked to the plate with the winning run on third. Bridwell lined Pfiester's first pitch into center field and McCormick scampered home with the winning run.

Giant fans immediately swarmed the field to begin a raucous victory celebration. Merkle was mobbed between first and second base and decided to retreat to the dugout for his own safety. At that point, chaos and confusion reigned. What happened next depends on who tells the story. Joe McGinnity, coaching first base for the Giants, saw the ball return to the infield and sail over the head of Cubs shortstop Joe Tinker. McGinnity out-wrestled Tinker for the ball and wisely threw the ball into a crowd of fans.

Rube Kroh then entered the drama and injected a comedic touch. Seeing the ball scooped up by a tall young fan in a derby hat, Kroh approached the fan and demanded the ball. When his request was emphatically denied, Kroh struck the young gentleman on the head, crushing his hat down over his face. The ball dropped to the ground where Kroh retrieved it and threw it to Tinker. Tinker turned toward second base and spied Johnny Evers standing on the bag waving his arms in the air and screaming for the ball. Instead of Evers to Tinker to Chance, this critical play went Kroh to Tinker to Evers.

Plate umpire Hank O'Day raced toward second base, and as Evers touched the bag, the ump declared Merkle out on a force play. The run did not count; the game was still tied 1-1. To circumvent further chaos, O'Day rather ingeniously declared the game suspended because of darkness. [8]

In a sense, the ruling was correct, but the interjection of a fan and two players not officially part of the game, should have caused the ball to be dead, and the play over. This play has been called the most controversial of all time. The Giants appealed but league president Harry Pulliam upheld the ruling on the field. The season ended 10 days later with the Giants and Cubs still tied for first place. The suspended game would be replayed on October 4 with the winner able to lay claim to the National League pennant.

The Cubs won the play-off and went on to defeat he Detroit Tigers in the World Series. Rube Kroh, the unsung hero of the Cubs' championship did not appear in the World Series, and was denied a share of winner's bonus. The Cubs' management felt that players who did not actually appear in a game did not deserve a financial reward. Kroh threatened to sue, and was eventually paid an equal share of $1,400. [9]

After his playing career, Kroh umpired in the Southern League for over 20 years until his health failed in 1943. He died in New Orleans, his adopted home, in 1944.

Rube Manning

Walter S. Manning was born in 1883 near Chambersburg, Pennsylvania, a small town nestled in the northern tip of the Blue Ridge Mountains. After spending his first year in professional baseball in equally rural Williamsport, he was acquired by the New York Highlanders and summoned to the Washington Heights section of Manhattan. As another young pitcher coming to the big city for the first time, the name Rube was an easy fit.

After joining the Highlanders in late August of 1907, he only toed the mound during one game, pitching a complete game loss. He evidently impressed New York manager Clark Griffith. Manning was invited back in the spring of 1908 and earned a spot on the Highlanders' roster. He and Happy Jack Chesbro were the workhorses of the staff, seeing action in 40 games each, and both logging ERAs under 3.00. Manning posted a 13-14 record, actually pretty good on a team that lost over 100 games and finished dead last in the American League.

The 1909 edition of the future Yankees was much improved and climbed to fourth place. Manning, however, did not show improvement in equal measure. He pitched in just 26 games and finished at 7-11 under the new field boss, George Stallings.

With an infusion of new pitching talent in 1910, Manning only started in nine of his 16 game appearances. Russ Ford, Hippo Vaughn, Jack Quinn and Jack Warhop started 116 games between them. His 2-4 record brought his major league total to 22-32. The writing was on the wall for Manning's career.

He was released after the 1910 season and found employment in the Tri-State League at Reading to begin the 1911 season. Over the next seven years he played for five different teams but could not get back to the big leagues despite a 20-12 season with Allentown in 1912. After the 1917 season with the Wilkes-Barre Barons, he called it quits at age 34.

In Ty Cobb's memoirs, he discussed his struggles fitting in with the Tigers in his early years in Detroit. As a loner who spent most of his spare time hiking or holed up in his room, he let his batting and fielding failures eat away at him. He particularly remembered being stuck out three times by Rube Manning. [10]

Rube Manning was on the mound on June 30, 1908, the day 41-year-old Cy Young pitched his third no-hitter in an 8-0 drubbing of the Highlanders at Hilltop Park. Young was on his way to his 15th and final season in which he notched 20 wins or more. [11]

Manning died in 1930 in Williamsport, Pennsylvania, the scene of his first baseball success in professional baseball. He was just 47-years-old.

Rube Ellis

George William Ellis signed his first professional baseball contract in 1905 at the age of 19. The lanky outfielder reported to his new team, the Los Angeles Angels of the Pacific Coast League as a bashful, socially awkward teen from nearby Downey, California. The area around Downey probably bore more resemblance to the California portrayed in the 1950s black and white Zorro episodes than the Los Angeles we know today. No sooner than opening his mouth with a naïve question, Ellis was branded with the name Rube, not unlike Zorro's swordplay victims who received three quick slashes in the shape of a "Z."

Ellis saw little action his first year, stepping to the plate just 18 times. But he left his mark with three singles and three doubles for a .333 average. He returned to the Angels the following year and barely surpassed the .200 batting mark. He remained with Los Angeles through the 1907 and 1908 seasons before catching the eye of a St. Louis Cardinal scout.

He made the Cardinals' roster in the spring of 1909, and soon became the everyday left fielder for Roger Bresnahan's struggling team. During his four years with St. Louis, he performed reasonably well, but never excelled at any facet of the game. During the 1912 season, he was called upon to play less and less, and eventually lost his spot on the roster prior to the 1913 season. October 6, 1912 would prove to be his last appearance in a major league game.

He was sold back to the Los Angeles Angels where he remained for the next nine years. In 1914, Ellis led the PCL in RBIs with 120, batting .310 for the year. He attempted comebacks in 1921 and 1925 but at age 40 conceded his skills to Father Time.

During his tenure with the Angels, Ellis played in the California Winter League, a popular venue for current and former big leaguers to earn some extra coin and keep their skills sharp. What made this league special was the decision to admit Negro players and later entire Negro teams. It was in this setting that Rube Ellis competed against the great Rube Foster. Foster had picked up the nicknamed because of his pitching skills a la Rube Waddell. Some say he named himself Rube after a pitching duel with Waddell. [12]

The loss of Ellis' major league career was eased by his return to his native California and success in the Pacific Coast League. He settled down in Pico River, not far from his birthplace. After his playing days had ended, Ellis served as the baseball coach at nearby Whittier College from 1924 through 1929.

The Proud Rubes

Baseball is overstocked with pitchers, great and average, who became known as Cy in honor of Cy Young. What young player would not be flattered to adopt that great name, even if it were dispensed mockingly in some cases? Similarly, a large group of players who accepted the nickname Rube did so because the name compared them to the great pitcher, Rube Waddell. These players, all pitchers, aspired to reach the same heights of their namesake. And, in some instances, the name Rube allowed them to escape such given names as Welton Claude (Ehrhart) and Otto Claude (Peters).

The roll call of aspiring Rube Waddells would sound like this: Rube Benton, Rube Ehrhart, Rube Foster (not the great Negro League founder), Rube Marquard, Rube Marshall, Rube Peters, Rube Schauer, Rube Walberg and Rube Yarrison. Rube Marshall was also called Cy Marshall, linking him with two of the era's best pitchers. Only Marquard lived up to the legacy of Rube Waddell.

Edward DeGroff falls into a sub-category all his own. He was nicknamed Rube because he once played in a game against Rube Foster. Though the nickname involved a very brief brush with the Negro League icon, the name stuck.

Rube Schauer deserves a special note as well. He was born in Russia in 1891 as Dimitri Ivanovich Dimitrihoff. He changed his name to Alexander John Schauer once in the United States. At some point in his early career, he picked up the nickname Rube, and his transformation into an American was complete.

Bumpus Jones

Charles Leander Jones was born in the small rural town of Cedarville, Ohio, in 1870 and made his big league debut in 1892. Had he burst onto the baseball scene 10 years later, he would have been a prime candidate to procure the nickname Rube. Like many of his 19th century contemporaries, Jones ascended directly from local/regional teams to the major leagues. The 22-year-old rustic found himself in the relative metropolis of Cincinnati with little experience in the ways of the city-folk.

The term bumpkin, or country bumpkin, had emigrated from Europe where it had been used for centuries to identify the unsophisticated commoners who dared mingle with their cosmopolitan betters. Bumpkin was converted to Bumpus and Jones had a new name for perpetuity.

Jones may have been a bumpkin, but he knew how to pitch and he also knew where to find a game and earn a few bucks. Traveling from one Ohio town to another, he became known as "an arm for hire." His peripatetic nature eventually put him in the right spot at the right time.

The big league Red Stockings were due to visit Wilmington, Ohio, to play an exhibition game against the locals. Jones was hired to join the team but did not get into the game until the seventh inning. The Cincinnati nine had built a comfortable lead but could not manage a single base hit against Jones. Manager Charlie Comiskey offered Jones a chance to pitch in the final game of the Reds' season. [13]

Our Mr. Jones joined the Cincinnati Reds on October 15, 1892. His rookie debut could not have gone much better. He pitched a complete game no-hitter against the Pirates in which he allowed one run and four walks. An error allowed an unearned run to score, denying him the shutout. His brief rookie season ended with a perfect 1-0 record and a 0.444 WHIP.

Jones and his team no doubt had great expectations for the 1893 season. Sadly, the Reds' opponents thoroughly thrashed him over a stretch of seven games and left him with a 1-4 record and an ERA of 10.05. One theory for his failure was a rule change moving the pitching mound from 50 to 60 feet from home plate. A serious beaning may have also contributed to the demise of his skills. For whatever reason, the magic was gone and so was Jones. He was sold to the New York Giants in midseason.

Sometimes a change of scenery can work wonders on an athlete's performance. That was not the case for Bumpus Jones. In his first game in New York he was given a starting assignment but failed to discover the general location of the plate. He walked 10 batters in four innings and surrendered five hits. The Giants bought him a train ticket home and the big league dream was over.

He was unable to find a professional job in 1894, but a year later he caught on with the Grand Rapids Gold Bugs in the Class A Western League. His 12-23 season did not impress the Gold Bugs and he was cast asunder again until securing a position with the Columbus Senators in 1896. The magic returned and the right-hander went 44-25 over the next two seasons.

No major league offers ever materialized, so he finished his career in the minor leagues with Fort Wayne, Wheeling, and the Cleveland Lake Shores in 1900. Cleveland was in the American League, which became a major league circuit the following year. Had Jones held onto his job for one more season he may have returned to the big leagues by default.

Although he finished his short career with a 2-4 record and 7.99 ERA, Jones secured his place in history by becoming the first and only pitcher to toss a no-hitter in his major league debut. Bobo Holloman pitched a no-hitter in his first big league start, but he had previously pitched in relief. Jones' no-hitter, coming on the last day of the season on October 15th, also stands out as the latest no-hitter ever pitched in a season.

Early Ohio census records listed Jones as a mulatto. His death certificate categorized him as white. Family genealogy research traced his ancestors back to Pocahontas in Virginia. [14] Where he belongs in the ethnic/racial spectrum is cloudy, at best. He could have emerged from baseball as Chief Jones or Nig Jones. Additionally, he was not big in stature, and could have qualified to be Skinny Jones or something similar.

Complications from a stroke claimed his life in 1938 in Xenia, Ohio, just a few miles from his birthplace in Cedarville. He was 68 years old.

Hick Cady

Forest Leroy Cady (nee Bergland in 1886) hailed from a small town in Illinois. Today, Bishop Hill, Illinois, is a sleepy rural village in the western-central part of the state. Swedish immigrants hoping to establish a utopian communal lifestyle founded the village in 1846. But it would be unfair to say that Cady grew up in the middle of nowhere. He grew up on the far side of nowhere, earning the nickname Hick.

Cady's first professional team was the 1908 Ottumwa Packers in nearby Iowa. He was on the bottom rung of minor league play. The following year he was promoted to the Evansville River Rats, a Class B team in the Central League where he became the starting catcher.

In 1911, he was catching for the Newark Indians in the Class A Eastern League when the Boston Red Sox came calling. One year later he was backing up first-string catcher Bill Carrigan for the pennant-winning Bosox. As a rookie, he had the honor of appearing in seven of eight games of the World Series against the New York Giants (there was a tie game). In fact, he started Game One as the battery-mate of Smoky Joe Wood and singled off New York's Jeff Tesreau. He also caught Smoky Joe in the decisive eighth game. Although he batted only .136 for the Series, he accomplished what very few rookies had done before, or have done since. During Game Four in the Polo Grounds, the Giants were batting in the seventh inning with John McGraw coaching third base. Art Fletcher doubled in a run to make the score 2-1 Boston. Fletcher then reached third base on a line drive hit by pinch hitter Moose McCormick. The ball had been knocked down by second baseman Steve Yerkes and rolled a few feet away. McGraw failed to see what the entire assemblage knew, Yerkes quickly recovering the ball. McGraw waved Fletcher toward the plate where Hick Cady watched in disbelief.

Fletcher knew he was a dead duck at home, but nobody disobeyed McGraw, ever. His only hope was to take a popular page from the McGraw playbook and try to bowl Cady over and spring the ball loose, somehow. Fletcher slid into the well-built Cady with spikes high, a la Ty Cobb, ripping into the catcher's chest protector. Cady held on to the ball until umpire Cy Rigler signaled the runner out, then spiked the ball near Fletcher's head and screamed, "You can't beat us playing ball so you try this horseshit? I should pound you into the dirt!" [15] The Red Sox held on to win the game 3-1. Cady chipped in with an RBI single.

Cady played a role in another interesting baseball anecdote from Game Three of the 1912 Series. He was batting with two outs in the bottom of the ninth inning, his Red Sox trailing by a run. He smacked a long drive into the late afternoon shadows in right-centerfield. Right fielder Josh Devore arrived in the general area of the ball's touchdown and stretched out in a desperate dive. He immediately jumped to his feet and made a dash for the locker room.

With no baseball in sight, the umpire ruled it a game ending catch and a win for the Giants. The following day, no fewer than three Boston fans claimed to possess the ball that had skipped untouched into the roped-in crowd. No one knows if Devore actually made the catch or just stole the game from the Red Sox.

In 1914, Cady caught for a 19-year old rookie pitcher named George Herman Ruth. The Sox finished in second place, but the stage was set for a Red Sox run that saw them reach, and win, the World Series three of the next four years.

In 1915, the Red Sox sent Rube Foster, Ernie Shore, Dutch Leonard, Joe Wood and Babe Ruth to the mound and edged out Ty Cobb's Tigers. Boston then rolled over the Phillies in the World Series 4-1. Cady played in 78 games and batted a career-high .278 for the season. In the Series, he caught four games and hit .333.

1916 was almost a repeat of the previous season for Cady. He appeared in exactly 78 games again, and helped the Sox to the pennant and a World Series victory over the Brooklyn Robins. He played a more limited role in this Fall Classic, a foreshadowing of the 1917 season.

Pinch Thomas and Sam Agnew caught most of the games during the 1917 season. Cady became the odd man out, appearing in only 17 games and batting well under .200.

The Red Sox traded Cady to the Philadelphia Phillies in the winter of 1918 for Stuffy McInnis. Cady remained a part-time catcher with the Phillies until his release in July of 1919. He did not return to the major leagues. He played four more seasons in the minor leagues before retiring at the end of the 1924 season at age 38. [16]

Cady, shedding the Hick moniker, umpired in the Pacific Coast League and Western League for several years after retiring as a player. In 1938, he moved closer to home by agreeing to umpire in the Three I League.

Cady holds the distinction of being one of only four Red Sox players who pinch hit for Babe Ruth. While still a pitcher, Ruth would occasionally smack the ball hard, but frequently struck out. The other three pinch hitters were Duffy Lewis, Delos Sheriff Gainor and Olaf Henriksen. Lewis was the only one who hit safely although Henriksen drew a walk. [17] Bobby Veach of the Yankees hit for Ruth, the outfielder, in 1925. (18]

Cady died in Cedar Rapids on March 3, 1946, as a result of a hotel fire. The blaze, probably started by a malfunctioning electric heater, was confined to one room. Cady was 60 years of age. [19]

Farmer Steelman

Five players have entered baseball history with the nickname Farmer. All were so-named for their agrarian roots. None of them played after 1910. Either the nickname lost its sting, or players took more umbrage to the name and pushed against it.

Morris James Steelman probably most deserves the name, and had no reason to reject it. In the off-season he actually was a farmer near Millville, New Jersey. [20] The town name suggests a manufacturing environment, but Millville was, and still is, a rich agricultural area known in the region as a major source of Jersey corn and tomatoes.

Steelman first played with the minor league Philadelphia Athletics in 1897, a Class B team in the Atlantic League. Two years later he made his big league debut as a backup catcher with the Louisville Colonels in the National League. The Colonels presented a perfect example of the stereotypical nicknames of the era. They sported a Chief (Zimmer), a Dummy (Hoy), a Doc (Powers), a Rube (Waddell), and a Deacon (Phillippe), among others. John Peter Wagner also appeared as a utility infielder. We know him today as Honus.

Steelman did not set the city of Louisville on fire, batting just .067 in four games, but the Brooklyn club saw potential and purchased him. After seeing action in only two games over a season and a half, he found himself unemployed in the middle of the 1901 season.

He joined the Eastern League's Hartford Indians and finally found his groove, batting .292 over 85 games. Before the 1901 season ended, he jumped his contract and signed with the Philadelphia Athletics, now a part of the new American League. [21] The Hartford Courant alleged that he "overdrew his salary here by $160," calling his action "reprehensible in the extreme." [22]

The bold move paid off, his new manager, Connie Mack, played him regularly for the rest of the season.

Sadly, 1902 was the "same-old-same-old" for Steelman and he languished on the Athletics' bench. He could not budge Ossee Schreckengost or Doc Powers out of the lineup. He took the field only 10 times, and five of those appearances were in the outfield. Following his last game in May, he was gone for good from the major leagues. He headed back to the Eastern League where he played for the Worcester Hustlers, Montreal Royals, and Rochester Bronchos before a one-year stint in the PCL with the Portland Browns in 1904.

After leading the PCL with 32 errors as a catcher, his West Coast adventure was over. [23]

He returned to Rochester for two more years, followed by Class B Utica for two years and finally Altoona in 1909. He batted just .226 over 11 minor league seasons and .218 over four major league seasons. One year he was launching a "can of corn" into the outfield, and the next year he was growing and selling corn to be canned. Steelman returned to New Jersey after his playing days and farmed until his death in 1944.

Farmer Vaughn

The first of the Farmers was Henry Francis Vaughn born in Ohio in 1864. His hometown was so rustic that the founders named it Ruraldale. The modern-day version of Ruraldale boasts 1,200 residents. While the city of Columbus is only 40 miles to the west, Ruraldale sits in a pocket of farmland bordered by I-70 to the north and Wayne National Forest to the south.

Vaughn joined the Cincinnati Red Stockings as a second-string catcher in October of 1876. He entered a game just one time and went hitless in three tries. The following spring he joined the newly formed New Orleans Pelicans of the Southern Association. No records exist of Vaughn's progress as a hitter, but he performed well enough to earn a contract with the big league Louisville Colonels of the American Association. He entered or started 51 games for the Colonels in 1888 but could not manage to reach the .200 batting level.

In 1889, he once again shared the Colonels' catching duties, but also had to share his nickname with Farmer (William) Weaver. The Colonels' also gave him playing time in the outfield.

In 1890, the Players' National League of Professional Base Ball Clubs, generally known a the Players' League, was formed with teams in eight cities, Boston (Reds), Brooklyn (Ward's Wonders), New York (Giants), Chicago (Pirates), Philadelphia (Athletics), Pittsburgh (Burghers), Cleveland (Infants) and Buffalo (Bisons). The new league set out to recruit players from the American Association and National League. Vaughn was caught in the Giants net and found himself in the metropolis of New York City. The backup catcher and outfielder had his best year with the Giants batting .256.

Sadly, the Players League could not sustain itself past the first year and dissolved into obscurity. Not until 1968 was it even officially recognized as a major league. The Boston and Philadelphia teams were absorbed into the American Association the following season.

Vaughn landed on his feet in 1891 with a job in his native Ohio. He signed with the Cincinnati Kelly's Killers as a back up catcher to King

Kelly himself. Correctly assessing his slim prospects of bumping Kelly from the starting position, he moved on to the Milwaukee Brewers in midseason. The following year he was back in Cincinnati, but this time with the National League Reds.

His career stabilized with the Reds and his performance improved greatly. By 1893 he was catching regularly and batting .280. Beginning with the 1894 season his hit near or above .300 each year until his final season where at age 35 he played part time and did not help the team offensively. He managed to raise his lifetime batting average to a very respectable .274, especially for a catcher.

This Farmer has left his mark in the record books. In 1894, he scored five runs in a game, tying him for second place with a long list of others. On the down side, he is tied in seventh place for the most passed balls in a season with 28.

Vaughn also made the Cincinnati Police blotter in 1895 when he reported the theft of one of his bats. The gendarmes quickly solved the crime when they discovered that a member of the visiting Chicago Cubs was the culprit. Malachi Kittridge returned the pilfered property and avoided arrest. [24]

Vaughn had his faults, as well. In 1890, he put a tag on hard-sliding Steve Brodie of the St. Louis Browns. He picked up the abandoned baseball bat and threw it at Brodie injuring his shoulder. He was ejected from the game and fined $25. [25]

After his nine years playing in Cincinnati, he made the Queen City his home until his death in 1914 at the age of 49.

Farmer Weaver

William B. Weaver was born in Parkersburg, West Virginia, in March of 1865, one month before General Robert E. Lee surrendered at Appomattox Court House effectively ending the Civil War. West Virginia had not yet celebrated its second year of statehood.

At the age of 23, Weaver signed with the Louisville Colonels of the American Association as an outfielder. He joined teammate Farmer Vaughn to create the only tandem of players named Farmer in baseball history (1888-1889). In 1889, Weaver crouched behind the plate in two games, making Weaver and Vaughn the only pair of catchers named Farmer to take the field for the same team at the same time.

Weaver, in his own right, became a regular on the Colonels until being sent to the Pittsburgh Pirates in 1894. He enjoyed a seven-year career and compiled a lifetime batting average of .278.

He played minor league ball from 1900 through 1910, bouncing from team to team. He called it quits after suiting up for the Lyons Lions, the Larned Wheat Kings, and the Great Bend Millers all in one season.

Weaver managed to stay under the radar for nearly a century until a modern day hitting feat resurrected his name. On April 15, 2009, Texas Ranger Ian Kinsler hit for the cycle and went six-for-six in a game against the Baltimore Orioles. The amazing Elias Sports Bureau determined that the last person to perform that tour de force was Mr. Farmer Weaver of the Louisville Colonels. Weaver accomplished his six-hit cycle against the Syracuse Stars on August 12, 1890, during a regulation nine-inning game. [26]

Weaver lived to the age of 77, passing away in Akron, Ohio, in 1943.

Farmer Burns

According to James K. Skipper, James Joseph Burns was given the nickname Farmer because of his country origins. An alternative source must be considered. Although Burns was born in rural Ohio in 1876, he may have been renamed in honor of a nationally known wrestler of the era, Martin "Farmer" Burns.

Burns, the wrestler, was born in 1861 in Cedar County, Iowa. Family poverty forced him to go to work at a young age. Physically demanding labor developed his musculature as a teenager. At the same time he became interested in wrestling and took on anyone who would challenge him. He studied the science of wrestling and developed techniques that enabled him to defeat many larger men.

In 1889, he hopped a cattle car to Chicago and soon noticed a sign that offered $25 to anyone who could last 15 minutes in the ring with Strangler Lewis and Jack Carkeek, champion wrestlers of that era. When Burns climbed into the ring in his bib overalls and stocking feet, he was ridiculed and called "Farmer." After holding his own against both opponents, the jeers turned to cheers. The newspapers hailed him as a hero.

Throughout his career Burns wrestled over 6,000 matches and was defeated only seven times. He earned the World Wrestling Title in 1895 when he defeated his old "friend" Strangler Lewis. He became known as "the father of scientific wrestling."

Farmer Burns, the ballplayer, achieved adulthood at about the same time Burns the wrestler was ascending to national prominence. The nickname Farmer may well have been derived from the combination of rural roots and the fame of wrestler Farmer Burns.

Burns first played professionally with the 1900 Toledo Mud Hens, appearing in the same pitching rotation with Pug Bennett, Snake Wiltse, and future star Addie Joss. He started two games for the Mud Hens and lost both despite allowing only one earned run in 13 innings.

In 1901, he signed with the St. Louis Cardinals and made his debut on July 6. He pitched the ninth inning allowing one run but did not figure in the decision. He never pitched again in the major or minor leagues. His lifetime ERA would forever be 9.00.

In 1898, he attended and pitched for Washington and Jefferson College in Washington, Pennsylvania. Little else is known about him, including when or where he died.

A man named James Joseph Burns died in 1961 in Black Hawk County, Iowa, not far from the birthplace of Martin "Farmer" Burns. Could it be our missing Farmer? Probably not, but an interesting coincidence if it was.

Farmer Ray

Robert Henry Ray was the fifth and last of the baseball Farmers. Born in Fort Lyon, Colorado, in 1886, he reached the majors in 1910 as a pitcher for the St. Louis Browns. He quickly became a starter and finished the season 4-10 with the last place Brownies, despite a decent ERA of 3.58.

Ray, like Farmer Burns before him, could last only one year in the city of St. Louis, and the major leagues. He bounced from Connecticut to Texas to Washington in the next six years.

He died in Electra, Texas, in 1963, near the town of Sherman where he played ball in 1914 and 1915.

Nig Cuppy

Throughout the history of baseball, 10 players acquired the nickname Nig because of their dark complexion. Incredibly, five of the 10 chose to use the name professionally. George Joseph Cuppy (nee Koppe) was the first. Of the nicknames that became common for players with a particular look, background or physical condition, Nig and Dummy were the most reprehensible.

This derivative of the modern day racial slur, Nig was not a product of an innocent age. By the late 1800s, the word nigger was almost always used in the pejorative. Abolitionists began using the word *colored* by mid-century, while southerners still preferred the insulting and contentious word nigger and the reaction it produced. [27]

Cuppy was the only Nig in the 19th century. He was born in the free state of Indiana in 1869, four years after the end of the Civil War. Several photos of Cuppy display a countenance more akin to a Native American than an African American.

He made his major league debut with the National League Cleveland Spiders in 1892. His rookie record of 28-13 was second on the team to a third-year pitcher named Cy Young who finished 36-12. Young's ERA was 1.93 and Cuppy finished at 2.51.

A major rule change occurred in 1893 that effectively "separated the men from the boys." The pitching mound was moved farther from home plate. Instead of pitching from 50 feet, Cuppy and his colleagues had to toss the ball 60 feet and six inches. Earned run averages jumped up all over the league. Cy Young was no exception, but he still managed to post a 34-16 record that year. Cuppy fell to 17-10. While he remained a prominent member of manager Patsy Tebeau's pitching staff for seven years, he never replicated his rookie record.

The hitters rejoiced at the decision to move the pitcher's mound. In 1892, National League batters averaged .245. The following year they improved to .280. In 1894 the mark jumped to .309 before settling back under .300 in 1895.

In 1899, Cuppy was sent to the St. Louis Perfectos (Cardinals) as a result of a disappointing year with the Spiders. The following year he was purchased by the Boston Beaneaters. After one season in South Boston, he jumped to the Boston Americans on the west side of town. He just could not conjure up the old magic from his Spider days. The Americans released him that same August and the ride was over.

Unlike many of his peers, he chose not to seek employment in the minor leagues. He left the game with a sparkling won-loss record of 162-98. He was a 20-game winner four times. In 1894, he not only pitched 29 complete games, he also served as a closer and led the league with 10 games finished. He led the lead with three shutouts that same year.

Derek Gentile ranked the top players all-time in his book *Baseball's Best 1,000*. Nig Cuppy is ranked #879. He is ranked among the top 10 best fastballs of the last decade of the 19th century. [28]

Cuppy was the first Spider pitcher to use a glove on the mound, and possibly the first in the big leagues. [29] He was also renown for being the slowest working hurler of his era, frequently requiring three hours to complete his games. [30]

During the off-season, Cuppy served as a clerk for a bridge construction company. His employers probably referred to him as George, not Nig. [31]

Cuppy died in 1922 in his native state of Indiana. He had recently observed his 53rd birthday.

Nig Fuller

Charles F. Fuller was born into the Furrer household in Toledo, Ohio during the spring of 1878. Like his predecessor, Nig Cuppy, he received his nickname from his dark complexion. He also changed his last name to Fuller. The arc of his baseball career was decidedly different from that of Nig Cuppy, however.

Fuller started in the minor leagues in 1901 as a catcher with the Fort Wayne Railroaders of the Western Association. He began the 1902 season with the Columbus Senators of the American Association and after 14 games was signed by the Brooklyn Superbas. The Brooklyn team may have been superb, but Fuller was not. He made his debut on

July 1 and played in his final game on July 12. During his three games with Brooklyn he batted 10 times with no hits. His main claim to fame was his sacrifice fly that accounted for his only career RBI.

Brooklyn sold him to Montreal of the Eastern League where he performed for the rest of the 1902 season. The rest of his professional life consisted of one-year, or shorter, stints in nine cities over the next six years. He called it "quits" in 1908 and returned to Toledo where he lived in relative obscurity until his death in 1937.

Nig Clarke

While Nig Cuppy may have looked like a Native American, Clarke was the real deal. Jay Justin Clarke was a Canadian player of Indian descent who immigrated to America in 1902 to sign as a catcher for Corsicana in the fledgling Texas League.

After one year in the seriously disorganized Texas League, he moved to the Little Rock Travelers of the Southern Association. Clarke would become one of the rare Native American players to avoid the nickname Chief. Arriving in the former slave state of Arkansas, his dark skin earned him the name Nig, instead. Perhaps his Canadian upbringing had not taught him the stigma of the name.

One year later, he ventured deeper into the southland to play for the Atlanta Crackers. The word cracker had become a disparaging term for a poor white person. The origin of the word is somewhat murky. Some claim that it was derived from the bullwhips used by slave owners. Others maintain that the name was given to poor white cattle herders whose bullwhips made the distinctive cracking sound. In any event, Nig became a Cracker in 1904.

He became the regular catcher for the Crackers and was soon purchased by the Cleveland Naps in August of 1904. He started the 1905 season with Cleveland but after five games was sold "on loan" to the Detroit Tigers on August 1, 1905. Eleven days later he was returned to the Naps, earning him the title of the Quickest Boomerang for any catcher in baseball history. Considering all positions, the 10-day bounce is the second quickest in MLB history.

In 1906, he batted .358 in a backup role and earned the starting position in 1907. Player manager Nap Lajoie used him as a backup catcher until

1907 when he took over the main catching duties, batting .269 in 120 games.

Clarke continued to catch for player-manager Nap Lajoie through the 1910 season before being traded to the St. Louis Browns in 1911. When the Browns released him late in 1911 he found work back in the minor leagues bouncing from team to team for the next five years.

When America became involved in World War I, Clarke joined the U.S. Marines and served proudly for his adopted country until 1919. Upon his return, the Philadelphia Phillies put him to work behind the plate backing up their starter Bert Adams. That job lasted only one season and he was put on waivers and selected by the Phillies' cross-state rivals in Pittsburgh. Three weeks into the 1920 season his big league career ended at age 37.

After several failed attempts to succeed in minor league ball, the 42-year-old Clarke retired.

As a major leaguer, he is regarded as being one of the first catchers to use shin guards. His lifetime batting average was .254 over nine seasons. He was considered to be one of the top defensive catchers of his day, but oddly had a reputation of possessing a weak arm. In his own defense he once said, "Anybody can throw a runner out stealing. I liked to pick 'em off first base while they were hanging around down there counting their money." [32]

His primary claim to fame came as a 19-year-old in the Texas League. He is credited with hitting eight home runs in one game. Some doubt still exists that the record is legitimate, despite sworn affidavits from three witnesses. But here is the story, some of it supplied by Clarke, himself, 45 years after the fact.

The hastily formed Texas League scheduled a game between Corsicana and Texarkana on June 15, 1902. In addition to not hiring umpires and writing official league rules, the schedulers overlooked the city of Corsicana's blue laws forbidding baseball on the Sabbath. Rather than reschedule the game, they moved it to the small town of Ennis, not far from Dallas.

A section of bleachers cut across the outfield not far behind first base, creating a right field dimension of 200 feet from home plate. Some witnesses maintain that the distance was much shorter. Clarke, a left-handed hitter, launched one fly ball after another into the prairie wind blowing out toward right field.

After his fourth home rum, Clarke claims that a wealthy cattleman approached him with a $50 bill. Clarke accepted it. After the fifth home run, a rival cattle baron bellied up to the catcher and jammed another $50 bill into his hand.

When the carnage had ended, Corsicana had a 51-3 win in its pocket. All 51 runs (and 53 hits) were charged to one pitcher, C. B. DeWitt. DeWitt was a first baseman making only his second pitching appearance. Why was he not pulled from the game? Some believe that he approached the manager and said that his father, the owner, wanted his son on the mound. Since the manager was not given permission to dismiss De Witt, the young man took his lumps for all nine innings.

After the game, the fans passed the hat and raised another $85 for Clarke. Local merchants later regaled him with enough hats, shirts and shoes to last for years.

The skepticism over the eight homeruns developed because the scorer "lost his mind" and stopped keeping score. Luckily, another official was keeping a box score, which bore out Clarke's version of the story, more or less.

In the absence of any credible evidence to the contrary, Nig Clarke holds the record for the most home runs in one game at any level of the sport.

Jap Barbeau

William Joseph Barbeau's last name is of French derivation, evolving from a type of fish called a *barbel*. Yet Barbeau did not garner the nickname "Frenchy." Instead he became known as Jap Barbeau. James K. Skipper, the godfather of nickname origins, claims that the nickname was given because of Barbeau's size and complexion. Barbeau was indisputably tiny at 5' 5" and 140 pounds. His complexion is hard to observe in black and white photos and highly colorful tobacco cards. He definitely did not have Japanese (or any Asian) facial features. In viewing a team photo of the 1906 Cleveland Naps, this author tried to identify Barbeau by his appearance. After choosing my suspect from the pictorial lineup, I learned that I had fingered Nig Clarke, instead.

Barbeau was born in New York City in 1882 of transplanted French-Canadian parents. During that period, Japanese culture was very idealized in America. Magazine articles and works of art displayed the delicate nature of Japanese women and beautiful exotic landscapes. [33] That may explain why Barbeau's nickname became Jap instead of the more commonly assigned "Chink."

His first professional gig occurred at age 23 when he signed with the 1905 Columbus Senators of the American Association. He was the Senators' everyday third baseman, coming to the plate 524 times. While he only batted .246, he earned a late season audition with the Cleveland Naps in the American League. Cleveland player-manager Nap Lajoie used Barbeau at second base to give himself a rest during the last weeks of the season. Barbeau took advantage of the opportunity and earned a spot on the 1906 Cleveland roster.

Barbeau had the distinction of becoming one of Ty Cobb's first victims in his strategy to terrorize infielders trying to tag him out on the base paths. Cobb was a starter toward the end of the 1905 season, his rookie year. Batting only .240, he was afraid that manager Bill Armour would bench him, jeopardizing his chances to remain a member of the Detroit Tigers. But Armour had instructions from owner Frank Navin to play the rookie. Navin liked Cobb's aggressiveness as demonstrated by the way Cobb "handled the matter of Bill 'Jap' Barbeau." Barbeau, playing second base for Cleveland, tried to put a tag on Cobb late in the game with the potential winning run on base. Cobb slid into Barbeau with spikes flashing and ripped up Barbeau's knees, sending the ball wildly into the outfield grass. Cobb was safe, the lead runner scored, Barbeau was bleeding, and a legendary style of play was born. [34]

The 1906 season was not a good one for Barbeau. He batted only .194 in 42 games and soon found himself back in the minor league with the Toledo Mud Hens. After two productive years in Toledo, the Pittsburgh Pirates came calling and Barbeau joined shortstop Honus Wagner on the left side of the 1909 Pirate infield. Pittsburgh manager Fred Clarke described Barbeau as a "difficult little monkey at the top of the batting order, " but traded him in late in the season for Bobbie Byrne, a solid third baseman with the Cardinals. [35]

After the trade to St. Louis, Barbeau performed well at the plate and in the field and retained his job for the upcoming 1910 season. History repeated itself in 1910, however. Just like his second season with

Cleveland, he could not push his batting average over the .200 mark and the Cardinals cut him loose. According to the New York Times, Cardinal manager Roger Bresnahan let Barbeau go because "he was a little smaller than the other infielders." [36]

By late spring of 1910 he was back in the American Association with the Kansas City Blues. He spent four seasons in KC then moved to the Milwaukee Brewers for the 1914 and 1915 seasons. He then bounced from team to team over the next four years before retiring in 1919 at the age of 37.

Barbeau died in 1969 in Milwaukee, Wisconsin, at the age of 87.

Chink Heileman

Around the time of John George Heileman's birth in 1872, a sea change was taking place in the way Americans looked at the immigrants arriving from Asia.

The first wave of Chinese immigrants to American began in the 1850's. Most of these were wealthy businessmen, merchants and hoteliers whose hard work and quiet lifestyles endeared them to the public. With the discovery of gold, followed by the expansion of the railroad system, the new wave of Chinese immigrants produced an influx of low-wage-seeking coolies who began to compete with Americans for many jobs. The attitude toward the Chinese took a decided turn for the worse.

Many Americans moving west to seek their fortune were poor southerners with a built-in prejudice for people who were different. Violence against the Chinese was common. Pressure on the political system produced the Naturalization Act of 1870 that restricted immigration to only whites and Africans. The Chinese Exclusion Act of 1882 further restricted the growth of the Chinese population. The male-to-female ratio of Chinese-Americans grew to 27:1, creating a virtual bachelor society among Chinese-Americans, further depressing their population. [37]

Heileman had Asian facial features and consequently became the first official "Chink" in baseball. [38] The fact that a pejorative nickname such as "Chink" was assigned to an individual would not be surprising. The acceptance of such a name by an individual points to a strong desire to fit into a group, however base that clique might be.

Heileman hailed from Cincinnati, Ohio. He joined the Cincinnati Reds in 1901 shortly before his 28th birthday. No record has surfaced to document his pre-1901 baseball exploits. He would have had plenty of time to pick-up the nickname playing for local or regional teams.

After he joined the Reds, he played only five games, four at third base and one at second base. It is possible that he was handed the name Chink with the Reds and never had a chance to repudiate it. He batted only .133 and his big league career in Cincinnati lasted just 13 days. When he left the field for the last time, he cemented his nickname in the annals of baseball for all eternity.

Heileman died in Cincinnati from heart disease in 1940. One of his post-baseball jobs was night watchman at a music hall. [39] One can assume that he spent the last 39 years of his life as John, not Chink.

Chink Taylor

C. L. Taylor was born in Burnet, Texas, in 1898. He secured his first minor league contract in 1921 with the Fort Worth Panthers in the Texas League. By the time he reached the Chicago Cubs in 1925, he had been dubbed Chink for his facial features.

He played for Fort Worth (twice), Paris, Beaumont and Shreveport in the Texas League before the Cubs drafted him in 1925. He came to spring training with a sterling minor league bating average of .324 the previous season in Beaumont where he contributed 37 doubles, 13 triples and 12 home runs.

His career with the Cubs was brief and disappointing. The outfielder played in only eight games and made just six plate appearances with zero base hits or walks. The only positive stat was in the "runs" column where he managed to score twice. Unless he reached base on errors, he probably was inserted into several games as a pinch runner and scored in that manner.

Following his expulsion from the Cubs, he returned to the minor leagues for five more years, retiring in 1929. Despite the fact that he hit .367 following his demotion, he did not get a second chance to impress the Cubs' brass. His total of eight seasons in the minors produced a .307 career batting mark.

Taylor died in Temple, Texas, in 1980 at the age of 82.

Chink Outen

The story behind the renaming of William Austin Outen seems to make little sense, but clearly displays the serendipity that leads to a nickname that can stick around for a lifetime. Growing up in North Carolina during the first decade of the century, Outen was called Willie by friends and family. As a teenager, he answered to Austin. But during a football game between North Carolina State and Clemson, that changed forever. He involuntarily became Chink.

Outen, an all-around athlete, was captain of the football and baseball teams for North Carolina State. In 1928, against the Clemson 11, Outen repeatedly smashed through the line for first downs. Clemson could not stop him. Their fans derisively began to chant "plunging Chink" over and over again. Why? No one knows for certain. Said Outen, "I suppose they thought I was a Chinaman." [40] Again, the question is, why? Perhaps the Clemson fans, viewing him through the leather helmet, misread his permanent squint. His last name certainly did not sound Chinese. His powerful physique also flew in the face of Asian stereotypes.

When baseball season arrived, the sportswriters had their nickname. Outen disliked the incongruous name and frequently requested that they desist. The burly outfielder hit for the cycle that spring against Virginia Military Institute and provided the sportswriters with more reasons to glorify the new nickname.

While still at college, Outen signed a contract with Charlotte in the South Atlantic League and accepted a $600 bonus to join them after his college career was at an end. He never did finish school, however. New York Yankee scout Johnny Nee came calling late in 1928 and offered Outen $1,200 and an invitation to spring training. Outen signed. [41]

Charlotte soon learned about Outen's deal with the Yankees and appealed to Commissioner Landis. The Yankees quickly paid off Charlotte and hoped the issue was resolved. Landis was not that easily mollified and he called a hearing in which Outen "outed" the Yankees for knowingly pursuing him. The Yankees were fined $500 and Outen was made to return the money he received from Charlotte.

The Yankees now had $1,700 invested in Outen and confirmed his invitation to spring training. It had to be a heady experience to rub elbows with Babe Ruth and Lou Gehrig. Despite a stable full of catchers on the roster, Outen played most of his spring innings behind the plate.

The Yankees sent Outen to the Asheville Tourists of the South Atlantic League (Class B) where he caught in 119 games batting .342. He started the 1930 season in Greenville where they switched him back to the outfield. He smashed 11 homers and batted .359. He was promoted to the Albany Senators where his power production ceased but he hit .329 and was again promoted, this time to Jersey City in the International League where the greater competition knocked his average down to .244.

He was back in Class B to start the 1931 season with Scranton. Once again he hit for power and average, and earned a promotion to Jersey City. He started the 1932 season still in Jersey City, but two things had changed. He was back behind the plate for the first time since his first year in the minors. Secondly, Jersey City was now affiliated with the Brooklyn Dodgers.

He continued to scorch International League pitching and turned in a stellar season with 15 home runs and a .337 record. The following spring he was a Brooklyn Dodger, the backup to first string catcher Al Lopez.

Outen's quest to escape the name Chink gained some traction during his second tenure with Jersey City. He suggested to the press that he preferred the name Chick to the unexplained and unwanted name Chink. Some of the New York Times sports writers began to refer to him as Chick in its write-ups of Jersey City games. They reported on August 31, 1932, "Reaching three Toronto Pitchers for 15 hits, Jersey City opened a three-game series today with a 12-7 victory. Chick Outen collected four of the victor's hits, two of them doubles, and drove in four runs." [42] Other writers, Roscoe McGowan for example, continued to refer to him as Chink.

During 1933 he played in 93 games with the Dodgers, getting regular mentions in the New York Times sports section, almost always as Chick Outen. He did not have a spectacular year, but performed well enough in the back-up role to earn an invitation to spring training in 1934.

The Dodgers decided to keep rookie Ray Berres and Clyde Sukeforth to back up Lopez. Outen was assigned to Buffalo and was back in the International League. The Miami News reported the assignment of Chink Outen. He never returned to the Dodgers or any other big league team.

After a short stint with Montreal, Brooklyn sent him west to the Pacific Coast League. He played for the Mission Reds/Hollywood Stars from 1935 to 1938, still operating exclusively behind the plate; and still batting over .300 every year.

Following the lead of the New York Times, the Los Angeles press continued to report his PCL exploits under the name of Chick. "Chick Outen, the bulky catcher from Brooklyn, blasted open the round with a line smash that caromed off the deep center-field screen for a triple." [43]

In 1939, he quickly spiraled down from AA to D level baseball, spending brief periods with minor league affiliates of the Phillies, Indians, and Athletics, all the teams in or near his native North Carolina. He left baseball after that season and joined the U.S. Army, later serving in World War II in Europe with the military police.

Outen 's efforts to leave the name Chink behind him seemed to be successful as he carved out a career in the PCL. When he returned to the Carolinas, the old name was waiting for him. "Chink Outen, built like a wrestler and probably as powerful, failed to impress railbirds because he ambled around and displayed little spirit as well as faring poorly in batting practice..." [44]

All official baseball records and statistics still reflect the name Chink Outen, an accidental nickname that the owner fought to eliminate, even to the extent of serving up a sound-alike alternative (Chick). Once a player's name begins to appear in box scores and newspaper reports, the cement is set and cannot easily be recast.

Lung cancer caught up to Outen and claimed his life in 1961. At the age of 55 he died in Durham, North Carolina, and was buried as William Outen.

Chink Zachary

When Albert Myron Zachary was given the nickname Chink for his Asian appearance, he was already inured to a change in his personal identity. He was born Albert Zarski in Brooklyn in 1914. The family name was Americanized to Zachary.

Zachary had the honor of receiving his nickname from his friend Casey Stengel. Stengel was managing the Boston Bees at the same time Zachary was in the Boston minor league system. Stengel was probably not the first person to observe Zachary's slant-eyed appearance, but he made the most impressing comment. Calling out to Zachary one day, Casey yelled, "Hey, ya Chink, whatcha doin'?" [45]

Zachary was comfortable on the mound as well in the batter's box. During his first professional season with the 1936 Dothan Boll Weevils in the Alabama-Florida League he batted 180 times as well as pitching 75 innings. He did not perform spectacularly in either role. The following year, Dothan manager Bobby Murray positioned him at third base and Zachary did not pitch one inning during the whole season. He batted only .242 and was sold to the Mayfield Clothiers. He was still in Class D, but Mayfield was affiliated with the St. Louis Browns.

Zachary showed the Browns some pop in 1938 as he hit eight home runs and eight triples while compiling a .272 average. His reward was an elevation to the Class C Utica Braves in the Canadian-American League. Zachary's life was becoming more interesting in Utica. Manager Mike Diffey platooned him at third base and gave him another shot as a pitcher. As the season neared its end, Zachary added another line on his resume', he was named interim manager to finish the season. [46]

Ernest Jenkins became the Utica manager in 1940 and named Zachary to his starting rotation. Zachary responded with a 15-11 season in 208 innings, recording a 3.29 ERA.

Instead of climbing the ladder up the Boston Bees minor league system, Zachary instead joined the war effort by entering the Army following the 1940 season. When he returned to civilian life in 1944, the struggling Brooklyn Dodgers signed him to join a pitching staff depleted by World War II enlistments.

Zachary had survived the war, but he could not survive the assault from National League batsmen. He started two games and relieved in two others. His Brooklyn career lasted fewer than 10 innings in which he surrendered 10 hits, seven walks and 10 earned runs. When the dust around home plate cleared, he owned an 0-2 record and a 9.58 ERA. Manager Leo Durocher had seen enough. Zachary was sent to the Dodgers' minor league team in New Orleans and then Montreal.

Zachary performed moderately well against the American Association and International League batters but never escaped the gravitational pull of the minor leagues. He remained in the Dodgers system until 1951 when he migrated to Oakland in the PCL to finish the season, and his career.

After his playing days were over Zachary served as a scout for the Milwaukee/Atlanta Braves. He toured the country talking to young players, regaling them with stories of his favorite players and coaches.

Zachary died in 2006 in Rome, New York, at the age of 92. He was buried in Utica, the scene of his greatest success in baseball. The nickname "Chink" was buried with him. He was the last player to be so nicknamed (officially or unofficially).

Earl "Chink" Yingling

Like Chink Heileman, Earl Hershey Yingling was born and raised in Ohio (Chillicothe). Unlike Heileman, Yingling did not have Chinese features. He did, however, have a name that sounded Chinese. Each syllable could have been a Chinese name, Ying or Ling. Yingling, though, is actually a variation of a German name, "Yungling" which means "young one." A nickname based on a twist of your last name would probably be easier to take than one reflective of your appearance. Even though early newspaper reports refer to Earl "Chink" Yingling, the name did not stick and allow him into the "Low Self-Esteem Club."

Heinie Meine

Henry William Meine was one of 22 players who answered to the name Heinie. Heinie Meine definitely fits into the category of Ethnic names because of his Germanic background. His name in the German language means "mine." Meine could have also been nicknamed Dutch, Germany, or Fritz. The choice of Heinie over the other options was no doubt based on a bit of verbal playfulness. Because of this, Meine's biography will be treated in full in the Wordplay section.

Dummy Hoy

Seven deaf players have "chosen" to be known by the commonly applied nickname of Dummy. During the late 19th century, the hearing impaired were labeled "deaf and dumb." This unfortunate choice of the word dumb evoked the negative connotation of stupidity, rather than the proper meaning, silent or refraining from speech. William Ellsworth Hoy was the not the first deaf player to reach the major league level, but he was earliest player to accept the nickname.

On June 2, 1883, Edward (Dummy) Dundon took the mound for the Columbus Buckeyes of the American Association. He is credited with being the first deaf player in a major league. He may have understood what his teammates were calling him, but he did not adopt the nickname as part of his personal identity. His career lasted two seasons and consisted of a 9-20 record.

Both Dundon and Hoy attended and played baseball for the Ohio School for the Deaf. Hoy graduated at the top of his class and after graduation, at the urging of his father, opened a shoe repair shop in his hometown of Houcktown, Ohio.

The next step in his baseball career was due to the rural habit of going barefoot in the summer. When his business slowed to a stand still, he encouraged kids to hang around his shop and play baseball. One day a traveler passing though Houcktown took notice of his skills, but kept going when he learned of Hoy's disability. On the return trip, the traveler stopped again, only this time invited Hoy to join his hometown team to help defeat a bitter rival. [47]

Playing locally on the weekends, his stellar outfield play caught the eye of Frank Selee, manager of the minor league Oshkosh (Wisconsin) team in the Northwestern League in 1886. Houcktown may have lost a capable cobbler, but the game of baseball gained a star player.

Hoy lost his hearing at the age of three from a bout with meningitis. He learned sign language and lip reading, but also could communicate in a squeaky voice that was often unintelligible.

Umpires at the time did not provide any visual signals to the players and fans; all calls were made verbally. Hoy found himself at a great disadvantage trying to determine whether a pitch had been declared a ball or strike. While he endeavored to make this determination, opposing pitchers would frequently quick-pitch him, producing a called strike three.

In order to combat this disadvantage, he worked out a system whereby the third base coach would flash an immediate ball or strike sign. The out and safe calls were soon added to the list of signals. Umpires later adopted these hand gestures, which are still used today.

After two seasons in Oshkosh, the last-place Washington Nationals came calling and purchased his contract. He quickly earned a starting outfield job and began stealing bases at a league-leading clip. He had one of the lowest batting averages on the team, but once on base, he began to terrorize the National league with his base running speed. When the 1888 campaign was over, he led the league with 82 stolen bases. He would never again match his rookie year tally of swiped bases.

Hoy's dazzling speed also allowed him to play a very shallow outfield. Opposing base runners soon learned that a base hit did not necessarily give them a free ticket to score from second base. In 1889, he became the first outfielder to throw out three base runners at the plate in a single game. The Washington catcher making the put outs was a character with the unwieldy name of Cornelius McGillicuddy.

Washington fans loved Hoy's daring outfield style and would applaud him by rising from their seats and waving their hats high in the air. The press called him "The Amazing Dummy." [48]

After four years of unsuccessful efforts to dismantle the reserve clause, the first players union, The Brotherhood of Professional Baseball Players, began to talk of a boycott. This labor unrest led instead to the formation of the Players' League in 1890. The eight-team league recruited many of the era's top stars. Hoy and Connie Mack landed on the Buffalo Bisons and once again found themselves on a weak last place team. The pain did not last long, however, as the league folded and players scrambled to find shelter back in the National League or American Association.

Charles Comiskey rescued Hoy and gave him a job with his St. Louis Browns in the American Association. The Browns were a sound, well-run club that finished near the top of the standings almost every year. Hoy responded by leading the league in walks and plate appearances while batting .292 during the 1891 season.

The term déjà vu was not yet in vogue, having just been coined by a French Psychic investigator. Nevertheless, the concept of "things already seen" would have been quite appropriate as Hoy watched the American Association collapse following his first season with the Browns. For two consecutive years he had played in a league that became extinct.

When the 1892 season opened the following spring, Hoy was a Washington Senator again. After two more years with the feckless Senators, Charles Comiskey came to his rescue again. This time, Comiskey managed the Cincinnati Reds. As the Reds gradually improved to a first division club, Hoy found a home. The Cincinnati fans loved the way he patrolled centerfield, calling him their "Flyhawk." [49]

After four years in Cincinnati, he was traded to the Louisville Colonels and later sold to the Chicago White Sox of the fledgling American League. Charles Comiskey now owned the Sox. In 1901, Hoy finally experienced the joy of a first place club, although the privilege of appearing in a World Series would elude him. The two leagues would not get together for a championship showdown until 1903.

During his single season in Chicago, he hit two home runs, both of them grand slams, and both of them in the same game. [50]

Despite the success of the 1901 ChiSox, Hoy jumped ship and returned to his beloved Cincinnati to play his final season. On May 16 of that year, the Reds faced the New York Giants at Cincinnati's Palace of the Fans. Dummy Hoy came to plate and faced Luther Dummy Taylor. This clash was the first and only time in history that a deaf-mute pitcher faced a deaf-mute batter. Although Taylor defeated the Reds 5-3, Hoy singled twice and scored a run.

Following the 1902 season, Hoy remained in Cincinnati and became a dairy farmer. After selling his farm in 1924, Hoy accepted a management position with the Goodyear Tire Company. [51]

In October of 1961, the Cincinnati Reds honored Hoy by inviting him to throw out the ceremonial first pitch of the Game Three of the World Series between the Reds and Yankees. Several weeks later, Hoy suffered a stroke. He died on December 15, about six months shy of his goal of celebrating his 100th birthday.

To the day he died, Hoy proudly carried himself with dignity, retaining a name given to him out of ignorance and cruelty.

Baseball reference books list Hoy's height at 5' 6". Some of his contemporaries report that he was even smaller in stature, perhaps as small as 5' 4" tall. Had he not been hearing impaired, he may have acquired one of the sport's sobriquets reserved for short players. He could have been known as Shorty, Stumpy or Skeeter Hoy.

Dummy Stephenson

Rueben Crandol Stephenson was the next deaf player to ascend to the major leagues. In Stephenson's case, his teammates and opponents called him Steve or Stevey. The fans and the baseball reporters called him Dummy. Further, his disability did not leave him a true mute. The *Trenton Sunday Advertiser* said of him, "Although profoundly deaf, Stephenson speaks very distinctly, and has learned to understand what is said to him by watching the speaker's lips." [52] Stephenson had a very strong opportunity to shake the negative nickname but failed to do so.

Like Hoy, Stephenson attended a specialized school for the deaf in his native New Jersey. Formerly a catcher for the Trenton school, he reluctantly accepted a centerfield spot on a semipro team in nearby Camden, New Jersey, in 1892. Meanwhile, across the Delaware River, Phillies outfielder Ed Delahanty suffered a late-season injury. With his star player projected to miss just a week or so of games, Phillies manager Harry Wright found a short-term solution and bought Stephenson's contract from the Camden club. Word had circulated that a young deaf player was crushing the ball in New Jersey.

Again, like Hoy, Stephenson without his impairment would have been a prime candidate for another nickname. A non-drinker, Stephenson did not fraternize with his teammates after ballgames. In fact, his manager at Camden actually released him during the summer of 1892 because he would not patronize a local tavern (co-owned by the manager). Clean-living players were often saddled with feminine names. With the first name Rueben, he might easily have become Ruby Stephenson.

Stephenson joined the Phillies on September 9 and subsequently played in eight games, walking to the plate 38 times. He acquitted himself quite nicely with 10 hits, including three doubles and five RBIs. When Delahanty returned, there was no room for Stephenson, despite his .270 batting average. In addition to Delahanty, the Phillies outfield featured Sam Thompson and Billy Hamilton. All three players became members of the Hall of Fame.

Following his experience with the Phillies, he played minor league ball for the next eight years in the Pennsylvania State league, New England League, Virginia League and New York State League. Despite his ability to hit the long ball as well as catch and play outfield, he never again put on a major league uniform. Stephenson claimed that a bad throwing arm prevented him from staying in the major leagues. [53]

Playing for Pawtucket in 1894, Stephenson came to plate seven times and hit the ball over the fence seven times. A strange ground rule, however, robbed the burly slugger of four home runs. A large tree stood just past the fence in left centerfield. The local rule declared that any ball that struck the tree and returned to the playing field would be a ground-rule double. Only three of his blasts managed to evade the leafy defender. [54] Seven home runs would have been a baseball record at that time, albeit destined to be eclipsed by Nig Clarke in 1902.

In 1898, he married a classmate and promised to quit baseball. The lure of the diamond was too strong and his pledge was broken, but he managed to limit his baseball activities to local teams. He relocated to Philadelphia and took a position with the gas company and continued to play for the YMCA and other company teams. He spent the latter part of his life working for a shipbuilder, an auto manufacturer and a state highway department.

Unlike Dummy Hoy, Stephenson created no lasting waves in major league baseball. But he did help make strides for the deaf. Serving with the New Jersey State Association for the Deaf, he tirelessly advocated for the hearing impaired. The *Silent Worker*, a nationally recognized newspaper from the New Jersey School for the Deaf, placed Rueben C. Stephenson's name on its short list of Who's Who in the Deaf World. [55]

Stephenson died in 1924 at the age of 55, his body ravaged by diabetes and tuberculosis. [56]

Dummy Taylor

Luther Haden Taylor came the closest to rivaling Dummy Hoy for success and notoriety among deaf ballplayers. Taylor was born in Oskaloosa, Kansas, of speaking parents. As a youth, Taylor discovered boxing and decided that he wanted a career in the ring. He worked out in the gym regularly and welcomed challenges from all comers. His parents vetoed that idea but approved his alternate choice of pitching a baseball.

He attended the Kansas School for the Deaf in Olathe. Despite graduating as valedictorian in 1895, he set out on a journey to become a professional baseball player. Many deaf mutes learned that the working world was tilted against them, except for sports. He spent the next three years learning his craft with various semi-professional teams spread over three Midwest states.

In 1899, a legitimate minor league team discovered Taylor. At age 24, he joined the Shreveport Tigers in the Southern League. His first year was not spectacular, but earned him an upgrade in 1900 to a club in Albany where George Davis of the New York Giants scouted him. By September of the same year, Davis had become manager of the Giants and signed Taylor to a major league contract. He made his debut on August 27 and appeared in 11 games. He sported a 2.45 ERA and secured a roster spot for the 1901 season.

The year 1901 was a breakout season for Taylor, even though he led the National League in losses with an 18-27 record. On the plus side, he also was the leader in games and games started. He had proven that his impairment was not an obstacle to becoming a valued member of a big league pitching staff.

The 1901 New York organization was so comfortable with the hearing impaired that no fewer than three deaf players, all named Dummy, dotted their roster. In addition to Taylor, the Giants signed (William) Dummy Deegan and (George) Dummy Leitner. All three "Dummys" were pitchers.

When Giants owner Andrew Freedman decided not to pay Taylor a salary equal to his proven value, Taylor jumped to the new American

League and signed with the Cleveland Bronchos for the 1902 season. The extroverted Taylor immediately regretted his decision. The Cleveland players felt no compulsion to learn sign language and Taylor felt alienated and alone. Freedman also regretted losing Taylor so he dispatched catcher Frank Bowerman to get him back. Each inning when Taylor walked to or from the mound, Bowerman would make an offer to Taylor using sign language. Taylor shook his head "no" until the bidding could no longer be ignored. He finally nodded "yes" and was back in New York the next day. He finished the season 8-18 on a disorganized and disheartened Giant team.

Toward the end of the 1902 season, John McGraw was promoted from player to player-manager and the eighth-place Giants' rebirth had begun.

The following year, McGraw and new owner John T. Brush rebuilt and reenergized the Giants and they climbed to second place behind the Pittsburgh Pirates. McGraw flushed out almost the entire 1902 team. Only Mathewson, Bowerman and Taylor survived the purge. Taylor contributed a 13-13 record, mediocre at best. But he was scrapper and a character; a perfect fit for a McGraw team.

In just his second full season as the manager of the Giants, McGraw jockeyed his team to the National League pennant. McGraw's offense batted only .262, but his pitching staff blew away the rest of the field. Taylor won 21 games and finished a distant third on his own team. Iron Man Joe McGinnity was 35-8 and Christy Mathewson right behind him with 33-12.

The Boston Red Sox won the American League title and expected to defend their 1903 championship crown. McGraw had other ideas. He hated AL President Ban Johnson and refused to pit his team against the champion of a "minor" league. The World Series was still a contest arranged by the two league winners, not yet an event authorized by Major League Baseball. Taylor thus missed his opportunity to be the first hearing-impaired pitcher to start a World Series game.

McGraw guided the Giants to the pennant again in 1905. Taylor chipped in with a 16-9 record and earned a shot at his first World Series start against the Philadelphia Athletics. He was scheduled to pitch in Game Three in Philadelphia. The rain pummeled Columbia Park and the contest was postponed until the next day. McGraw figured Mathewson was rested and gave him the ball instead of Taylor. Matty shutout the A's for the second time to put the Series at 2-1 New York. McGinnity took his turn the next day and likewise blanked Philadelphia 1-0. Mathewson pitched again in game five and ended the Series with another shutout 2-0. All of the five games were shutouts. Philadelphia's only win came at the hands of Chief Bender in Game Two. Taylor would not get another chance to represent the deaf community on baseball's most prestigious stage.

He played three more years with the Giants going 17-9, 11-7, and finally 8-5 in 1908. Following his release from the Giants, he bounced around the major leagues for seven years before calling it quits in 1915 at the age of 40.

Taylor was ejected from several games in his lifetime without ever saying a word. On one occasion, he and manager John McGraw were enjoying a running critique of umpire Tim Hurst via sign language. Neither Taylor nor McGraw were aware that Hurst had a deaf relative and had become proficient in signing. Both player and boss were ejected from the game. [57]

Another time, while pitching, Taylor became so incensed at the ball and strike calls that he began to silently cuss out the umpire. His lips were moving but the umpire had no idea what Taylor was trying to communicate. Finally, Taylor walked to the plate, got face-to-face with the ump, and slowly and clearly formed his lips into an unmistakable diatribe. He quickly received an invitation to leave the premises. After the game, the umpire explained to the press, "Even if I wasn't a good lip reader, I knew Taylor wasn't saying his prayers. For a guy who can't hear, he's picked up some nasty words. Why, he actually called me some names I'd never heard before." [58]

While coaching first base, Taylor would emit a loud screeching noise designed to upset the opposing pitcher. Teammate Mike Donlin compared it to "the crazed shrieking of a jackass." One day umpire Hans Zimmer heard enough and ejected Taylor from the field, making Taylor the only deaf mute thrown out for making too much noise. [59]

The one time he did make a comment, the umpire never suspected a deaf-mute and tossed a nearby teammate instead. Umpire Bill Klem was not blessed with a Hollywood countenance. He had full lips and large mouth. The players and coaches called him Catfish behind his back, a name that he despised. Any player ready to exit the game needed only to address him accordingly. Taylor's teammates laboriously taught him to say the word "catfish" and waited for the perfect opportunity to spring their joke on Klem. When the umpire's back was turned, Taylor spoke the forbidden name. Klem spun around and tossed Mike Donlin from the game. Taylor repeated the name and Klem spun around again, still incredulous that Dummy Taylor could utter his dreaded nickname. Taylor remained in the contest. [60]

After his playing days were over, Taylor worked with deaf students at the Kansas School for the Deaf before eventually settling down for over 20 years at Illinois School for the Deaf. He served as coach, teacher and administrator until he was in his sixties. During the 1950s Taylor patrolled Illinois and Indiana as a scout for the New York Giants.

Taylor married three times but had no children.

Dummy Taylor was an ebullient personality who fought hard to be accepted by his teammates, and for the most part he succeeded. But off the diamond, away from the clubhouse, he still had to deal with the many prejudices and insults of strangers. A clown and jokester on the baseball field, he reacted with restrained fury when treated poorly.

He seemed an unlikely candidate to accept the name Dummy. The deaf community was incensed that the sporting world continued to assign the name to all deaf athletes. The Silent Worker reported, "The highest salaried deaf man in the United States is the much heralded Dummy Taylor – I say Dummy only to serve to show how contemptible the epithet looks." [61] When asked about the name in 1945, he told Baseball Magazine, "In the old days Hoy and I were called Dummy. It didn't hurt us. It made us fight harder." [62]

Luther Taylor gave up the fight in 1958 at the age of 83. He was buried in Baldwin City, Kansas, beside his first wife.

Dummy Leitner

George Michael Leitner was the fourth deaf player to enter the major leagues with the nickname Dummy. The 30-year-old pitcher's acclimation to the big leagues was undoubtedly made easier by the presence of Dummy Taylor who preceded him on the Giants roster by one year. Taylor's determination to teach his teammates sign language provided a much softer landing for Leitner.

Leitner, listed at 120 pounds, is the co-holder of the lightest major league player on record, which he shares with Candy Cummings and Sparrow McCaffrey. Standing only 5' 7" tall, Leitner would have easily qualified for another nickname had the default name of Dummy not been applied.

Unlike Hoy and Taylor, Leitner left us only a faint and broken trail to follow. The path begins in the minor leagues at Norfolk in 1901. By June of the same year he was a member of the fledgling Philadelphia Athletics. One game later, he was gone from Philadelphia and had become a member of the New York Giants. He started, completed and lost two games for the 1902 Giants.

The following year, like Taylor, he was on the roster of the Cleveland Bronchos, very likely after Taylor's sudden departure (and reverse jump back to the Giants). After just one start, an eight-inning no-decision effort, he was sold to the Chicago White Sox. In Chicago, he entered a game and threw the last four innings, yielding six runs, in a 21-6 loss to the Orioles, severely crippling Chicago's quest to win the first American League championship. [63] That would be his last appearance in a big league game. His two-season career would consist of only fives games in which he compiled (if that is the right term) an 0-2 record with a 5.34 ERA.

Four years later, his trail is spotted again, this time in Baton Rouge of the Cotton States League. The Class D Cajuns gave him a good shot and he responded with a 5-4 record in 15 games. No record exists of any further experience with a professional team.

The years between his 1906 season in Baton Rouge and his death in Baltimore in 1960 are a blank.

Dummy Deegan

William Joseph Deegan made his major league debut with the New York Giants in 1901, the same year as Dummy Leitner. Deegan and Leitner, along with Dummy Taylor, were all pitchers on the 1901 Giants. As with Leitner, Deegan's tenure with the Giants was brief. He appeared in just two contests, one as a starter (a complete game) and one as a reliever. According to the Deegan family genealogy site, Giants manager John McGraw felt that Deegan was a bad influence on Dummy Taylor, and was purged from the team for that reason. Neither his 6.35 ERA nor 0-1 record helped his chances of remaining on the Giants' roster.

Prior to his debut with the Giants, Deegan did not play for any recognized minor league teams. He honed his pitching skills while attending the St. Joseph's Deaf and Dumb School in New York City. [64]. His name also appears on the roster of the Young Men's Catholic Lyceum, a skillful team based in North Tarrytown, New York, in the 1890's. [65]

After his dismissal by McGraw, Deegan's name does not resurface in the baseball world until 1907 when at age 32 he pitched in six games with the Jersey City Skeeters in the Eastern League. Despite a WHIP of .897 and an ERA under four, his record was just 2-4.

Later that same year, the Reading (PA) Eagle announced that Dummy Deegan would pitch for the Reading Red Roses against Allentown in an Atlantic League Contest. [66]

No trace of Dummy Deegan has been discovered since 1907. Dummy Deegan, the ballplayer, was gone. Bill Deegan the welder would be is his new identity. He died in 1957 in the Bronx, where he was born. He was 83-years-old.

Dummy Murphy

The arc of Herbert Courtland Murphy's baseball career was not dissimilar to most non-impaired players; minor league experience, promotion to the major leagues, followed by a return to the minor leagues prior to retirement. His tenure in the major leagues, however, closely paralleled that of the deaf players that preceded him. He spent just 23 days with the Philadelphia Phillies.

Murphy, a shortstop, saw action in just nine contests and batted a meager .154. He reached base five times on four singles and one double. He navigated the base paths around to home plate a single time.

Murphy was born in Olney, Illinois, in 1886. It would be expected that Murphy attended a school for the deaf. The Illinois School for the deaf was located near Springfield, reasonably close to Murphy's hometown. No evidence that he matriculated there has surfaced.

Murphy first appears on the baseball radar in 1912 playing for the Class D Greenwood (Mississippi) Scouts in the Cotton States League. He was tall for a shortstop at 5" 10". Offensively, his first year was mediocre (.260) and his defense poor (63 errors).

The 1913 season found him in Georgia still playing at the Class D level with the Thomasville Hornets. His .338 batting average propelled him all the way to the big leagues in Philadelphia to begin the 1914 season. Within a month he was back in the minors with Class AA Jersey City in the International League.

Beginning in 1915, he migrated to the Pacific Northwest where he played for Spokane, Portland, Salt Lake City, Los Angeles, and Seattle over the next four years. He left the game at age 32 in 1919.

Murphy left no discernible trace for the next 43 years of his life. He died in Tallahassee, Florida. in 1962. He was buried in Thomasville, Georgia, the scene of his best year in professional baseball.

Dummy Lynch

Matthew Daniel Lynch was born in 1926, 12 years after the end of Dummy Murphy's career. His first professional job was with the Waco Pirates in the Big State League in 1948. Late in September of the same year he signed to play second base with the Chicago Cubs, his only year in the majors.

By that point, 34 years had slipped by since that last player was designated as a "Dummy." Even though the era of racist, ethnic and insulting nicknames was entering its final decades, the old prejudices still lingered in the shadows. Had the hearing-impaired Lynch been a cobbler or a plumber, he would still today be known as Matt or Matthew Lynch. His brief sojourn into baseball made him forever Dummy Lynch.

How did baseball and society at large become so callous as to denigrate the handicapped, the dark-skinned, the foreign born and even those who chose more wholesome pastimes than drinking and womanizing?

Researcher Robert E. Bionaz suggests that a cultural paradigm of masculinity and virility at the turn of the twentieth century reflected an opinion born in 1893. The federal Civil Service Commissioner was a man named Theodore Roosevelt. Roosevelt warned his fellow citizens of a danger to "a peaceful and commercial civilization" of placing too little emphasis on virile virtues such as vigorous, manly sports." Roosevelt said further, "The true sports for a manly race are sports like running, rowing, playing football and baseball, boxing and wrestling, shooting, riding and mountain climbing."

Bionaz: "...Roosevelt's rhetorical linkage of sports with manliness resonated with many American men." [67]

When Teddy became president in 1901, his manly exploits underscored his words and the nation adopted and elevated the value of manly activities and physical strength.

During that period in our history, baseball was the only truly organized sport, and its participants lived up to the ideals of virility and masculinity. Players that failed to join their mates at the bars and brothels were given mock feminine and religious nicknames.

On the other hand, the wild and crazy personalities were rewarded with names that glorified their eccentricities, such as Cuckoo and Dizzy.

A player could bring great skill sets to the game, but still had to be reminded that he was shorter, thinner or fatter than his masculine teammates.

So it was no surprise that players with physical handicaps needed to be designated as such. Bionaz wrote, "Such labeling emphasized the players as distinctly different from their non-disabled, more masculine counterparts although the Deaf community viewed (Dummy) Hoy and (Dummy) Taylor very differently. Both were seen as 'heroes who were both deaf and All-American.' Even though the Deaf community viewed Hoy and Taylor as 'normal' they accepted with little protest, the largely insulting term "Dummy." [68]

Above: left – Nig Cuppy   right – Nig Clarke
Below: left – Dummy Hoy   right --Hick Cady

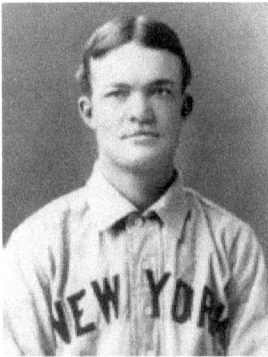

Chapter Five – Word Play

Yo-Yo Davalillo

Pompeyo Antonio Davalillo was not as accomplished as his brother Victor Jose Davalillo. Younger brother Vic had a 16-year career in the big leagues, compiling over 1,100 hits and playing in the 1965 All-Star Game. Pompeyo spent just the 1953 season with the Washington Senators where he managed only 17 hits. But the older of the two siblings claimed one of the craziest nicknames in baseball, Yo-Yo.

The word yo-yo, of course, refers to the classic toy that has been around in some form since 500 B.C. The toy was patented in 1866 and named a "bandelore." In 1928, Pedro Flores opened the Yo-yo Manufacturing Company in California and the name was born. Donald Duncan entered the picture a few years later and bought out Mr. Flores and the rest is history, as the saying goes. [1]

Davalillo did not acquire his nickname because he had a penchant for, or skill with the yo-yo, but the nickname never could have taken root without the popularity of the toy. His name did not evolve because he "yo-yoed" back and forth between the minors and the majors. No, his nickname was the result of the sound of his full name when spoken aloud. Pompeyo Antonio Davalillo rolls off the lips as "Pom-pa-YO An-tone-ee-YO Da-vah-lee-YO. By all rights, he could have been called Yo-Yo-Yo.

A more pejorative meaning of the word yo-yo puts Davalillo into this project. A very popular slang definition refers to a yo-yo as a stupid, foolish, or incompetent person. Perhaps Davalillo, born in Venezuela, was not familiar with the American slang meaning of his new name.

Putting aside the 3' 7" Eddie Gaedel, the shortest MLB players on record were 5' 3" tall. Davalillo, at 5' 3" and 140 pounds, shares this distinction with 11 others.

Davalillo's career flashed onto the radar screen in 1953, at age 22. Drafted by the Yankees, he was released and signed by the Washington Senators who dispatched him to the Class B Charlotte Hornets. The flashy shortstop immediately hit for average (.305) and earned an August call up to the big league team. Unlike many players who moved quickly to the parent team and failed to perform, Davalillo continued to hit and impressed HOF manager Bucky Harris.

A serious injury in August of 1953 cost him a longer career in the major leagues. He missed the entire 1954 season. When he recovered from his injuries he played for the Havana Sugar Kings who were a part of the International League in 1955. He spent 1956 with two stateside teams before returning to the Sugar Kings for the next few years. He returned to the U.S. after the Cuban Revolution and played for the Jersey City Jerseys for the remainder of the 1960 season and all of 1961.

Fear of flying also contributed to his truncated major league career.

As the years worn on, his place of employment moved ever southward; Mexico from 1962 to 1964, then back home to Venezuela where he played and coached for many years.

Yo-Yo passed away in his home country of Venezuela in 2013. His brother Vic is still living at the time of this writing.

Heinie Meine

Eeny, meeny, miney moe, catch Heinie Meine by the toe. No, that's not the way the child's counting rhyme goes, but it illustrates the playfulness that resulted in Henry William Meine's nickname. He was one of 22 players who answered to the name Heinie. He could also fit into the category of ethnic names because of his Germanic background. His name in the German language means "mine." Meine could have also been nicknamed Dutch, Germany, or Fritz. The choice of Heinie over the other options was no doubt based on the rhyming of Heinie and the last name Meine. So, here he shall reside in the Wordplay section.

The German word "meine" is actually pronounced my-nuh, but fortunately for the wag that coined this nickname, the player pronounced it my-nee. [Author's note: Marge Mesplay of Heine Meine Field in St. Louis confirmed the pronunciation]

Meine was also known as the Count of Luxemburg, not because he had roots in the Grand Duchy of Luxembourg, but because he made his home in the village of Luxemburg, Missouri.

Meine was born in St. Louis in 1896. He did not land a professional baseball job until he signed with the Beaumont Explorers of the Texas League in 1921. At some point in his early career, the right-hander learned to throw the spitball, and pitched well enough to earn an audition with the big league St. Louis Browns in 1922. His cup of coffee in St. Louis was somewhat bitter. Because he was not on the list of exempted pitchers when the spitball ban was enacted, he had to rely on his "dry" repertoire. He was knocked around for three runs in four innings and was handed a train ticket back to the Texas League.

From 1923 through 1926, he worked to develop his traditional pitches in the minor leagues. He managed to compile a 54-39 record during those four seasons, but detected no interest from the major leagues. In 1927, he quit baseball to open a bar in the Lemay section of St. Louis.

During the next two years, Meine did more than draw beers and pour shots. He worked on a variety of "junk" pitches and eventually succumbed to the suggestions of his patrons to give baseball another try.

In 1929, the Pittsburgh Pirates, led by the Waner brothers and Pie Traynor gave Meine the opportunity he needed. He contributed seven wins as a reliever and spot starter and contributed to the Pirates second-place finish.

The 1930 season was not as successful, the Pirates dropped to fifth place and Maine had a losing 6-8 record. But better things were just around the corner in 1931. The 35-year-old Meine became the elder statesman, and eventually the ace of the Pirates' pitching staff. Throwing an assortment of off-speed pitches, he led the league in innings pitched at 284. To the amazement of most everyone in the National League, he won 19 games, tied for the league lead with Jumbo Elliott of the Phillies and Bill Hallahan of the Cardinals.

During the off-season, Meine joined the Waner All-Stars barnstorming team, playing clubs like the House of David (featuring Pete Alexander) and the Kansas City Monarchs (with Satchel Paige), who had been displaced by the collapse of the Negro National League. [2]

While he failed to repeat his 19-win season, he compiled a 27-17 record over the next two seasons. At age 34, he closed out his career in 1934 with a winning record (7-4).

He retired to his St. Louis tavern where he continued to host many baseball luminaries, such as Dizzy Dean. Adjacent to the tavern was a nine-acre tract of land which was developed by the Lemay Baseball Association in 1949 to provide organized youth teams. The field was named Heine (sic) Meine Field in honor of Henry Meine. [3]

Bevo LeBourveau

Some doubt exists as to the derivation of the nickname Bevo LeBourveau, but there can be no argument with the proposition that some very lyrical wordplay is involved. DeWitt Wiley LeBourveau has something in common with Yo-Yo Davalillo. One has to say the name aloud several times to fully appreciate the sweet sound that these five syllables produce. Bee-vo Le- Bor-Vo. The name could easily belong to an exotic dancer or silent film star.

One theory claims that Bevo was a malt beverage produced during Prohibition and accounted for the name. Unless Mr. LeBourveau was a committed devotee of this beverage, Bevo was still used as a play on his last name, sending it into the word play category.

Another suggestion concerns the abbreviation of LeBourveau that appeared in the box scores, "LeBo." Lebo LeBourveau could have morphed into Bevo LeBourveau just because it sounded better. [4]

LeBourveau was born in Dana, California in 1896. He played in the outfield for Santa Clara University, a regular supplier of players to major league baseball. Today, Santa Clara boasts 54 alumni who have gone on to greater glory in the big leagues. LeBourveau's ascension to the Philadelphia Phillies outfield occurred rapidly. A season and a half in the minor leagues culminated in a September call-up to the Quaker City in 1919. He made the best of his opportunity by hitting .270 in 17 games.

New Phillies manager Gavvy Cravath kept him on the roster in 1920 as a back up to an outfield consisting of Casey Stengel, Irish Meusel and Cy Williams. He did not display a lot of power but hit enough to keep his seat on the Phillies bench.

In 1921, he enjoyed his best year in baseball, batting .295 in 319 plate appearances. He contributed 23 extra base hits including six home runs. Another managerial change brought Kaiser Wilhelm to the helm in 1922, and LeBourveau did not see as much action during that campaign. When the season ended, the "Beeve" had to leave. He had lost his place on the Phillies roster.

He began 1923 with the Nashville Volunteers in the Southern Association but ended the season in Little Rock. He batted a combined .333 and launched a string of seven consecutive years with a .300 plus batting average. Still, no major league team came calling until Connie Mack invited him back to Philadelphia for the Athletics' stretch run in September of 1929. The 32-year-old outfielder played an important role in lifting Philadelphia to the American League pennant with a .313 batting average during the 12 games he entered. The A's defeated the Chicago Cubs four games to one in the World Series, but LeBourveau saw no action.

Mack had no further need for LeBourveau's services in 1930 and he retrenched to the minors where he spent the last five years of his playing career, hitting over, or near, .300 every year but his last, finishing with a stellar .349 lifetime minor league batting average. His major league average of .275 was not as spectacular, but solid, nevertheless.

He amassed over 2,000 hits in the minor leagues while batting .349 over those 14 seasons. During his four seasons with the Toledo Mud Hens, he compiled an average of .380, the highest of any Toledo player. [5] In Toledo, he was reunited with his former teammate Casey Stengel, now the manager of the Mud Hens. Despite LeBourveau's success, Stengel tried to sell him to other teams several times, but always had to take him back when the outfielder's emotional problems were discovered. During slow games he would stand in the outfield stewing about some issue. Once he left the field, his emotions would erupt into very intense argument with teammates. This condition very likely prevented him from returning to the major leagues until 1929. [6]

LeBourveau died in 1949 in Nevada City, California. He was only 51 years old.

Pickles Dillhoefer

Many of the nicknames in this category were puns based on the first or last name. Most of these names must have been assigned early in life. William Martin Dillhoefer, as an example, could not have escaped grade school without a classmate calling attention to the dill pickle reference of his last name. In some cases, a family name so strongly suggests a pun that a nickname passes from one generation to the next. Most likely, Dillhoefer emerged from Cleveland, Ohio with the name Pickles firmly in place. Pickles' father was also named William Martin Dillhoefer and his mother's name was Delia Butter. [7] This raises the possibility that junior also had bread-and-butter pickle connection.

Our friend Pickles was basically a back-up catcher most of his short career with the Cubs, Phillies and Cardinals. He was a throw-in to the trade that moved Grover Cleveland "Pete" Alexander from the Phillies to the Cubs. World War I beckoned and pulled Pickles off the diamond for most of the 1918 season.

Shortly after his wedding in 1922, Pickles died of typhoid fever contracted following surgery for injuries sustained in an off-season game. [8] His funeral service was held in the same Alabama church as his wedding. [9]

The Sporting News in 2001 ranked the all-time great baseball nicknames and declared Pickles Dillhoefer the winner. Perhaps the most prestigious award garnered by Dillhoefer is the Number One Peculiar Pickle Name as determined by the Pickle Preservation Society on their web site.

His obituary lists no offspring, so the great Pickles family nickname was buried with him.

One other cool cucumber left in the jar is George Pickles Gerken. Gerken only receives honorable mention because he is not officially listed as Pickles Gerken, choosing instead to be known as George. Apparently, Gerken had no great sense of humor.

Kaiser Wilhelm

The next batter in the Word Play lineup is Irvin Key Wilhelm. Coming of age during the reign of Kaiser Wilhelm II, the nickname Kaiser would have been a natural. Little Irvin was probably not called Kaiser around the Wilhelm family dinner table, so he probably gained his sobriquet in the minor or major leagues.

The European version of Kaiser Wilhelm was the last Emperor of Germany and King of Prussia. He was right in the middle of the conflict that led to World War I. In 1918, in the midst of a revolution by his troops, he abdicated the throne and escaped to the Netherlands.

Irvin Kaiser Wilhelm was born in Wooster, Ohio, in 1884. He joined the Pittsburgh Pirates in 1903, subsequently pitching for the Boston Beaneaters, followed by the Brooklyn Superbas. Kaiser also pulled an abdication of his own in 1914 by jumping to the Federal League and playing for the Baltimore Terrapins during their two years of existence. During 1914, Kaiser would have played across the street from the minor league Baltimore Orioles where George Herman Ruth was starting his career as a pitcher.

In 1921, Kaiser joined the Philadelphia Phillies as a player-manager, replacing Wild Bill Donovan in mid-season. The Kaiser was both relief pitcher and manager. When on the mound in the middle of a rally, did he have to walk to the dugout and return to give himself the hook? Did he pat himself on the fanny before turning the ball over to the next pitcher?

He abdicated again in 1915, when he gave up his player status and stayed in the Phillies dugout. Art Fletcher replaced him in 1916 following two losing seasons.

He ended his pitching career with a 56-105 record and his managerial career with an 83-137 record. He died in 1936 in Rochester, New York.

Chicken Hawks

Nelson Louis Hawks no doubt gained his nickname because of his last name. While research has not revealed when this nickname was assigned, common sense would dictate that teammates at Santa Clara College or one of his early minor league teams so regaled him. Because he chose to go down in history as Chicken, rather than Nelson (or Nellie, Louis, Louie, etc), we must assume he felt some affinity for the name.

But why Chicken Hawks? Why not embrace something more manly such as Night Hawks? In the wild, the chicken hawk is actually a very aggressive bird more correctly known as the Cooper's Hawk. This crow sized raptor feeds mostly on other birds.

Our baseball Chicken Hawks came out of college and signed with the Oakland Oaks of the Pacific Coast League where he performed for two years as a third baseman and outfielder. He joined the New York Yankees in 1921 and served mostly as a pinch hitter because of his poor fielding record. Despite a decent .288 batting average, the Yanks set the Chicken Hawk free.

After laboring in the minors for three years, the Phillies gave him a shot at playing first base where he batted .322 in 90 games. Despite his offensive numbers, he found himself back in the minor leagues in 1926. (Throughout baseball history, it is amazing how many players finished their major league careers with the Phillies). Chicken Hawks could not fly high enough to reach the majors again. He died in 1973 at the age of 77.

Pol Perritt

William Dayton Perritt was born in 1891 in Arcadia, Louisiana. The transition to Pol Perritt is a bit of a stretch, but here we go. The name Perritt is very similar to the word parrot. A very common name for a parrot in the latter part of the 19th century and early 20th century was Polly. The name Polly became so synonymous with parrots, that the bird was often called a Polly-parrot or a poll-parrot.

William would have likely objected to being named Polly Perritt, but the less-feminine Pol Perritt apparently suited him. Unlike many of the Deadball-era players who affected unusual nicknames, Perritt was a very successful pitcher, helping John McGraw's Giants win the National League pennant in 1918. All told, Perritt spent 10 years in the major leagues, seven of them with the Giants. From 1916 to 1918 he compiled a 53-31 record.

Perritt spent his first three seasons with the St. Louis Cardinals. After a 16-13 record in 1914, he was traded to the New York Giants the following February. Rather than report to the Giants to begin the season, Perritt signed with the Pittsburgh Rebels of the rival Federal League for a $1,000 pay raise. According to an article in a New London (Connecticut) newspaper, McGraw was so incensed that he dispatched top scout Dick Kinsella to intercept Perritt and bring him back alive. Kinsella met up with Perritt somewhere near Augusta, Georgia, where the Rebels were convening for spring training, and invited him to sit down and enjoy a sarsaparilla.

Kinsella probed and discovered that Rebels owner Reb Oakes was going to pay Perritt $8,000 for the upcoming season. Kinsella, acting on McGraw's determined quest to keep his player, offered Perritt $9,000 per season for three years. Perritt replied, "The terms are suitable to muh (sic), but before I move from this here spot I wanta know what Jawn (sic) McGraw thinks about 'em. If he fusses about it I'll go right along on my way to the Feds' camp." [10]

"Jawn" gave his blessings and Pol Perritt got his crackers, $27,000 worth. Perritt was the rare bird that was able to successfully negotiate salary with a baseball team official.

After a partial season with the Tigers in 1921, he retired back to his native Louisiana and entered the oil business. [11] He left this world in 1947.

Red Bird

James Edward Bird may have entered the Hall of Nicknames through two different doors. The name Red Bird could easily be a reference to the color of his hair, and is definitely a play on words using his last name. Research has yielded no explanation of his nickname. What we do know is that Red Bird landed briefly in Washington D.C. in 1921, pitched five credible innings and batted one time. On the mound he surrendered three runs on five hits and struck out two batters. At the plate he struck out.

While Red Bird appears to be the quintessential "cup of coffee" player, a deeper look reveals an odd circumstance. His seven-year minor league career occurred almost entirely after his major league experience. He hailed from Stephenville, Texas, near Dallas. Like the fictional Roy Hobbs, he was invisible until the age of 31, and then appeared at A-level Shreveport in the Texas League. A 17-12 record somehow propelled him to the Washington Nationals for one game. The next year he was back at Shreveport. He bounced around the minors through 1927, never rising above Class A ball.

He was able to reminisce about his "cup of coffee" for many years. He died in 1972 at age 82 and was buried in Stephenville near his birthplace.

Sugar Cain

When Merrit Patrick Cain graduated from high school in Macon, Georgia, around 1925, he was already known as Sugar Cain. His high school buddies had sweetened his image and he never looked back. He was forever after known as the right-handed pitcher Sugar Cain.

His first professional baseball job did not occur until age 23 when he signed with the Class D Carrollton Champs in 1930. His stats were not outstanding, but he earned a promotion to the Class B Harrisburg Senators where he rubbed elbows with a dozen other future major leaguers, including the wondrous Snake Henry. One year later he was sharing the dugout with Connie Mack and his Athletics.

Cain turned in a 13-win season in 1933, the last decent year for Connie Mack's A's before they sank into the bowels of the American League for two decades. His best year (15- 11) came in 1936 after being traded from the St. Louis Browns to the Chicago White Sox.

Sugar Cain is frequently credited with a role he did NOT play, pitching to 3'7" Eddie Gaedel in Bill Veeck's classic promotional stunt. Pitching that day in 1951 was Bob Sugar Cain for the Detroit Tigers. Bob Cain had picked up the nickname Sugar Cain but did not officially adopt it. The real Sugar Cain had retired in 1938, long before Veeck's famous gag.

Cain died in Atlanta in 1978 two days before his 68th birthday.

Frank Kane (1915-1919) and Tom Kane (1938) were also called Sugar but did not embrace the name professionally.

King Cole

One would think that Leonard Leslie Cole picked up his nickname at an early age, but history tells us that he arrived in Chicago in 1909 as Leonard Cole and left as King Cole, thanks to Ring Lardner. [12] Lardner had made the obvious connection to Old King Cole from the nursery rhyme hall of fame, but he very likely was working on a double pun, since Cole had become the Cubs "ace", or "king of the hill" with his league-leading 20-4 record in 1910 and 18-7 in 1911.

By 1914, his star had fallen and he was available in the Rule V Draft. The New York Yankees selected him and opened the door for his greatest claim to fame. On October 2, 1914, he allowed the opposing Red Sox pitcher to reach second base on a double, thereby giving up the first base hit of Babe Ruth's career.

King Cole might have someday been able to call the Babe his teammate, but he contracted a serious disease in 1915 and could no longer play baseball. He was dead within a year. The cause of death has been speculated to be malaria, TB, or even syphilis. He may, or may not, have been a merry soul, but he certainly met an unhappy ending.

Cookie Cuccurullo

Arthur Joseph Cuccurullo was a Jersey boy who rose out of the minor leagues to pitch for the Pirates during World War II. His was a 20-game winner with Albany in 1943 and earned his promotion to the talent-thin major leagues. When the war ended, he found himself back in the minor leagues where he spent the last five years of his professional career. His claim to fame was being the losing pitcher when Rogers Hornsby McKee became the youngest modern era player to pitch a complete game. McKee was 17 years and 17 days old when he started for the Phillies against the Pirates on October 3, 1943, the last day of the season. Cuccurullo was making his major league debut that day.

Cookie's nickname was derived from the pronunciation of his last name. The fact that he accepted the name Cookie professionally might indicate that he may have carried the nickname from his childhood. Cookie's lyrical nickname always reminds me of a fictional Italian named Arthur "Fonzie" Fonzarelli. While Fonzie grew up in Milwaukee in the 1950's, not Asbury Park in the 1940's, they might have become great pals.

Another Cookie, Harry Arthur Lavagetto, lent broader fame to the nickname. This Cookie also started with the Pirates but gained fame by virtue of his exploits with the Brooklyn Dodgers.

Rags Faircloth

James Lamar Faircloth was another player who enjoyed a very brief major league visit. The word "career" would hardly seem to fit. It would be safe to say that he picked up his nickname Rags before he reached the Phillies in 1919. He made his pitching debut on May 6 and his last appearance on May 15.

The name Rags was a play on his last name. Not the most imaginative, but an interesting choice all the same. Faircloth attended Mississippi State University in 1911 and 1912. His minor league career started in 1913 and ended in 1916. The missing years of 1917 and 1918 indicate a detour caused by World War I. As it turned out, he was more valuable to the U.S. war effort as a baseball player than a warrior. He played for the Great Lakes Naval Air Station team along with future major leaguers George Halas and Red Faber.

When arm troubles ended his career, he went to work for Westinghouse and helped the St. Louis Browns with some scouting. He died in Arizona in 1953 at age 61.

King Lear

Charles Bernard Lear was accorded a royal nickname befitting a Princeton graduate. *King Lear*, of course, was one of Shakespeare's better-known plays. The latter-day Lear pitched for the Princeton Tigers from 1910 to 1913. King Lear jumped from the Ivy League directly to the National League, joining the Cincinnati Reds in 1914. His career lasted just one more year.

According to the Allison-Antrim Museum, Lear invented the knuckleball. If not the first knuckleballer, he was among the pioneers. [13]

Lear is part of another historical footnote. He was on the mound when Rogers Hornsby walked to the plate for his first at bat in 1915. Hornsby went hitless in two tries. [14]

Lear did not descend into madness like his regal namesake. He lived until the age of 85 and was buried in the town of his birth, Waynesboro, Pennsylvania.

Noteworthy Unofficial Word Play Nicknames

The following players were commonly known by nicknames but chose not to allow the new monikers to become part of their official identity.

Bob Ach Duliba

Nineteen-year-old pitcher Bob Duliba joined the Peoria Chiefs in 1954 with no clue that he would leave Peoria with one of the zaniest nicknames in baseball. His manager, Whitey Kurowski, could not say his new player's name without recalling the Viennese folk song *Ach du lieber Augustin*. [15]

The song title translates to "O my good friend Augustin." What sounds like a happy drinking song was actually a reference to an incident that took place during one of Vienna's darkest hours. The bubonic plague, ravaging most of Europe, reached Vienna in 1679. The death count became so great that the city employed a "corpse patrol" to rid the street of victims each morning. One evening a chap named Augustin enjoyed his wine and company late into the night and passed out on the walk home. At dawn he was scooped up with the other bodies and thrown into the pit that served as a mass grave. Augustin awoke to the horror of infected corpses and considered himself doomed. The deadly buboes never appeared and Augustin survived the ordeal. Rumors washed over the continent that wine was a cure or a preventative measure to combat the plague.

Duliba must have researched the song himself and decided not to embrace the name. Some historical records include his nickname, while others do not. His career was unremarkable. He spent six seasons in the major leagues serving strictly as a relief pitcher for the Cardinals, Angels and Red Sox.

In 1967, Kansas City owner Charlie Finley promoted him from Vancouver in the Pacific Coast League to the parent club. He appeared in seven games and accumulated enough time to qualify for his pension. [16] There are many stories that cast Finley in a bad light, but this is not one of them.

"Ach du lieber Bob Duliba."

Hank Bow Wow Arft

Hank Arft was a first baseman who made the St. Louis Browns roster in 1948 at age 26. When considering the source of his nickname Bow Wow, the word that comes to mind is "duh". While there is no written record of other names, his teammates undoubtedly piled on other sobriquets such as "Doggie", "Mutt", and myriad other canine related terms.

Arft was a Brownie when Bill Veeck took over the ownership in 1951. In addition to the legendary Eddie Gaedel promotion, Arft witnessed the game in which Veeck allowed the fans to "manage" the game using placards. Said Arft of his Veeck years, "The Brownie fans were the best...although Veeck should have owned a circus instead of a ballclub." [17]

After retiring from baseball after his 1954 season with PCL Portland Beavers, Arft returned to his native Missouri and founded a funeral home with his wife and brother-in-law. It seems that you *can* teach an old dog new tricks. Incidentally, they did not name the establishment the Bow Wow Funeral Home. Artf died in 2002 at the age of 80.

Johnny Hippity Hopp

He could have easily become Bunny Hopp or even Bad Hopp. He was, in fact, really nicknamed Cotney, a bastardization of cottony, a description of his hair color. But the nickname-gods blessed him with the great moniker of Hippity Hopp. His 1949 Bowman baseball card designates him as Johnny "Hippity" Hopp.

Hopp was a very underrated player who enjoyed a 14-year career beginning with the 1939 Cardinals. He entered the 1952 season with a lifetime average of .300. Splitting the year with the Yankees and Tigers, he batted under .200 and lost his chance to retire as a career .300 hitter, finishing at .296.

In 1944, the Cardinals traded Johnny Mize to the Giants and gave Hopp a shot at centerfield. He responded by hitting .330 and knocking in 72 runs and led all NL fielders with a .997 fielding average. The Cardinals triumphed in the World Series that year. In 1946, playing for the Boston Braves, he was voted onto the All-Star team.

On May 18, 1949, Hopp was traded by the Pittsburgh Pirates to the Brooklyn Dodgers for outfielder Marv Rackley. Dodger officials stated that Hopp was an insurance policy for first base. [18] Three weeks later the trade was voided and both players bounced back to their former teams. Even though Rackley was hitting over .300, Pirates president Frank McKinney complained that Rackley had injured his arm in spring training and had hidden it from the Dodgers. Since Johnny Hopp had gone hitless in 14 tries, the Dodgers agreed to void the trade. [19]

Hopp died in 2003 in his native Nebraska at the age of 86.

Poison Ivy Andrews

Ivy Paul Andrews, the pride of Dora, Alabama, eschewed the promise of a college education and possible medical career to pursue his true love, baseball. Following high school graduation in 1926 he learned that a young man could make a living pitching for the local industrial teams. His lively fastball earned rave notices while laboring for the Sloss Mine, Pratt Fuel and Bessie Mine teams. He spent five years in the minor leagues before getting his first taste of the majors with the New York Yankees in 1931. His first win was fueled by a Babe Ruth home run. [20]

He moved to the Boston Red Sox, St. Louis Browns, and Cleveland Indians before retuning to the Yankees in 1937 and 1938. He had the distinction of being Joe DiMaggio's roommate during his second stint with the Yanks.

Andrews struggled with arm troubles through most of his career, and was forced to develop an impressive arsenal of slow pitches to survive. He featured a menu of pitches that included sliders, screwballs, knucklers and sharp breaking curves. Said one writer of Andrews, "He drives batters crazy with a meat ball they can't carve." [21]

While Poison Ivy is a nickname mentioned often in short biographies, early accounts of his exploits refer to him as Paul Andrews, or Ivy Paul. Admirers and friends speak of Ivy Andrews while others call him Paul. In Joe DiMaggio's nomination letter to the Alabama Hall of Fame, he fondly refers to him as Paul. Poison Ivy, then, was likely a name given by newspaper writers and not something that resonated with the player himself.

Johnny Gee Whiz

Had his last name been Smith or Jones, the sight of a 6'9" 225 pound giant looking down from the mound might still have evoked a "gee whiz" from cowered batters. But his name was Gee and Gee Whiz could not have been a better fit. After his baseball career ended, Gee joined the NBA with the Syracuse Nationals (they became the Philadelphia 76ers in 1963). His height not only provided him with two years employment in basketball, but also allowed him to remain a civilian during World War II. The government declared him 4-F and he enjoyed three years of playing time that might have otherwise been spent carrying a rifle. [22] Further, the scarcity of quality players in 1943 gave him his only opportunity to become a regular starting pitcher with Pittsburgh.

Gee died on January 23, 1988 at the age of 72. A brief obituary in the New York Times declared him to be the tallest pitcher in major league history. That distinction held for only eight months. On September 15 of the same year, the pitcher destined to become the Big Unit made his debut with the Montreal Expos. Randy Johnson stood 6'10" but never made an NBA roster.

Dave Kong Kingman

Dave Kingman was a big man (6' 6" and 225 pounds) with a big strike zone. When the bat found the ball in that zone, Kingman trotted around the bases. From 1971 through 1986 he sent long mortar shots into the stands at a pace that would warrant the reference to King Kong. When the bat and ball resided in different planes, Kingman took a walk back to the dugout. Despite his low lifetime batting average of .236, the ballpark came to life when he walked to the plate. Kong gave the fans what they came to see, long, towering homeruns, 442 of them, in fact. Kingman also collected the nickname Sky King, a reference to his name, his proclivity for the long ball, and the flying cowboy of 1950's television.

Without checking Kingman's records, one remembers that he bounced around the big leagues quite a lot. The facts say otherwise. Discount the 1977 season, and Kingman had a fairly stable career. Most of his stops were three plus years in duration, except as noted in 1977. That year he began the season with the Mets and was traded in June to the Padres for Bobby Valentine and Paul Seibert, not exactly the premium players a power hitter would attract. On September 6, the Padres placed Kingman on waivers and the Angels claimed him. Nine days later the Angels cashed in their cheap investment by trading him to the Yankees for Randy Stein.

Kingman finished the 1977 season with the Yankees and contributed four homers and seven RBI's in just 24 at-bats. Nevertheless, the Yankees granted him free agency in November and he signed with the Cubs. During the course of that single year he belonged to five different organizations. From the chaos of his travels came one note of distinction. He became the first player to hit a home run for four different teams in one season.

Kingman was known as a "difficult teammate" and he feuded with the press, once sending a rat to a female reporter. Chicago columnist and humorist Mike Royko publicly changed his loyalties from the Cubs to the White Sox, explaining, "I'd prefer an owner with a wooden leg to a left fielder with a wooden head." [23]

The Cubs found gold, however, when they signed Kingman. After a decent 1978, he broke loose in 1979 for a league leading 48 home runs to go with his 113 RBI's. If the reader assumes that playing in Wrigley Field contributed to Kingman's success, consider that all of the other starters combined barely exceed Kingman's home run total.

In 1984, Kingman was voted Comeback Player of the Year with the Oakland A's. Oakland had signed him as a free agent following a down year with the New York Mets. Kingman was a three-time All-Star, 1976, 1979 and 1980.

HENRY (HEINIE) MEINE

Above: left – Pickles Dillhoefer   right – Heinie Meine
Below: left – Pol Perritt   right – Johnny Gee Whiz

Chapter Six -The Miscellaneous and Unknown Sources

Piggy Ward

The leadoff batter for this category must be Frank Gray Ward, also known as Piggy. Ward surely can lay claim to the most egregious of all unflattering nicknames. The source of Frank Ward's alter ego has been lost to history. The thumbnail photo of Ward on Baseball-Reference.com shows a man with a receding hairline, small eyes and an over-size moustache. The nose is not flat and wide, nor does it feature prominent pig-like nostrils.

The name may have emanated from Ward's physique. He was 5' 9" tall and weighed around 200 pounds, although not exactly porcine dimensions. Perhaps his eating habits reminded teammates of a barnyard animal, either in appetite or lack of table manners. He may have squealed like a pig when excited or agitated. The only certainty is that Ward felt some kind of affinity for the name; at least enough to not push back against it.

The fact that Ward allowed himself to be saddled with such an uncomplimentary nickname may produce the assumption that he was a passive personality who would not resist his teammates name-calling. That assumption would not hold water. Ward was reputed to be very muscular in build, and a genuine "tough guy" on the field. [1]

He was also a verbal agitator to opposing players. He was described as having "a tongue like a rattail file." [2] A rattail file is thin and round with small sharp teeth on most of its surface.

Ward was born in Chambersburg, Pennsylvania, in 1867. In June of 1883, at the age of 16, he emerged from the obscurity of southern-central Pennsylvania to appear as a third baseman for the Philadelphia Quakers of the National League. He successfully handled two chances in the field but failed to hit safely in five at bats. The Quakers defeated the Cleveland Blues 4-3. Shortly after his debut, he was sent back to whence he came, most likely a local team playing in, or around, Chambersburg.

The trail goes cold after his cameo appearance in Philadelphia. Four years later, he joined the Johnstown entry in the Pennsylvania State

League. Now 20 years old, he held down first base for the Johnstown team until they folded in mid-season. He signed on with the Shamokin Maroons in the Central Pennsylvania League, where he played first base, right field and catcher. Cupid Childs played second base for the Maroons.

In 1888, Childs was promoted to the Quakers while Ward disappeared off the radar screen. The following year, Ward joined the Quakers for the 1889 season but hit a disappointing .160 in seven games and lost his job again. After a year in the minors with Galveston in the Texas League, he ascended again to the majors with the Pittsburgh Pirates in 1891.

His third tour in the big leagues was successful. He played the next four years with the Pirates, Baltimore Orioles, Cincinnati Reds and Washington Senators. Following his release from the Senators, he accepted work back in the minors where he flourished for another nine seasons, compiling a lifetime batting average of .310 over 12 seasons.

Ward's claim to fame on the field was his 1893 streak of 17 consecutive times reaching base. The oddest fact relating to Ward's three-game performance is that he was traded during the streak. After nine successful trips to the plate with the Baltimore Orioles, he was suddenly dispatched to the Cincinnati Reds for Tony Mullane. Once he donned the Reds uniform, he stepped to the plate eight times in his first game and recorded two hits, five walks, and one HBP. That is also a record.

In his second game for Cincinnati, he stroked four singles and a walk in five at-bats, bringing his total to 17 straight. Ward managed seven singles, a triple, eight walks, and one hit-by-pitch.

An additional oddity about these two records is that it took over a 100 years for the feats to be recognized. In 1997, Chicago's Frank Thomas reached base 15 times in a row. Researchers delved into the record books and determined that Ted Williams held the record of 16, which he set in 1957.

In 1998, researcher Trent Collier published his study on Piggy Ward and the revelation that Ward, not Williams, deserved the credit for this record.

Ward suffered a fall in 1912 and never recovered. He died at the age of 45 in Altoona, Pennsylvania. He might have derived a small comfort had he known that he held two major league records.

Ward's claim to fame off the field is his name. Two other players were later known as Piggy, but Pat Paige and Walter French preferred their given names, so Frank Ward goes down in baseball lore as the one and only Piggy.

Pussy Tebeau

Charles Alston Tebeau was born in 1870 in Worcester, Massachusetts, and grew up in nearby Pittsfield. He is sometimes referred to as a brother of Patsy and George Tebeau of the infamous Cleveland Spiders of the 1890s. Patsy and George were born and raised in St. Louis, Missouri. The possibility exists that they were related to the New England Tebeau family but no proof has been shown to substantiate that.

Pussy Tebeau must join the list of players whose nickname source is unknown or unproven. Brian McKenna of SABR's Baseball Biography Project theorizes that newspaper articles reported on the performance of C.A. Tebeau, leading to the acronym C.A.T. that morphed into Pussy, as in pussycat.

Pussy might also be a feminine name assigned to Charles for refusing to join his namesakes in brawling, swearing, cheating, drinking and womanizing. If Pussy Tebeau does not owe his nickname to Patsy Tebeau, he certainly owes his brief major league career to the Spiders' player-manager. He may have detrained in Cleveland as Charles, but he returned to Worcester as Pussy when his brief stay with the Spiders ended.

During the spring of 1895, Charles was an unknown semi-professional playing for several independent leagues in New England. When his team in Lowell, Massachusetts, disbanded he signed to play second base and outfield for the Portland entry in the New England League. His plans changed drastically when a better offer suddenly appeared. Tebeau boarded a train for Cleveland, not Portland, and he soon became the third Tebeau playing for the Cleveland Spiders.

Patsy Tebeau may have known about Pussy's recent successes in New England. More likely, he saw an opportunity to make some mischief by importing another Tebeau to confuse Cleveland's opponents.

Once he put on the Spiders uniform, he played in just two games, acquitting himself nicely with three hits and two walks in eight plate appearances. He scored three times, drove in a run and stole one base. His fielding was perfect in his two games, yet he never set foot on a major league field again. Did Patsy tire of his little name game? Quite the contrary; jilted Portland manager Frank Leonard filed a grievance with the National League and Tebeau was suspended until a hearing could be held. The arbitrator declared him to be property of the Portland team to the dismay of a bitter Patsy Tebeau.

Pussy Tebeau did not rejoin Portland to finish the 1895 season. He later signed and rejoined them in 1896. After just nine games he was batting .143 and was released. He had to travel all the way to Alabama to find another employer. He joined the Birmingham Bluebirds of the Southern Association and appeared in three games without a hit. He finished the 1896 season batting .080.

During a preseason game the following spring, he was beaned and lay unconscious near home plate for a quarter of an hour. He emerged from the hospital two weeks later 25 pounds lighter and effectively retired from baseball as a player.

The following year he accepted a manager's position in his hometown of Pittsfield. The new league folded and Tebeau reinvented himself as machinist and spent the rest of his working-life employed by General Electric.

He was a father of eight and grandfather of many until his death at age 80 in Pittsfield.

Oyster Burns

Of all the creatures in the world, the oyster may be one of the last choices for a nickname, yet that slimy, unattractive mollusk came to signify Thomas P. Burns. How that name attached itself like a barnacle to Tommy Burns has been the subject of debate over the past century.

Lee Allen asserts that Burns had a real fondness for oysters, and was named accordingly. Bill James claims that Burns was commonly called

Tommy and not renamed as Oyster Burns until after his death, primarily to distinguish him from a contemporary named Thomas Everett Burns, who somehow evaded the assignment of a nickname. [3] The two claims are not mutually exclusive and combined may provide a complete explanation.

On the other hand, the Dodgers Encyclopedia states that the nickname was derived from an offseason job selling seafood.

A similar claim stated that he worked for an "oyster farm" when not playing baseball. The fact that his obituary did not refer to him as Oyster Burns would tend to support Bill James' postmortem theory.

Burns was born in 1864 (or 1862 depending on your source) in Philadelphia while the Civil War was still raging. He grew up to be stocky but fast, and excelled at the plate and in the field. As he matured he added a handlebar moustache to his appearance.

The teenaged Burns first appeared in a major league uniform with the Wilmington Quicksteps in 1884. Wilmington was a late-season addition to the nascent Union Association, replacing the defunct Philadelphia Keystones. The league collapsed during its first season. Burns, however, was sold to the Baltimore Orioles of the American Association before the ax fell on the Union Association. One of the most versatile players of his era, he played every position in the infield, plus many games in right field. He even pitched occasionally.

He survived the 1884 season with Baltimore but struggled in 1885 and was released. He found a temporary home at Newark in the Eastern League where he exploded into stardom in 1886 with a .385 batting average, 10 home runs and 22 steals. The Orioles observed his success and said "Come on down." Back in the big leagues again in 1887, he continued playing at a high level, leading the A.A. in triples with 19 while posting a .341 average.

The following year the Brooklyn Bridegrooms, also in the American Association, purchased him in midseason. In 1890, Brooklyn joined the National League and Burns joined their roster of star players, leading the league in home runs with 13 and RBIs with 128.

Burns became a favorite of Brooklyn fans, playing there through 1895, helping them to win pennants in both the American Association and the National League. According to the Dodgers Encyclopedia, the denizens of Flatbush called him "Erster Boins." If author William McNeil is correct, the nickname Oyster must have been used prior to Burns' death, contrary to the assertions of Bill James. [4]

During the 1895 season, Burns was sold to the New York Giants to finish the season and his big league career. The Giants then sold him to the Newark Colts of the Atlantic League. He ended his baseball career on a high note in 1897 when he joined the Hartford Bluebirds of the same league. He played in 126 games and batted .324 for the Bluebirds.

His 11-year career produced 1,451 hits and 869 runs scored. The stocky Burns also swiped at least 263 bases (1884 and 1885 stolen base stats are missing). In 1890, he was the first Brooklyn player to hit for the cycle. [5]

On an anecdotal note, he was involved in one of baseball's oddest plays of all time. Playing at Brooklyn in 1893, Burns was on second base and catcher Con Daily was on third base. When the batter hit a grounder to shortstop, Daily took off for home and Burns broke for third. Half way home, Daily made a sudden u-turn and sped back to toward third base. When he arrived at the bag, Burns was already occupying the base. Without hesitation, Daily continued running until finding safe harbor at second base. The confused umpire called both runners "safe" creating the first (and probably last) time that two base runners ever switched bases. Daily was now on second and Burns on third. After regaining his senses, the umpire declared Daily out and Burns safe at third.

After his playing days he made Brooklyn his home until his death in 1928. One can assume he enjoyed many oysters until his demise.

Noodles Hahn

There are many possible reasons how a person could be nicknamed Noodles by teammates or sportswriters at some point during a long career. Frank George Hahn, however, belongs to that group of players who carried a nickname into professional baseball from childhood. He was born in Nashville, Tennessee, in 1879. As a kid, Hahn had the task of bringing his father's lunch to the piano factory where he worked. Quite frequently, the lunch included a hot offering of noodles, cooked by Mrs. Hahn. [6] His father's co-workers probably assigned the name to him. There are alternate stories surrounding the nickname, but they all revolve around his involvement with noodles as a boy.

In 1896, at the age of 17, he signed a contract to play for the Mobile Blackbirds in the Southern Association. Far away from home, he could have left his food-based moniker behind. He could have given his teammates the privilege of finding a new handle for him. As a southpaw, he qualified to become a card-holding member of the *Lefty Club*. But no, the name Noodles traveled south with him.

His first season was quite remarkable for a teenager, finishing the year with a 1.44 ERA and a 7- 4 won-loss record. He earned a promotion to Class A baseball and went north to play for the Detroit Tigers of the Western League. He went 17-16 against the tougher competition and made the Tigers roster for the upcoming 1898 season.

Ironically, the 1898 season, split between Detroit and St. Paul, was his worst in professional ball, but he received an invitation to spring training by the Cincinnati Reds. He made the team because the Reds owner, John Brush, over-ruled manager Buck Ewing who wanted to send him down.

Brush's decision turned out better than he could have imagined. Hahn exploded for 23 wins against only eight losses to become the ace of the Reds staff at the age of 20. He led the National League with 145 strikeouts. A possible reason for the miraculous improvement was Hahn's decision to clean up his personal life. The pitcher explained, "This year shows me what I can do when I'm not drinking. I'll never again indulge in any kind of strong drink." [7]

The poor performance of the Cincinnati team caught up with Hahn in 1900. Despite leading the league in strikeouts and shutouts, he had a losing record of 16-20 to show for his efforts.

In 1901, the Reds were even worse, and Hahn was even better than the previous year. He posted a 22-19 record for the eighth place Reds. No modern era pitcher had won 20 games again for a last place team until Steve Carlton produced his remarkable 27-10 year with the woeful 1972 Phillies. Hahn claimed 42% of his team's victories, Carlton 46%.

Hahn went 23-12 in 1902 and 22-12 in 1903 as the Reds claimed fourth place both years. During his first five years in the major leagues he sported a combined 106-71 record. At the age of 23 he was already a 100-win pitcher. With some good luck and good health, he could have expected another 10 years on the mound and a shot at 200 to 300 wins.

His luck betrayed him in 1904, and his health in 1905. Despite an ERA of 2.06 in 1904, he suffered a losing record of 16-18. The following year an arm injury deprived him of his velocity and the Cincinnati Reds released him in August with a 5-3 record. [8]

After resting his arm for six months, Hahn secured a tryout with the New York Highlanders in the American League. He made the team and by early June had a winning mark of 3-2. Hahn knew that he did not have his former "stuff" and he requested to be released. He pitched for a few years at the semi-professional level but never returned to the major leagues. He did not blame the fates for the sudden loss of his career. In an interview with the Sporting News in 1901, his words were prophetic; "I am wise enough to know that I cannot last forever and that I am greatly shortening my career by pitching as I did last season (375+ innings)." [9]

Hahn fired a no-hitter against the Phillies on July 12, 1900. In his career, he completed 212 of his 231 starts. His arm had probably become noodle-like by 1905.

Noodles kept in touch with the Reds over the years, pitching batting practice when he could. The Cincinnati Reds enshrined him into their Hall of Fame in 1963. He would have greatly appreciated the honor had it occurred three years earlier. He died in 1960 in at the age of 80.

Spud Chandler

Spurgeon Ferdinand Chandler may have enjoyed a side dish of potatoes on a frequent basis, but his nickname was not related to a food preference. The name Spud was derived from his unusual first name. Newspaper articles trumpeting his college football exploits with the Georgia Bulldogs refer to him as Spurgeon. [10] Almost all articles reporting his major league performances call him Spud. Sometime between his collegiate years and his elevation to the New York Yankees in 1937, Chandler's teammates decided how to deal with an odd name. They compressed Spurgeon into Spud and Chandler went along with it. [11]

Chandler was born in Commerce, Georgia, in 1907. Several years after graduating from nearby Carnesville High School he matriculated to the University of Georgia and quickly became a three-sport star for the Bulldogs. While still attending classes, Chandler was offered a chance to play professional football with the New York Giants. The baseball

Cardinals and Cubs also tempted him with offers to pitch for their organizations. He stayed in school instead and earned a degree in agriculture in 1932. [12]

The New York Yankees were the team he really wanted to join. In 1932, they made his wish come true. The Yankees sent him to the Binghamton Triplets in the New York Penn League and his professional career was launched. After winning eight of nine decisions, the Yanks elevated him to the Springfield Rifles of the Eastern League. He went 4-0 with Springfield and the Yankee Stadium pitching mound did not seem far off.

Beginning in 1933, tougher competition and injuries slowed his progress. In 1937, at the age of 29 he started the season with the Newark Bears of the International League. The Newark roster was filled with future and former big league pitchers.

Despite a pedestrian 1-2 won-loss record, the Yankees called his name and he debuted with the big club on May 6, 1937. His rookie season went very well as he managed a 7-4 record with an ERA of 2.48. That performance was good enough to secure a roster spot to begin the 1938 season. While his ERA shot up to 4.03, he won 14 games and contributed to the Yankees' successful pennant drive. Manager Joe McCarthy employed a three-man rotation of Red Ruffing, Left Gomez and Monte Pearson in the World Series. The Yanks rolled over the Cubs in a four-game sweep as Chandler watched from the sidelines.

Injuries slowed Chandler in 1939. He pitched in only 11 games, none as a starter, and won all three of his decisions. During 1940 and 1941, he regained his starting role and posted a combined 18-11 record. He started Game Two of the 1941 World Series against the Brooklyn Dodgers. Despite yielding only two runs on four hits, he was outdueled by Whit Wyatt and lost the game 3-2.

He stepped into the limelight in 1942 season, finishing 16-5 with a 2.38 ERA. Only Tiny Bonham, with a 21-5 season, won more games for the Yankees that year. Spud Chandler was now an All-Star. He pitched in Game One of the World Series against the St. Louis Cardinals and "saved" the only game the Yankees would win (saves were not an official statistic in 1942). He started Game Three and lost 2-0. He gave up only one run in eight innings but was bested by Ernie White who allowed the Yanks nothing.

The following year would be even nicer for Spud. He became the ace of the 1943 team, helping the Yankees claim their third straight pennant. He led the American League in wins, (20), winning percentage (.833), ERA (1.64), complete games (20) and shutouts (5). He was named the MVP of the AL, garnering 12 of the 24 first place votes, beating out Luke Appling for the top spot.

His fantastic 1943 season extended to the World Series wherein the Yankees had a chance to payback the Cardinals for the previous year's defeat. He started and won Game One by a score of 4-2. In Game Five, with his team holding a 3-2 edge in games, he allowed the Cardinals to nick him for 10 base hits. Not one Cardinal base runner could return to home plate, however, and the Yankees prevailed 2-0 and clinched the Series. Chandler had negotiated the dangerous Cardinal line up over 18 innings and surrendered only one run, good for an ERA of 0.50.

After pitching just one game to start the 1944 season, Chandler joined the armed forces. World War II gained another soldier while Yankees lost their top pitcher. He returned a year and a half later to squeeze in four games late in the 1945 season.

During the war, many people felt that individual baseball deeds were somewhat tainted by the thinned-down talent pool left in the major leagues. Chandler in 1946 eradicated the suspicions about his 1943 season. With many big leaguers back in baseball uniforms, Chandler duplicated his career high with another 20-win season (20-8). The Yankees finished a distant third in the AL to the Boston Red Sox. Chandler would not have the opportunity to prove that his triumphant 1943 World Series was not a fluke.

With Joe McCarthy gone, and Bucky Harris at the helm, the Yankees reclaimed first place in 1947. While Chandler was a valuable contributor, he was no longer the ace. Allie Reynolds claimed that honor, with Spec Shea right behind him. Chandler was 9-5 with a 2.46 ERA.

The Yankees again faced the Brooklyn Dodgers in the World Series. Again, the Yankees would prevail, but Chandler did not play a major role. Harris brought him into Game Three to pitch the fourth and fifth innings after the Dodgers blew-up Yankees starter Bobo Newsom. Chandler allowed two runs on two hits. He would never throw another official pitch to a major league batter. The Yankees eventually defeated the Dodgers in seven games. They released Chandler at the conclusion of spring training in 1948. He descended from stardom to unemployment in less than two years.

He remained in baseball after retirement, coaching for the Kansas City Athletics in 1957 and 1958. He also scouted for many years with both the Cleveland Indians and Minnesota Twins.

His entire playing career was spent with the Yankees, which may help explain why he is not more highly acclaimed. So many superstars have shone in the Yankee firmament, that outstanding performers like Chandler pale by comparison. Let it be known that Spud Chandler, four-time All-Star, still holds the all time major league record for winning percentage (.717) among pitchers with 100, or more wins.

Chandler died in 1990 at the age of 82. He remains the last player to carry the name Spud.

Greasy Neale

Earle Neale was born and raised in Parkersburg, West Virginia, and became a football star at West Virginia Wesleyan College. He spent eight seasons in major league baseball, mostly with the Cincinnati Reds. He also played professional football in the early days of the NFL. He later coached football at the college level, and eventually earned entry into the NFL Hall of Fame as the long-time coach of the Philadelphia Eagles.

Many sports writers have attributed his nickname to his elusiveness as a ball carrier on the football field. They said he slipped through the line as though he had been "greased." Why then, is Greasy not in Chapter Three with the players whose names derived from a certain skill set or style of play? The answer: the story is not true. If not for a cocktail party conversation, the "greased runner" myth may have become an unchallenged falsehood.

At a National Football League sponsored reception, Neale was reminiscing with past teammates and colleagues when an admirer and his son stepped forward to meet the legend. After a brief conversation about baseball and college football, the young man asked about the nickname Greasy. His reply:

"I'll tell you how that came about. There was a boy I grew up with in Parkersburg, W.Va., and he was a kind of Huckleberry Finn. His

parents didn't pay him much mind or discipline him in any way. He wasn't too particular about his appearance, and one day I called him 'Dirty Face' or 'Dirty Neck' or some such thing, and he got even by calling me 'Greasy' because I had worked for a time as a grease boy in a rolling mill. The other kids picked it up and it stayed with me for life. Of course, some sportswriters wrote that the nickname referred to my elusiveness as a ball carrier in football, or a base runner in baseball. But it was the boy back home who gave me the name." [12]

Twenty-year-old Neale launched his baseball career with the 1912 London Tecumsehs of the Canadian League. The young outfielder played baseball while still attending college. After four years in the minors, he made his breakthrough with the 1916 Cincinnati Reds. He was never a spectacular hitter but he played his position well and frequently led his team in stolen bases. Neale stole second, third and home in one game during the 1919 season. [13]

In 1919, he played in 39 games for the Reds, and played eight games against the Chicago Black Sox in the World Series. A lifetime .259 hitter, he rose to the occasion during the Series and batted .357 with a triple, double and eight singles. He drove in four runs.

When baseball season ended, he put on his football coach's hat for West Virginia Wesleyan, Marietta College, and Washington and Jefferson. After his baseball career ended in 1924, he coached at the University of Virginia and then West Virginia University. [14]

When Neale joined the coaching staff at Yale University in 1934, he was asked to drop the name Greasy. He declined the suggestion and told the media, "Yale or no Yale, if you fellows want to call me Greasy, go ahead." [15] Neale's boss and mentor, Raymond "Ducky" Pond, must have had a good laugh when considering that a Ducky and a Greasy would coach the Yale gridders.

Neale's resume is chocked full of highlights, most of which involve football:

- He played along side Jim Thorpe for the pre-NFL Canton Bulldogs using an alias.

- He led his Washington and Jefferson team to the Rose Bowl in 1922 where his team tied the heavily favored squad from the University of California.

171

- He coached the Philadelphia Eagles from 1941-1950 and led them to two NFL championships.

- He introduced several defensive innovations, including the 4-3 defense that is still used in the NFL today. [16]

- Neale was inducted into the Pro football Hall of Fame in 1969.

- He was inducted into the College Football Hall of Fame in 1967.

- In baseball, he led the 1919 Reds in batting in the World Series against the Chicago Black Sox.

- Neale is the only man to play for a World Series champion as well as coach an NFL championship team.

Neale passed away in 1973 in Lakeland, Florida, a few days shy of his 82nd birthday. He was buried in his hometown of Parkersburg, West Virginia.

Mule Haas

George William Haas steps forward with two unexplained nicknames. Playing on local teams in his native New Jersey, the teenaged Haas was already known as Eggs Haas. No definitive explanation of that early moniker has been established. The second and everlasting nickname of Mule was handed to him prior to his major league debut. In 1925, the Pittsburgh Pirates summoned Haas from the Birmingham Barons in the Southern Association. An article in the August 14, 1925 edition of the New York Times is headlined: *Pirates Recall Mule Haas.*

Several explanations have been presented to demystify the name, none of which seem very substantive. One possible reason can be eliminated straight away; Haas was not a slow runner. Ken Schlager, writing for the New Jersey Monthly, calls him "the mule who could run like a deer." [17]

We must face the fact that a mule is not a pretty animal, except in the eyes of another mule. Any comparison of Haas' appearance to this beast of burden could have easily prompted him to jettison the nickname. Haas seemed comfortable with the name. His long face and sad eyes could have contributed to the nickname. Another account sites his large ears as the reason, but photos of Haas do not bear out that physical comparison. Some photos show him to sport a large mouth with protruding teeth, a very mule-like characteristic.

Other theorists pin the name on his personality, too stubborn to accept defeat. A last explanation is metaphorical in nature. A sportswriter in Atlanta predicted that Haas "would put a kick in our ballclub" when the Mule joined the Atlanta Crackers. [18] One problem exists with that reasoning, Haas already had the nickname for at least a year before his tenure with the Crackers began.

By whatever name, Haas was arbitrarily the biggest baseball hero of 1929. Following his call up to the Pirates in 1925, he descended back to the minors in 1926 with Atlanta. After his second successful season as a Cracker, the legendary Connie Mack signed him to a contract to join the Philadelphia Athletics. Mack's star-studded outfield corps consisted of Ty Cobb, Al Simmons, and Bing Miller. The ever-canny Mack had just signed 40-year-old Tris Speaker as a back up, but now secured a set of young legs in the person of 24-yer-old Mule Haas. The A's had a great year but could not unseat the New York Yankees from atop the American League.

When the 1929 season rolled around, both Cobb and Speaker were gone from the game. Haas became the everyday centerfielder replacing Cobb. The club also had Jimmie Foxx at first base, Mickey Cochrane catching, and lefty Grove on the mound. The "Mack Men" proceeded to annihilate the American League, cruising to an 18 game margin over the second place Yankees.

In the World Series against the Cubs, Haas' day in the sun occurred in Game Four. The Cubs had an 8-0 lead in the seventh inning and were threatening to even the Series at two games apiece. Haas blasted a three-run inside-the-park home run to rally the A's to a 10-8 victory. Two games later the Cubs once again held a 2-0 lead in an effort to tie the Series at three games each. This time Haas smashed a clutch ninth-inning home run to tie the game 2-2. Bing Miller later doubled in the winning run and Philadelphia captured the World Series. The Mule had carried the A's on his back and was the undisputed hero of the 1929 season.

He played in the 1930 and 1931 World Series as well, but did not come close to his 1929 performance. Following the 1932 season, Mack began the dismantling of the A's and Haas was sold to the Chicago White Sox. He spent the next five years with the Sox, rotating between first base and the outfield, before returning to the Athletics in 1938 for his final season in the majors. He ended his 12-year career with a .292 lifetime batting average.

He is the current record holder for most years (six), and most consecutive years (five) in leading the league in sacrifices. [19]

Haas managed in the minor leagues in 1939 before rejoining the White Sox as a coach in 1940. He coached and managed in the minor leagues for two more years before becoming an Athletic Consultant at Ft. Monmouth (New Jersey). He died at the age of 70 on June 30, 1974, while visiting his son in New Orleans. He was buried in his hometown of Montclair, New Jersey. [20]

Goat Anderson

Edward John Anderson sprung fully named from the South Bend Greens in 1907 to try out for the Pittsburgh Pirates. A spring training article in the Pittsburgh Press in March of 1907 identifies him as Goat Anderson. After an outstanding season in South Bend, he had a shot to replace Bob Ganley who was jettisoned by player-manager Fred Clarke after a disappointing rookie season. The Pirates and the local press were impressed with Anderson's skill and speed in the outfield during spring training in Hot Springs, Arkansas. [21]

Anderson turned in a very poor offensive performance batting just .206 with an even more pathetic slugging average of .225. Manager Clarke flexed his quick trigger finger and the Goat was no longer a part of the Pirate menagerie. Clarke, however, may have missed the big picture. Anderson broke (and still holds) the record for the highest OPS by any player with a slugging percentage under .250. Coincidentally, the top 10 in that list includes another Anderson, Sparky, for his efforts with the 1959 Phillies.

Because Anderson never made it back to the Pirates or any other big league team, he also qualified to play in the "One Year Wonder" competition. He set the NL standard for most steals (27) and most runs scored (73). Even more impressively, he set the MLB record for walks (80). [22]

Anderson was just one in a long line of Pittsburgh rookies who distinguished himself but could not live up to their freshman performance. In 1899, Jimmy Williams had a rookie season for all time. On his way to a .354 batting average, he banged out 27 triples to lead the league and set a record that no rookie has matched in over a century. Williams enjoyed a productive 11-year career but never duplicated his rookie season. In 1936, Bill Brubaker collected 102 RBIs in his first year and never exceeded half that number again. In 1938, Johnny Rizzo eclipsed Brubaker with 111 RBIs plus set a franchise-high for rookie home runs. He never approached the century mark again, either. [23]

What about the Goat? What was the source of that lovely nickname? While no research has yet unlocked the secret, several clues exist. Pittsburgh sportswriter George Moreland said this when spotting Anderson on the playing field for the first time, "Anderson is not the little midget that he has been pictured (as), although he is not a large man, either." [24] Anderson's short compact physique may have reminded some creative minor league teammate to bestow upon him this unflattering nickname.

Perhaps the name was an attempt to describe a stubborn or surly personality. During his tryout with the Pirates in 1907, he missed a signal and returned to the dugout to receive a rookie scolding by his manager. When Clarke's critique morphed into caustic sarcasm, Anderson abruptly shouted, "Ah, shut up. You don't know everything!" While his teammates waited for Clarke's fuse to burn down to an explosion, nothing happened.

Clarke finally said, "Son, you got spirit. I like you." Obviously, that admiration wore off by the end of the season. [25]

The name Goat may have evolved from an incident where Anderson was made the scapegoat for an incident in amateur or minor league baseball. Taking into account, his apparent low tolerance for criticism, he would not likely embrace the accusation or the nickname.

Tragically, Anderson died from cancer in 1923 at the young age of 43.

Toad Ramsey

Much has been written about Thomas H. Ramsey, but the derivation of his nickname remains a mystery. His countenance displays no toad-like features. Neither his pitching delivery, nor his gait has been described as containing a hop or a leap. Some writers speculate that Toad was a play on his name Tom. Perhaps an early teammate likened the movement of his pitch to the hopping of a toad.

Ramsey was born in Indianapolis one year before the Civil War ended. At the age of 20 he signed with the Louisville Colonels of the American Association. His first year in the majors proved to be very ordinary in terms of his 3-6 won-loss record. But his 1.94 ERA and 9.5 strikeouts per nine innings signaled better things to come as he learned to control his pet pitch, a "drop curve."

Ramsey and Mordecai Brown traveled down the same road early in their careers. Brown lost part of his right index finger in a farming accident. Ramsey lost the use of a tendon in his left middle finger when a load of bricks fell on his hand. Both pitchers were forced to alter the way they gripped a baseball. Both developed a pitch that neared the plate and danced merrily out of the strike zone. Mordecai became known as Three-Finger Brown and pitched his way into the Hall of Fame (posthumously). Ramsey chose alcohol and drank his way into relative obscurity. The qualifier "relative" is used because many baseball historians consider the lefthander the "father of the knuckleball." Additionally, he still ranks second in strikeouts in a single season (499) before 1893.

In 1886, Ramsey's second year in Louisville, he won 38 games against 27 losses with 66 complete games. His knuckle curve bedeviled hitters to the tune of 499 strikeouts. He pitched a no-hitter in Baltimore, as the Baltimore Sun box score showed no Oriole base hits. At some unknown point in history, a hit was credited to one of the Oriole hitters and Ramsey lost his membership in the no-hitter club. [26]

The 1887 season was just as successful. Despite the rule change that now allowed hitters four strikes instead of three, Ramsey still finished the season with another 37 wins against 27 losses and 217 strikeouts. Louisville manager Honest John Kelly, a notorious penny-pincher would not increase Ramsey's salary going into the 1888 season. Ramsey reacted by becoming a full-time drinker and part-time pitcher, frequently disappearing for days. In 1888, he lost 30 games, winning only eight. On July 28, 1888, he was arrested for avoiding a large, well overdue bar tab. [27]

The 1889 season began much as it had ended for Ramsey. With a 1-16 record, Ramsey was traded to the St. Louis Browns. Despite the horrendous record and reputation, the Browns had a problem child of their own to unload. Nat Hudson was under a one-month team suspension for malingering. [28]

Once in St. Louis, Ramsey swore off alcohol and finished the season 3-1. He admitted that he had hung out with a bad crowd in Louisville. Nat Hudson never did report to his new team.

From a distance, the 1890 season appeared as though Ramsey had turned his life and career around, as he won 23 games. A closer examination would prove otherwise. During July, Browns owner Chris Von der Ahe accused Ramsey of being drunk during a game, cursing him in German. Ramsey had a few choice words of his own and was rewarded with a suspension. After the pitcher returned to action, Von der Ahe began to scold Ramsey whenever he lost. Someone with such a magical pitch should never lose a game. When Ramsey finally got angry and tried to straighten out the boss, he was cut from the team.
Ramsey no longer had a reason to deny his fondness for drink. He began a downward odyssey that led him to one minor league town after another and one bar after another. He eventually lost his "money" pitch and took up umpiring until deciding to return to bricklaying.

Ramsey may be remembered more for the creation of his favorite drink than for any accomplishments on the baseball field. Reportedly, he consumed three *Ramsey Cocktails* per day. Ramsey would pour a pint of whiskey into a pitcher of beer. Associates were welcome to join him if they secured their own pint and full pitcher. [29]

In 1906, he was laid to rest in Indianapolis at the age of 41. His life, like his career, was cut short by the debilitating effects of excessive alcohol consumption.

Possum Whitted

George Bostic Whitted was a "good ol' boy" from North Carolina. He was born in Durham in 1890. As a youth he loved to regale his friends with stories, real and otherwise, about his possum hunting exploits. Despite the reference to one of nature's ugliest creatures, Whitted was obviously pleased with the nickname and carried it throughout his life. After his death, his survivors elected to drop the nickname from his tombstone. [30]

His professional career was launched in 1910 with the Savannah Indians of the South Atlantic League. Playing first base, the 20-year-old was used sparingly and did not make much of an impression. The following year, with the Jacksonville Tarpons, he played just well enough to retain his spot on the 1912 Jacksonville roster. He moved to third base and found his hitting stroke. His .307 average earned him an invitation to join the St. Louis Cardinals in September. Manager Roger Bresnahan gave his rookie a shot to play, using him in 12 games. Whitted acquitted himself well with a .261 average and a spot on the 1913 roster.

The Cardinals hired Miller Huggins to manage the 1913 team. Huggins loved Whitted's versatility and played him at every position except catcher. He hit only .220 but served the team well in his utility role.

After a disastrous start to the 1914 season, he was traded to the Boston Braves along with outfielder Ted Cather. The Cardinals needed a pitcher and Hub Perdue was acquired. Whitted returned to form with the Braves, again batting .261 for Boston. The Braves won the National league pennant and faced the mighty Philadelphia A's in the World Series. Connie Mack's team featured Home Run Baker, Eddie Collins, Stuffy McInnis, Chief Bender, Bullet Joe Bush, Eddie Plank and Bob Shawkey.

The underdog Braves shocked the Athletics in four straight. Whitted played in all four games and contributed three hits that produced two RBIs. He tripled off Chief Bender in Game One to give the Braves a 5-1 lead.

The trade to Boston was a fortuitous one, but the following February he was on the move once again. The Braves coveted the Phillies' star outfielder/first baseman Sherry Magee. Whitted was the "player to be named later" in the deal. At first the trade probably looked like a bad deal for Whitted, leaving a pennant winning team for a second division club. The move turned out to be a blessing. The Phillies had assembled a very good team and jumped from sixth place in 1914 to win the 1915 National League pennant. For the first time in his career he was an everyday starter, playing along side Bill Killefer, Gavvy Cravath, Dave Bancroft, Eppa Rixey and Grover Cleveland "Pete" Alexander.

The Phillies were headed for their first World Series against the Red Sox while the Braves and Cardinals finished second and sixth respectively. In Game One of the Series, Whitted singled in the bottom of the fourth inning to give the Phillies a 1-0 lead in a game they eventually claimed by a 3-1 score. The Red Sox stormed back to sweep the remaining four games and the championship, but Whitted played in all five contests, taking the collar four times for a .067 average.

While the Phillies were unable to return to the Fall Classic after 1915, Whitted enjoyed a productive tenure in Philadelphia until August of 1919. He was traded to Pittsburgh for a right fielder named Charles Stengel who went by the name Casey in honor of his birthplace, Kansas City. Stengel was making a stink over his salary with Pirates owner Barney Dreyfuss who preferred to dump the troublemaker rather than deal with him.

Stengel immediately pressed Phillies owner William Baker for a raise. His demands refused again, Casey decided not to report to the Phillies. Instead, he returned home to Kansas City and organized a barnstorming team for the remainder of the 1919 season. [31]

Meanwhile, Whitted hit .389 for the balance of the season, and later performed well for the Pirates over the 1920 and 1921 seasons. Prior to the 1922 season, he was sold to the Brooklyn Robins. He batted one time in Brooklyn and failed to get a base hit. He would never appear in a major league game again.

His final career line shows 14 seasons and a .269 lifetime batting average; not bad for a possum hunter from the hills of North Carolina.

In 1962, he took a spill and suffered a severe hip injury. He died a short time later. He was 72 years old.

Whitted served his country during War World I missing most of the 1918 season and part of 1919. His military service entitled him to be interred in the Wilmington (North Carolina) National Cemetery, not too many miles from his birthplace.

Kewpie Pennington

The derivation of George Lewis Pennington's nickname is a mystery. He was born in New York City in 1896. He was a right-handed spitball pitcher who ascended to the St. Louis Browns in 1917 after three years in the minors. He pitched just one inning for the Browns before being dispatched to the Newark Bears in the International League. The reason for his demotion is not clear. He allowed no runs on just one hit. He did not walk or strike out a batter. He will travel through all eternity with a spotless 0.00 ERA.

Once he arrived in Hartford in the Eastern League in 1920, he appeared on the radar screen frequently in newspaper articles in the Hartford Courant, referred to as George "Kewpie" Pennington. Since he only had a cup of coffee in St. Louis, the nickname either arrived before or after his big league cameo appearance.

Before speculating on the source of the nickname, a brief history of the Kewpie Doll is in order. In 1909, the Ladies' Home Journal began printing illustrations of an angelic looking baby. The dolls drew their name from the word cupid, whom they resembled, without the wings and bow and arrow.

The illustrator was Rose O'Neill, born in Wilkes-Barre, Pennsylvania, raised in Nebraska and relocated to New York City. The popularity of the cartoons led to the decision to produce paper cutout baby-dolls. When demand continued to surge, the next marketing step was the creation of an actual doll in the likeness of the cutouts. Production was set up in Germany and soon the bisque dolls were being shipped around the globe. Not surprisingly, a cheaper celluloid version appeared and carnival games of chance had their most famous prize offering. [32]

Perhaps Mr. Pennington reminded someone of the cupid-like doll. As an adult, he stood 5' 8" tall and weighed 165 pounds. At the age of 14, Clark Griffith and the Washington Senators gave him a tryout. His appearance at the tryout may have been occasion for the Kewpie Doll connection. This physical resemblance scenario is more likely than a cupid-like personality. When he played for the Hartford Senators he was a repeat hold out for more money, and once was suspended for reporting to spring training out of shape. [33]

During a minor league career that spanned 10 years he compiled a won-loss record of 90-89. Before posting two losing seasons at the end of his career, his record stood at a very respectable 80-64.

Following his baseball years, Pennington was in management for the Bankers Indemnity Insurance Company of Newark, New Jersey.

Kewpie Pennington died in 1953 at the age of 56 after a lengthy illness. The New York Times obituary listed him as simply George L. Pennington. They also miscalculated his age to be 57. [34]

Leech Maskrey

Essentially, Samuel Leech Maskrey brought his nickname with him onto the baseball field. Leech was his middle name. The mystery is why he would forsake a solid, respectable name like Samuel to assume the identity of an ugly blood-sucking worm. Certainly, his appearance did not suggest such a resemblance. He was slightly built but quite handsome. No evidence exists that he was a human parasite, leeching money and equipment from his teammates. No, it was just his unusual middle name that spurred others to call him such a repulsive name.

Maskrey was born in 1854 in Mercer, Pennsylvania, located near the Ohio border just south of Erie. The *History of Mercer County* lists a number of residents with the last name Leech, suggesting that Maskrey's middle name honored his mother's side of the family.

The same history mentions that a Leech Maskrey served as a Mercer town councilman from 1907 through 1909, indicating that he maintained the appellation beyond his playing days.

Maskrey began his professional career with the Louisville Colonels in 1882. The outfielder played regularly in his rookie season despite an anemic .226 batting average. He remained with Louisville until the middle of the 1886 season when his .158 average motivated the team to sell his contract to the Cincinnati Red Stockings. He was unable to boost his average into the .200 neighborhood and lost his place on the Reds' big league roster. After five full seasons, his lifetime batting average stood at .225.

In 1890, an attempt was made in Britain to start a baseball association. The Brits enlisted the aid of Albert Spalding to help them get their endeavor off the ground. Spalding, co-founder of the National League and sporting goods entrepreneur, sent one experienced manger, Jim Hart, and several players to Britain to launch the fledgling project. The British goal was to convert soccer playing athletes into baseballers. Spalding's goal was to expand his market for sporting equipment across the Atlantic.

Britain's modern-day love affair with soccer and the virtual non-existence of baseball would suggest that Maskrey's team failed. The athletes that may have eschewed soccer to become baseball players gravitated to the game of cricket instead. But the American contingency did forge a movement that peaked just before World War II.

During the last decade of the 19th century, baseball took root in the form of the National Baseball league of Great Britain and Ireland. Mackrey served as player-manager for the team in Preston. The Derby County Baseball Club initially overwhelmed the other teams and was forced to resign its championship due to employing too many American players. The Derby County boys survived until 1898. Baseball in the U.K. also survived, peaking in the 1930's when large crowds numbering in the thousands turned out for the games.

Great Britain actually won the first World Baseball Cup held in 1938. The fact that only two teams participated did not diminish the victory because the silver medalist was the United States. The Brits to this day have yet to win any other medals in this competition.

While Maskrey played no big part in the history of American baseball, he did help start a movement that may have flowered in Europe had Adolf Hitler not decided to conquer the world. As Britain struggled to rebuild after World War II, the game of baseball lost all momentum and never recovered.

Following his return from England, he traveled west and joined the Pacific Coast League as a manager and part-time player with Tacoma. After Tacoma, he returned to Mercer, took a wife, and joined his brother in running several hotels in Mercer County. He continued to manage local and regional teams over the years.

He died on April 1, 1922, from a heart attack. He had suffered for months from congestive failure before the last fatal cardiac arrest. He was 68 years old. His obituary named him "a man of fine character and ability--a true gentleman."

Maskrey was unusual in that he entertained interests beyond sport. During his tenure with the Colonels, a Louisville publication described him as "a man of more than ordinary literary attainment. He is also a finished artist at the easel, and a musician of no mean ability. He reads Dickens, Thackeray and Bulwer almost constantly during the week."
[35]

Granny Hamner

The nickname Granny is usually employed to chide someone who is fussy, slow moving, or wearing "old person" clothing. More often than not, Granny is a temporary moniker abandoned shortly after the precipitating incident has ended. For Granny Hamner, the name stayed with him for most of his life. Granville Wilbur Hamner was not guilty of any granny-like behaviors; he simply had a haughty first name that begged to be knocked down a peg. Granville reminds one of a stiff, blue blood character similar to Judge Smails from the movie Caddyshack. Actor Ted Knight played the part perfectly.

Granny Hamner, a shortstop, signed with the Phillies as a teenager in 1944. The manpower shortage brought about by World War II allowed Hamner to jump from high school baseball directly to the Phillies. He appeared in 21 games that season and recorded a .247 batting average. He began the 1945 season in Utica playing for the Blue Sox. For the next three years he would bounce between Philadelphia and Utica. In 1948, he nailed down the shortstop position for the Phillies, joining the core players soon to be known as the Whiz Kids.

Hamner was an All-Star from 1952 through 1954. In all but two of his 17 years spent in the major leagues, he wore a Phillies uniform. He played briefly for the Cleveland Indians in 1959 and concluded his career with the Kansas City Athletics in 1962.

He died of a heart attack in his hotel room in Philadelphia in 1993. He was scheduled to join a Whiz Kid reunion and memorabilia show. He was 66 years old.

His older brother Garvin played for the Phillies in 1945. There is no evidence that Garvin acquired a nickname during his baseball career.

Noodles Hahn   P

"MULE" HAAS

Above: left – Noodles Hahn   right – Mule Haas
Below: left Greasy Neale   right -- Oyster Burns

Chapter Seven - How Did They Avoid a Nickname?

The following names are real. Despite the well-documented propensity of baseball players to conjure up nicknames, these players somehow escaped without a new identity. Perhaps they used all of their resources to shake off the renaming process to retain the name on their birth certificates.

Gene Krapp

Eugene Hamlet Krapp was born in Rochester, New York, in 1887. The word "crap" meaning dung, or to defecate, came into popular usage in 1846. During the four previous centuries, the word referred to items cast off, or having no value. [1] At the time of Krapp's birth the word already carried a negative connotation. That may explain the choice of a classy Shakespearean middle name to balance the equation.

By the time Krapp reached professional baseball in 1907 he would have been easy pickings for mischievous teammates or opponents. The sad fact is that no word or words added to the name Krapp can possibly sound professional. At some point in his career he did acquire a nickname that mercifully did not bear any association to toilet activity. Krapp, a right-handed pitcher became known as Rubber Arm Krapp.

Krapp, a right-handed pitcher, joined the Cleveland Naps in the spring of 1911 and posted an impressive 13-9 record for a rookie. In 1912, he struggled to a 2-5 record and lost his spot on the Cleveland roster. After a year in the minor leagues with the Portland Beavers of the PCL, he made a comeback with the 1914 Buffalo Buffeds of the Federal League. His 16-14 record and 2.49 ERA secured a slot on the 1915 team.

The 1915 season was not kind to ol' Rubber Arm. He finished the season at 9-19 and the Federal League collapsed. No American or National league team offered him a position in 1916, so he signed with the Chattanooga Lookouts in the Southern Association. With his "stuff" gone, he retired after a 2-6 season. Over four big league seasons he compiled a 40-47 won-loss record.

After baseball, he settled in Detroit as the principal owner of Krapp Brothers Auto Sales. One must ask if the name Krapp was the best choice for an auto sales business.

In 1923, at the age of 35, he died from intestinal cancer.

Bert Hogg

Wilbert George Hogg was a city boy, born in Detroit, Michigan, in 1913. His city roots may have contributed to his success in avoiding any porcine nicknames such a Piggy or Sooey. The cartoon character Porky Pig was introduced in 1935 and did not become well known until after Hogg's career ended. Otherwise the name Porky would have been a no-brainer for teammates to bestow on him. The nickname that is associated with him is Sonny, very commonly a family moniker, frequently used to differentiate a junior from his father.

In 1933, Hogg became a Duck, a Dayton Duck, that is. The third baseman batted .263 in his first year of professional baseball. The following year, he earned a June call up to the Ducks' parent club, the Brooklyn Dodgers. In two games with the Bums, he batted just one time and failed to reach base. His big league career spanned just two days.

He finished the 1934 season with the Richmond Colts where he hit just .221. He played in the minors for two more seasons and faded from view.

Had Bert Hogg been born 50 years later and played baseball in the early 1980s, there is little doubt that somebody would have nicknamed him Boss Hogg, from the popular Dukes of Hazzard TV show.

He died in Detroit in 1973 at the age of 70.

Tony Suck

This guy really asked for it. He was born Charles Anthony Zuck but changed his last name to Suck. The vast majority of people desiring to improve the name Zuck would look in the direction of Smith or Jones. Leaving aside all of the vulgar and slangy connotations of the word "suck," even the traditional definitions create a reason to avoid calling oneself Mr. Suck.

Suck was born before the Confederate States were formed and played in the very early days of organized baseball. He broke in with the Buffalo Bisons of the National League in 1883. Since the use of the word "suck" to describe a sexual act did not appear until 1928, and the usage of the word to denote something disgusting, the range of possible nicknames is not as vast as it first appears. Still, a teammate with a creative bent could have played with the word to comic effect.

Hanson Horsey

Horsey was born in 1889 in Galena, Maryland. Galena is a small crossroad town closer to the Delaware border than any of Maryland's population centers. With a normal name, a kid from a rural area was subject to a name chosen from a menu that included Hick, Farmer, or Rube. His last name, however, should have resulted in some form of equine related nickname. How he escaped being "Whoa" Horsey, "Giddyup" Horsey, or something similar, seems a miracle.

Horsey entered professional baseball in 1910 with the Class B Reading Pretzels of the Tri-State League. The rookie right-hander struggled but blossomed in his second season with the Pretzels. His 22-10 record was rewarded with a roster spot on the 1912 Cincinnati Reds. He made his debut on April 27 and pitched four innings in relief. By the time Horsey entered the game, the Pirates had a 13-0 lead. The Pirates torched him for 10 more runs and 14 more hits. Reds manager, Hank O'Day, allowed Horsey to finish the game, a 23-4 blowout, then put him out to pasture permanently. He never pitched another major league inning, ending his career with a 22.50 ERA.

The Reds sent him packing back to the minors where he languished for seven more seasons before calling it quits.

He died in 1949 in Millington, Maryland, a few miles south of Galena. He had lived to the age of 60. His biggest claim to fame was allowing a triple to Chief Wilson on his way to a major league record of 36 three-baggers.

Dick Braggins

Richard Realf Braggins was a right-handed pitcher for the Cleveland Blues in the inaugural season of the American League in 1901. He posted a 1-2 won-loss record and fell from the major leagues and never returned.

The slangy word "dick" has been around for centuries with various meanings, thanks to the creative genius of the British. The word has meant a riding whip, cheese (see spotted dick), an apron, a policeman, a detective and an oath. Around 1890, the word picked up a new meaning which has remained popular to this day, a crude renaming of the penis. [2]

With discretion remaining the better part of valor, no suggested nicknames for Mr. Braggins will be offered.

Johnny Dickshot

John Oscar Dickshot did pick up a nickname in his baseball travels. His teammates called him "Ugly." If the new name seems cruel, consider that teammates were reacting to Dickshot's claim to be the "ugliest man in baseball." How he managed to escape a cruder name or double entendre is a mystery. See the short treatise on the slang word "dick" under the Dick Braggins section. As with Mr. Braggins, no suggested names will be forthcoming.

Dickshot was born in Waukegan, Illinois, in 1910. He claimed his professional start at age 20 with the Dubuque (Iowa) Tigers of the Mississippi Valley League in 1920. He started hitting for average in Dubuque and did not stop until making the major leagues in 1936.

After three consecutive years hitting over .300, the Pirates found a place for him on their roster to start the 1936 season. After visiting the batter's box just 10 times in nine contests, he hit only .222 and was demoted to the Buffalo Bisons of the International League. He dominated IL pitching to the tune of .354 with 17 triples and 17 home runs.

The Pirates brought him back for the 1937 season and he batted .254 in 82 games. He had a diminished role with the Bucs in 1938 and was traded to the New York Giants in 1939 where he played sparingly.

He was back in the minor leagues after his release from the Giants in 1939. He logged five more years in the International League and Pacific Coast League batting .320. He began the 1943 season with a 33-game hitting streak for the Hollywood Stars. The Chicago White Sox purchased his contract from Hollywood and put him in their outfield in

1944. The following year was his high water mark when he batted .302 over 130 games.

When the 1946 season rolled around, the entire pre-war outfield of the White Sox returned to Chicago to claim their jobs. Taffy Wright, Thornton Tucker, Bob Kennedy, Ralph Hodgin, and Whitey Platt combined to bump Dickshot back to the minors. He retired in 1947 with a lifetime batting average of .318 over 14 minor league seasons. His big league average was a very credible .276.

After baseball, he returned to Waukegan and opened a tavern fittingly named *The Dugout*.

He died in 1997 after siring five children, 14 grandchildren and four great-grandchildren. The actor John Ducey was his grandson. Ducey appeared in numerous television shows from *Will and Grace to Desperate Housewives*.

One last musing on his name; he was not born with the name Dickshot. Either he, or his family changed it from Dicksus to Dickshot.

Elmer Sexauer

Elmer George Sexauer was born in 1926 in St. Louis County, Missouri. After graduating from Riverview Gardens High school, he joined the U.S. Army where he served in the Philippines. He then attended Wake Forest University and joined Tommy Byrnes in the alumni club of Demon Deacon ball players who made the major leagues.

He left a very faint footprint in professional baseball. He showed up in 1948 as a pitcher for the Danville Dodgers in the Three I League. His 11-7 record and low ERA earned him a call up to Brooklyn in September. The 22 year-old right-hander pitched in two games and was not touched for a base hit. The only problem is that he walked two batters and one of them scored leaving him with a 13.50 ERA. The trail ends there, as far as minor or major league baseball history is concerned.

Had he stuck around a bit longer, he stood a good chance of acquiring a nickname associated with the first syllable of his last name. Not surprisingly, he did not escape locker room teasing. A favorite prank in Danville involved a straight man inquiring, "Do we have a Sexauer

here?" The comic would answer, "We don't even get a coffee break."
[3]

Although his tenure with the Dodgers was short, he did have a memorable first day in the major leagues. The Dodgers were playing the Braves in Boston and home plate umpire Jocko Conlin was on the receiving end of a lot of static from the Dodger dugout. Following another called third strike on a Brooklyn hitter, an anonymous Dodger mockingly tossed a white towel onto the field signifying their surrender to a force beyond their control.

Conlin marched to the dugout and addressed manager Burt Shotten. "OK, Burt, somebody has to go. Since I don't know who threw the towel, you pick him." [4]

Shotten assessed the situation and chose a rookie pitcher who had virtually no chance of entering the game. Conlin ordered "the kid" to exit the field. The innocent Sexauer had no clue what was happening and had to be told that he was just ejected from the game. The Braves' fans booed Sexauer lustily as he crossed the field to the locker room runway.

Sexauer finished the 1948 season and returned to the St. Louis area to marry Marilyn Mansfield, his high school sweetheart. [5]

The following year he pitched in spring training for the Dodgers, but did not make the squad. The Dodgers cut him loose and the Phillies claimed him. There are no official records showing that Sexauer played for any Phillies minor league club, although newspaper accounts show Sexauer being assigned to Wilmington in the Interstate League in the spring of 1950. The Phillies released him in late April of the same year. He played semi-pro ball in his hometown area well into the 1950's

Sexauer died in 2011 in Atlanta, Georgia, at the age of 85.

George Harvie Burpo

George Burpo was born in Jenkins, Kentucky, in 1926. According to the Online Etymology Dictionary, the word "burp" first appeared in the American vocabulary around 1932. By the time Burpo reached the minor leagues in 1939, this new and humorous term for belching would have spread through the culture and reached the baseball locker rooms. The very sound of a belch could produce the word "burp." Any number of gas eructation terms could have been stamped onto this young pitcher from the hills of southern Kentucky. Further, the letter "o" on the end of his last name would create entertaining combinations such as "Gaseous Burpo".

Additionally, a cultural phenomenon known as the Marx Brothers exploded in the 1930s. Groucho, Chico. Gummo, Zeppo and Harpo became household names. After spending 1939 through 1942 in the minors, Burpo joined the U.S. Navy to serve his country during World War II. When George Burpo made his debut with the Cincinnati Reds in 1946, he might well have been called Burpo Marx.

As a result of two disastrous outings with the Reds, Burpo's major league career lasted four weeks and consisted of just 2.1 innings in which he allowed four earned runs, issuing five walks. He spent the remainder of 1946 and two more seasons in the minor leagues before dropping off the grid.

Burpo was a flamethrower but was never sure where the ball was going. During a game in a military league, he struck out 19 of the 21 batters he faced. [6] More frequently, his control problems got him in trouble and cost him dearly. During his seven minor league seasons, he averaged almost eleven walks per nine innings. His minor league career record was 30-41.

After baseball, he worked for the Moore Business Form Company in Albuquerque. [7] He passed away at the age of 85 in 2011 in Atlanta.

Harry Chozen

Chozen was a Jewish catcher born in Winnebago, Minnesota, with a prophetic name. Why was Harry Chozen not nicknamed "The Chosen One?" Perhaps the answer lies in his length of major league service, one game. He joined the last place Cincinnati Reds in the waning days of the 1937 season. He was inserted behind the plate by manager Chuck Dressen against the seventh place Phillies. Chozen stroked a single in four trips to the plate. He was not chosen to appear in any more games. He was not chosen to rejoin the Reds in 1938. He was not chosen to play on any big league team ever again.

Teammates in the Southern Association did have ample reason to anoint him as the chosen one, however. In 1945, he set a league record for hitting safely in 49 consecutive games with the Mobile Bears.

He retired from baseball in 1952 after 17 years in the minor leagues. He relocated to Lake Charles, Louisiana, and became an executive in the insurance business.

Chozen may not have earned the name the Chosen One, but many McNeese State University students have become a "chosen one." Each year, a student-athlete is awarded the Harry Chozen Baseball Scholarship. Chozen passed away in 1994, but his name lives on in the hearts of McNeese students year after year.

Art Doll

Arthur James Doll could have easily been given a feminine nickname based on his last name. Fortunately for the Chicago native, he picked up the very masculine nickname of Moose. Standing 6' 1" tall and weighing in at almost 200 pounds, he certainly had the qualifications to join the "Moose Club."

Doll signed with the Class B Richmond Colts in the Piedmont League in 1934 as a 21-year-old catcher. One year later he was in the major leagues with the Boston Braves. He batted just .100 and was returned to the minor leagues to begin the 1936 season. While in Class B baseball, Doll decided to try his hand at pitching. When the season was over in Columbia, he had complied an 8-7 record as a pitcher and batted .263. He was summoned back to Boston for another cup of coffee, this time as a pitcher. He started one game and pitched eight credible innings in which he allowed just three runs. He batted twice and failed to reach base.

Once again, Boston sold him back to the minor leagues, this time to Scranton in the Class A New York Penn League. After going 7-14, he was moved to Hartford in the Eastern League for the 1938 season. Serving strictly as a pitcher, he won 17 games and boarded the train for Boston once again. Manager Casey Stengel used Doll as a reliever. He performed in just three games and sported a 2.25 ERA over four innings of work.

Doll was sent back to the minors in 1939. He played at that level for another five years until World War II called him into service. After his discharge from the military, he returned to minor league baseball in 1946. For the next four years he pitched and caught until retirement in 1949.

Doll was a rare bird in that he logged major league service as both a pitcher and catcher. His career stats show three big league seasons in which he caught three games and pitched in four. As a pitcher he went 0-1 and as a batter he hit just .154. He died in 1978 in Calumet City, Illinois. He was just a few weeks shy of his 65th birthday.

John Boozer

Boozer pitched in relief for the Phillies from 1962 to 1969. Historical records fail to reveal any nicknames ever assigned to him, officially or otherwise. If his last name didn't produce a nickname related to excessive alcohol consumption, an eccentric pastime in the bullpen or dugout definitely should have warranted a designation such as Bugs, Crazy, Dizzy, etc. Whenever he, or a teammate, captured a large bug or worm, Boozer would pop it in his mouth and wait for the reaction of shocked bystanders.

Boozer passed away in 1986 at the very young age of 47. One must wonder if his diet led to his early demise.

Fernandes Eunick

Eunick was sometimes called Dutch, but baseball history mostly remembers him as Ferd. Ferd does not exactly roll off the tongue in a euphonious manner, but the name beats the heck out of any derivative of Eunick.

Ferd appeared in just one contest for the 1925 Cleveland Indians before his career was cut short by circumstance or the absence of talent.

John Wesley Glasscock

Glasscock was generally described as the best middle infielder of the 19th century. He went by the name Jack, though informally referred to as Pebbly Jack for his habit of patrolling the infield to pick up small pebbles and removing them from the playing field. Glasscock labored for nine teams over a very productive 17-year career (1879-1895).

We will conclude with just one more. Benjamin Bowcock played 13 seasons in the minor leagues and one in the majors with the St, Louis Browns (1903), picking up nothing worse than Benny as a nickname.

Above: left – George Burpo   right – Johnny Dickshot
Below left – Harry Chozen   right – Art Doll

Chapter Eight - We Don't Need No Stinking Nicknames

Bird Blue

What were his parents thinking? At least Bird Wayne Blue was given a normal middle name. One can only imagine what they would have named a child if their last name had been Brown or Green. Bird was born in Bettsville, Ohio, in 1877. He grew up to be a very large man at 200 pounds and 6' 3" in height. Had he grown up in the era of Sesame Street, he probably would have garnered the nickname Big Bird. As it was, he eventually went by the name Bert, conjuring up another Sesame Street character.

Bird labored as a catcher for seven years in the minors before the St. Louis Browns chose him in the Rule V Draft from the Columbus Senators in 1907. He made his major league debut for the Browns in 1908. After squatting behind the plate in just 17 games, the Browns traded him to the Philadelphia A's in midseason. His .375 average in St. Louis did not transfer to Philly. He batted .175 for Philadelphia and Connie Mack released him. He resurfaced with the minor league Newark Newks in 1911, and then dropped off the charts forever.

'Tis a pity the Browns did not send him across town to the Cardinals. The trade would have made an interesting headline, "Blue Bird Now a Red Bird."

Bird passed away in 1927 in Detroit, Michigan, at the age of 51.

Lu Blue

Luzerne Atwell Blue was called Lu Blue. Not much chance of creating a better name than that. He was born in 1897 in Washington D. C. Blue frequently found himself black and blue from visits to the proverbial woodshed. The young Blue would play hooky to attend Washington Nationals games, especially when his idol, Ty Cobb, was in town. The harsh punishments meted out by his father did not greatly alter Blue's future behavior. Following high school, his father packed him off to a military school for both educational and disciplinary reasons. [1]

Blue's father did not know that a former baseball player, Sid Lodge, operated Briarly Hall Military School. Lodge not only tutored his new student on the game of baseball, he used his contacts to get Blue a deal with the minor league team in Martinsburg, West Virginia, in 1916. Blue's parents objected to their son's vocational aspirations, feeling he was wasting his life. If the woodshed could not alter the kid's dreams, another parental censure would prove futile.

Five years in the minors sculpted Blue into a good defensive first baseman with decent power at the plate. Blue signed a contract to join the 1921 Detroit Tigers, joining his hero Ty Cobb. Cobb, elevated to player manager that year, made Blue his starting first baseman. The 24-yearold rookie responded by batting .308 with 75 RBIs.

Blue spent the next six years with the Tigers holding down the first base job. His best year was 1925 when he batted .306 for the Tigers and knocked in 94 runs. Blue found that idolizing Cobb from afar was much easier than dealing with the foul-tempered curmudgeon on a daily basis. Cobb frequently lambasted Blue, and others, in public for their misdeeds. Following the 1927 season, he and Heinie Manush were traded to the St. Louis Browns for Harry Rice, Elam Vangilder and Chick Galloway.

Blue had developed a keen knowledge of the strike zone by the time he arrived in St. Louis. During his three years with the Browns, he averaged over 100 bases on balls per season. The Browns were going nowhere in the American League, finishing sixth in 1930. They put a $15,000 price tag on Blue and sold him to the Chicago White Sox.

In 1931, Blue proved worthy of the purchase price and batted .304 with 127 walks to go with 16 triples. The following year, age caught up to the 35-year-old and he fell off to a .249 average.

The Chicago White Sox front office declared Blue in 1932 to be the best fielding first baseman in baseball." A few months later they gave him his release. [2]

Within weeks, Dodger manager Max Carey announced the signing of Lu Blue. Blue reported to the Dodgers on April 20, 1933. [3] After just nine days as a Bum, he was released. He walked to the plate just one time and failed to hit safely. He fielded two throws and was credited with two putouts. His 13-year career was over. He had complied a .287 batting average, but more impressively, a .402 on base percentage. By comparison, Joe DiMaggio would later end his career at .398 OBP.

Blue retired to Virginia and raised chickens for a living. He died in 1958 of complications from his long bout with arthritis. He was interred in Arlington National Cemetery. He had been drafted and served briefly in the Army in 1918 to earn his place in Arlington.

Blue's mother, Ida Blue, made news in 1928 by becoming the only blue, silver and gold star mother in the United States. She had already won four blue stars for sending her four sons into war. The discharge of one son from a veterans' hospital qualified her for a silver star. She had previously been named a gold star mother for the son she lost in battle. The American War Mothers honored her by choosing her to lay a wreath under the statue of General Lafayette. [4]

Orval Overall

Born in Farmerville, California, in 1881, Orval (no middle name) Overall was a right-handed pitcher who attended the University of California from 1900 to 1903. He starred on both the Golden Bear football and baseball teams. He was named as an All-American because of his skills at three positions. He played guard, fullback and handled the punting chores. Growing up in a wealthy family, he disappointed his father when he chose baseball as a career.

The year after leaving college he joined the Tacoma Tigers of the Pacific Coast League where he won 32 games in his first professional season. He was on his way to the big leagues.

Overall was a big man for his time, standing 6' 2" tall and weighing 215 pounds. A nickname relating to his physique would not have been out of the question. Later in his career he was sometimes call the Big Groundhog because of his February 2nd birthday. [5]

Following his spectacular season in Tacoma, he joined the 1905 Cincinnati Reds where he became a 20-game loser at 18-23. The following year he was acquired by the Chicago Cubs at the request of manager Frank Chance, a fellow Californian. Chance felt the rookie had been overworked and focused on the 2.86 ERA rather than the 23 losses. [6] Overall made Chance look smart by contributing 12 wins for the first place Cubs. In the World Series against their Southside Chicago rivals, Overall pitched 12 innings of very effective relief, allowing just two runs. The White Sox prevailed in six games.

In 1907, Overall won 23 games for the pennant winning Cubs. In Chicago's World Series sweep of the Detroit Tigers he started two games and allowed just two runs in 18 innings for a 1-0 record.

The Cubs conquered the National League again in 1908. Overall went 15-8 during the regular season, but was even better in the World Series against the Tigers. He started three games, wining two against no defeats. He finished the post-season with a sparkling .098 ERA.

Although the Cubs finished second in 1909, Overall led all National League pitchers with 9 shutouts and 205 strikeouts. He recorded his second 20-game season with a 20-11 mark and a 1.42 ERA.

Dark clouds began to drift into his life in 1910. The Cubs once again ascended to the National League pennant. By the time the World Series was set to start, Overall was fighting a nagging sore arm. For the first time in his career he failed to start 30 games. Even though Mordecai Brown and King Cole were 20-game winners, Frank Chance gave Overall the ball to start Game One against the Philadelphia A's. Chance felt that Overall had earned the honor. After just three innings, the truth was there for all to see, Overall's arm was dead. The Athletics touched him for three runs on six hits. He suffered his only defeat in eight World Series appearances. He was scratched from the rest of the Series, which Philadelphia captured.

Overall returned to California and worked in a gold mine that he purchased along with teammate Mordecai Brown. Efforts to resuscitate his right arm were disappointing. A two-year hiatus convinced him that he his well-rested arm was ready to be tested again. He rejoined Chance and the Cubs. His comeback lasted 11 games. He was not a bad major league pitcher at 4-5, but he just was not the pitcher he had been during the previous decade. The Cubs sold him to the San Francisco Seals of the Pacific Coast League where he finished out the 1913 season. His 2.14 ERA looked good, but his lost more games than he won (8-9). The writing was on the locker room wall. Overall pulled the plug on his baseball career.

After retirement he took over his deceased father's citrus farm and became wealthy from the sale of the farm's real estate. He ran for Congress in 1918 and was not elected. [15] In 1922, he entered the banking business with the First National Bank of Vidalia, near his birthplace. He rose to the rank of vice-president for the Fresno branch of the Security First National Bank in Los Angeles. [7]

Overall claimed 108 victories with just 71 losses during his foreshortened seven-season career. He had the distinction of being a 20-game loser (1905 Reds) and a 20-game winner (1907 and 1909 Cubs).

In World Series play, he saw action during four different campaigns (1906, 1907, 1908, and 1910) all with the Cubs. He boasted a 3-1 record with a 1.58 ERA. At the plate, he stroked four World Series hits for a .250 average.

For over half a century, Cincinnati fans listed his trade to Chicago Cubs as the worst in franchise history. Cincinnati sent Overall and $2,000 to the Cubs for pitcher Bob Wicker. Wicker spent a single season in Cincinnati and won just six games. The Frank Robinson trade in 1966 pushed the Overall trade down to number two.

Overall died of a heart attack in 1947 at age 66. In 1987, he was admitted posthumously to the University of California Sports Hall of Fame. The website spells his first name as Orville. No other source uses this spelling. [8]

Angel Bravo

Angel Alfonso Bravo came to us from Venezuela in the early 1960s and eventually made his debut with the 1969 Chicago White Sox. The outfielder with a made-for-the-cinema name spent three years in the big leagues with three different teams, moving from the Sox to the Reds and then the Padres.

His name conjures up a World War II battle scene. A beleaguered group of soldiers hunker down in a foxhole calling on their radio for air cover. "This is Angel Bravo Charlie Company calling for help."

Yes, the real call letters are Alpha, Bravo, Charlie, but why ruin the imagery with facts?

While in the minors, Bravo led his league twice in fielding percentage for outfielders. On the offensive side, he led the Pacific Coast League with a .342 average in 1969 while playing for the Tucson Toros.

Bravo, born in 1942, lives in his native Venezuela in the city of Aracaibo.

Guy Sturdy

With no middle name to dilute the image, Guy Sturdy entered the world in 1899. Records do not indicate what the parents named the first girl baby in the family, but Girl Sturdy would fit the pattern. Luckily, our Guy grew up to be a good physical specimen at 6' 0" tall and 185 pounds. Had he developed into a small, lightweight model, the last name might have motivated teammates to brand him with a name such as "Small But" Sturdy.

Sturdy plied his trade in the minor leagues for eight years before the St. Louis Browns gave him a shot at first base in the fall of 1927. The 27-year-old rookie tore the hide off the ball for the remaining five games of the season, and fashioned a .429 batting average. The Brownies brought him back for the 1928 season, but Sturdy hit only .222 and could not displace Lu Blue from the first base sack. The Browns sold him to the Milwaukee Brewers in August and he stayed submerged in the minors for the next 12 years before ending his career in El Dorado (Arkansas). Like the explorer Pizarro, Sturdy found no city of gold, just a conclusion to a minor league career that lasted 19 seasons. His longevity and lifetime batting average of .321 proved that he was a Sturdy guy in every sense of the word.

He died in Marshall, Texas in 1965, at the age of 65.

Urban Shocker

The pitcher with a name that sounds like a movie tagline was born in Cleveland, Ohio, in 1890. The name on his birth certificate read Urbain Jacques Shockor.

Shocker was an intense, stern individual whose teammates would have composed nicknames behind his back but would not have had the temerity to anoint him publicly.

Originally a catcher, Shocker's strong arm earned him a transfer from one end of the battery to the other. As he progressed through the minor leagues, he developed his signature pitch, a spitball. He used the spitball sparingly, which made the pitch even more effective, a wet change up, so to speak.

His major league career began with the Yankees in 1916. Shocker pitched well for a Yankees team that was still laboring in the shadow of the Red Sox and White Sox. After two winning seasons at 4-3 and 8-5, he was traded to the St. Louis Browns.

The Browns, like the Yankees, were trying to rise out of the American League's second division. As the Brownies slowly climbed up the standings, the Yankees were always just a little bit better. Shocker's development mirrored that of the Browns. He won 20 or more games four years straight, leading the American League in 1921 with a 27-12 mark.

In 1925, he was traded back to the Yankees for Bullet Joe Bush and two other players. His arrival coincided with one of New York's worst seasons ever, a seventh place finish. In 1926, he finally discovered the joy of pitching for a pennant winning team. The Yankees lost the World Series to the St. Louis Cardinals in seven games. Shocker started Game Two and was bested by Pete Alexander, 6-2.

In 1927, Shocker was instrumental in the Yankees repeat pennant. He contributed 18 wins, losing only six. New York manager Miller Huggins started Waite Hoyt, George Pipgras and Herb Pennock in the first three games of the Series against the Pittsburgh Pirates, all Yankee victories. Instead of turning to the well-rested Shocker in game four, he gave the ball to Wilcy Moore who nailed down the Yankee sweep.

He came back to the Yankees for just three games in 1928, and then retired to run a radio shop in St. Louis. Later in the year he traveled to Denver to pitch in an exhibition game. During the trip he contacted pneumonia and never recovered. In fact, he never got well enough to leave Denver, dying one month later from a weakened heart. He was just weeks shy of his 38th birthday.

Urban Shocker is not a household name despite the fact that he won 187 games and lost only 117, a .615 percentage. He also accomplished something that many great pitchers cannot claim; he never had a losing season during his 13-year career.

Clyde Kluttz

Clyde Franklin Kluttz was born in 1917 in Rockwell, North Carolina, and attended Catawba College in nearby Salisbury. He signed his first professional contract in 1938 to play for the Johnson City Soldiers in the Appalachian League. Four years later he made his debut with the Boston Braves.

He caught for six different major league teams during his nine-year tenure (1942 to 1948 and 1951 to 1952). After his major league playing career ended, he served as a scout for the Yankees. He signed the young Jim "Catfish" Hunter for the Oakland Athletics and is credited with persuading Hunter to sign with the Yankees when he became a free agent. Kluttz later served as the Director of Player Development for the Baltimore Orioles. [9]

The name Kluttz sounds exactly like the word *klutz*, which means a clumsy, awkward person, or worse, a stupid or foolish person. The name comes from the Germans who originally spelled it Klotz. Ironically, the name Klotz in the German language means awkward or clumsy. The German Klotzes immigrated to America during the early 18th century. Various spellings of the name exist throughout the United States. [10]

Catchers were generally not the most graceful players on the team, so 6' tall 195 pound Kluttz may have actually nicknamed himself without even trying.

In 1946, during his only year with the St. Louis Cardinals, he was the backup to rookie catcher Joe Garagiola and contributed to the Cardinals' successful pennant drive. Sadly, when the World Series was played, Del Rice rotated with Garagiola behind the plate and Kluttz did not see action in the victory over Boston in seven games.

A career .268 hitter, he also played for the New York Giants, Pittsburgh Pirates, St. Louis Browns and Washington Senators.

He died in 1979 in Salisbury, North Carolina, where he had attended college as a young man. He was 61 years old.

Drungo Hazewood

On September 2, 1959, the Hazewood family of Mobile, Alabama, welcomed a baby boy into the family. They celebrated by naming the child Drungo LaRue Hazewood. Baby Drungo grew up to be a solid young man standing 6' 3" tall and weighing over 200 pounds. He learned to make a baseball disappear into the distance and was rewarded by the Baltimore Orioles as a first round draft pick in 1977.

The name conjures up visions of Mongo, the brutish character from the movie *Blazing Saddles* played by former NFL star Alex Karras. One can imagine a minor league manager looking down his bench and calling out, "Drungo, grab a club and get ready to hit."

The dictionary contains no entry for the word drungo. Drungo, the surname, does appear in news archives, albeit infrequently. Hazewood's parents might have had some ancestors with that name and wanted to honor them.

The 17-year-old Hazewood struggled in rookie ball with the Bluefield Orioles. His sophomore year in Miami was not much better. But once he arrived in Double-A Charlotte in 1979, his power began to evolve. He smacked 48 home runs in the next two seasons and earned a September audition with the Baltimore Orioles in 1980.

The American League pitchers immediately put him to the ultimate test for rookie hitters. Could he handle a big league curve ball? He could not. Five times he came to plate and five times he took a quick seat back in the dugout, fanning four times. The highlight of his brief Oriole stint was entering a game in the ninth inning against the Cleveland Indians as a pinch runner and scoring on a single by Pat Kelly. (11]

When the 1981 season arrived, Hazewood was back in the minors where he would spend the next three seasons. He never had another shot in the majors. He died in 2013 at the age of 53.

Van Lingle Mungo

Van Mungo pitched for the Brooklyn Dodgers from 1931 until 1941. He finished his career with the New York Giants in 1942, 1943 and 1945. He achieved moderate success from 1932 through 1936 when he won 81 games for the second division Dodgers. Often referred to as a "fireballer" he led the league with 238 strike outs in 1936.

With a melodious name like Van Lingle Mungo, one would expect a quiet personality and a professorial appearance. Van Mungo was an animal. He was a brawler, a drinker and a womanizer. He short fuse and bad temper were legendary. Casey Stengel managed Mungo from 1934-1936. Casey described how he handled his mercurial hurler, "Mungo and I get along fine. I just tell him I won't stand for any nonsense, and then I duck." [12]

The legendary Burleigh Grimes took over the Dodgers' helm in 1937. Before his seat in the dugout was even warm, Grimes had to suspend and fine Mungo $1,000 for drunkenness and fighting. On May 22, Mungo returned to his St. Louis hotel around 3 a.m. He broke into the suite of teammates Woody English and Jimmy Bucher and "went on a rampage." This marked the third time in the past year the pitcher had to be disciplined by the Brooklyn club. [13]

During spring training in Cuba in 1941, Mungo was caught in a compromising situation by a jealous husband and was attacked with a machete or large knife. Dodger officials had to sneak him onto an airplane and off the island minutes before the murderous cuckold discovered the escape.

Mungo had no publicly known nickname, but was likely called many things, behind his back, of course.

Despite his success and public reputation, Mungo drifted toward obscurity by the late 1960s. The Jackie Robinson and Sandy Koufax led Dodgers teams pushed him into the shadows. In 1969, a songwriter named David Frishberg composed and sang a song that brought Mungo back into the limelight. Frishberg, who had penned songs performed by Blossom Dearie, Rosemary Clooney and Mel Torme, fashioned a jazzy bossa nova number using just the names of baseball players from the 1940s. Each stanza ended with the name Van Lingle Mungo, which was also the song's title. Mungo was invited onto the Dick Cavett TV show where Frishberg performed the song for him.

Mungo died in his hometown of Pageland, South Carolina, in 1985. His obituary in the New York Times read: "Van Lingo Mungo, 73, Dies; Colorful Pitcher For Dodgers."

Loren Babe

Sixteen former MLB players have joined George Herman Ruth to officially bear the nickname of Babe. Another dozen or so used the name informally along with countless minor leaguers. Loren Rolland Babe is the only player who can claim the name on his birth certificate.

Actually, Babe did acquire a nickname. Early in his career, a teammate with a sense of humor dubbed him as "Babe-Babe". Eventually, that name was shortened to BeeBee.

Babe was born in 1928 in the tiny Iowa town of Pisgah. At some point in Babe's life, someone must have twisted that word into a joke of sorts.

Like the Bambino, Loren Babe played for the Yankees, debuting in 1952 as a third baseman. Despite a lack of success at the plate (.095), he returned to the Yanks in 1953 but was sold to the Philadelphia A's after five games. Later in the same season, he was traded back to the Yankees but never again set foot on a major league field. He labored in the minor leagues until retiring in 1961.

Babe managed in the minor leagues from 1962-1966 before rejoining the New York Yankees as a coach and later as a scout. In 1983, he was working in the Chicago White Sox organization when he was diagnosed with cancer. The White Sox brought him to the parent club as a coach so he could gain the 57 days of service that he needed to qualify for MLB pension benefits. [14]

Sadly, the disease claimed him in 1984 at the age of 56. He is buried in Omaha, Nebraska, 30 miles south of his hometown.

Jim Bowie

James R. Bowie was born in Tokyo, Japan, in 1965. He entered professional baseball in 1986 well after the era of baseball nicknames had ended. Had he been born a century sooner, a nickname would still have been totally unnecessary. The name Jim Bowie is legendary now, as it was a 150 years earlier.

Bowie's major league career lasted just nine days in 1994. He played six games at first base for the Oakland A's. He singled three times in 14 plate appearances for a .214 average.

A great ending to Bowie's biography would be a last at-bat in San Antonio, Texas, near the Alamo, but sadly, the facts will not support that storybook ending. He retired from baseball after playing for the 1997 Mobile Bay Bears in the Southern Association Mr. Bowie is still living, at last report, in Suisun, California.

Above: left – Orval Overall   right – Van Lingle Mungo
Below: left -- Loren Babe   right – Lu Blue

Chapter Nine - Smart Move, Brother! Players Who Resisted Their Nicknames

The ballplayers in the earlier chapters of this book embraced demeaning, insulting and just plain weird nicknames. This section is a tribute to the men who had the good sense to ignore or reject the new names that were pinned on them. They may have tolerated the names to some degree, but were smart enough not to become known officially by them.

Bill "Little Eva" Lange

This is the story of William "Bill" Lange and *Uncle Tom's Cabin* coming together to create a classic baseball nickname. First of all, Lange was not a little man. He stood 6"1" and weighed 190 pounds. He was not assigned a feminine name because of a clean-living lifestyle. Lange had an unusual gait that amused his teammates. They told Lange that he walked like a little girl. [1] They could have chosen from hundreds of girls' names, but they designated him as Little Eva. Harriet Beecher Stowe now joins the drama.

In 1852, Stowe published an anti-slavery novel called *Uncle Tom's Cabin* that became the topselling book of the entire 19th century. Uncle Tom was a slave who was sold by his goodhearted owner to raise needed cash. While on a riverboat headed for the slave auction, Tom rescued a young white girl named Evangeline St. Clare from drowning. Evangeline, called little Eva by her family, convinced her father to buy Tom.

Lange's contemporaries would have been very familiar with the plot, the characters, and the fateful impact that the book had on America. When Stowe met Abraham Lincoln during the Civil War, he said to her, "So this is the little lady who made this big war." [2]

Lange was born in 1871 in San Francisco, California. At the age of 20 he was signed to play in the Pacific Northwestern League with the Seattle Reds. He spent one more year in the minors before joining the Chicago Colts of the National League in 1893. Cap Anson, a confirmed bigot and racist, was his first big league manager. While there is no evidence to support the idea that Anson coined the Little Eva name, he would obviously be included among the "persons of interest."

Lange played his entire career with Chicago, spending time in both the outfield and at second base. In 1898, the Colts changed their name to the Chicago Orphans, a reference to the loss of Cap Anson's services. (In 1902, the franchise became known as the Chicago Cubs.) Lange's last year in baseball was 1899. Lange fell in love and wanted to get married, but his sweetheart's father refused to condone a marriage to a lowly baseball player. There is no way to know how many players left baseball for the love of a woman, but Bill Lange was one of them. The marriage also opened doors for him to enter the profitable world of real estate. [3]

The marriage did not long survive, but Lange turned down all offers to return to the diamond. The Orphans offered him $3,500 to sign, an amount that would make him the highest paid player in the league. He stayed in the real estate business and prospered.

He retired with a lifetime batting average of .330. His high water mark was .389 in 1895. Lange may have walked like a little girl, but when he took off running, he could fly. He stole 400 bases in just over 800 games, leading the National League in 1897 with 73 swipes.

He died in 1950 at the age of 79. Had he lived until 1962, he would have been amused to witness the hit song *The Loco-motion* by Eva Boyd, recording under the stage name of Little Eva, another reference to Harriet Beecher Stowe's sympathetic character.

Joe "Horse Belly" Sargent

Here is a nickname that conjures up a disturbing visual, the swayback horse with a prominent low hanging belly. Chances are good that Joe Sargent's nickname exaggerated the infielder's physical shape, but there is little doubt that he fully earned his name. Sargent was a 27-year-old infielder on the 1921 Detroit Tigers. Repudiating this name would have given Sargent a new lease on the life, the opportunity to lose weight and develop a more attractive persona.

He was born in Rochester, New York, in 1893. He played in the minor leagues from 1913 until his promotion to the Tigers in 1921. His .304 season with the Buffalo Bisons propelled him to Detroit. He descended to the minors in 1922 via a trade to Portland in the Pacific Coast League. He hung up the cleats after the 1924 season.

His lifetime minor league batting average over eight seasons was .260. During his single year in the majors, he hit .253 while filling in at all infield spots but first base. The rest of his Tiger mates hit well over .300 that year, putting his trade to Portland in a clearer perspective.

The search for positive exploits in Sargent's career yields very little, prompting the conclusion that his only claim to fame was his colorful nickname.

He died in 1950 at the age of 56. If nothing else, he could sit around the cracker barrel and regale his friends with stories of playing with Ty Cobb.

Charlie "Piano Legs" Hickman

Charles Taylor Hickman was reputed to have very thick legs, hence the comparison to furniture legs. He carried the reputation of a slow runner, yet his statistics show 72 career stolen bases and 91 triples.

Hickman, a turn-of-the-century infielder, led the National League in base hits with 193 while playing for the 1902 New York Giants. He logged 12 big league seasons frequently bouncing from team to team, primarily because of his defensive shortcomings. The record for errors in a game by a second baseman is five, co-held by Nap Lajoie (April 22, 1915 with Cleveland) and Charlie Hickman (September 29, 1905 with Washington). [4] He played on seven different teams and was a member of the Cleveland Naps three separate times. His peripatetic ways did not have a negative effect on his demeanor. In addition to "Piano Legs" teammates also referred to him as "Cheerful Charlie."

Hickman was born in 1876 in Taylortown, Pennsylvania, a small burg near the West Virginia border. Following high school, he matriculated at nearby West Virginia University and starred on the baseball team, beginning as a catcher then converting to a pitcher. Although not the first Mountaineer to reach the major leagues, he still retains the top spot in major league at bats among all WVU alumni.

He played most times at first base, but frequently appeared at second base or in right field. He also took the mound occasionally. In 1899, he started nine games for the Boston Beaneaters and finished the season with a perfect 6-0 record. A contemporary player with Hickman's statistics would be considered a star player by today's standards, yet he is more remembered for his quirky nickname than his accomplishments.

Following his playing career, he returned to his alma mater to take the reins of the Mountaineer baseball team from 1915 to 1917. He then settled down in Morgantown and successfully ran for mayor. He later served in the West Virginia department of justice and later as sheriff of Monongalia County. Heart disease cut short his life in 1934 at the age of 58. [5]

Frank "Dodo" Bird

Frank Zeprin Bird was born in Spencer, Massachusetts, in 1869. His parents were not nearly as creative as those of Bird Blue, or they may have named him Blue Bird. Baseball was deprived of having a Blue Bird and a Bird Blue in its archives.

The nickname Dodo was a no-brainer. Frank Bird's repudiation of the nickname was likewise an easy decision. The dodo bird is undoubtedly the most famous example of a species sinking into extinction. The flightless bird was clumsy and unafraid of humans when Europeans began to show up on the Island of Mauritius in the Indian Ocean. Dodos were easy prey for the dogs, pigs and cats that accompanied the visitors. Dodos quickly slipped from view and quietly disappeared forever.

A new connotation of the word dodo became popular during Bird's lifetime, a person who was dull-witted; slow afoot, or blatantly out of date. Bird's teammates, opponents, fans and sportswriters would have had a license to make bad jokes at his expense. Bird, a catcher who stood almost six feet tall and weighed close to 200 pounds, was probably not the fastest moving player on the field. But there is strong evidence that he was not slow-witted; he maneuvered himself away from a lifetime of answering to a pejorative nickname.

In retrospect, Frank Bird's career did somewhat parallel the infamous bird. He made the spring roster of the 1892 St. Louis Cardinals and shared the catching duties with 33-year-old Dick Buckley. Two months and 17 games later, Frank Bird became extinct as a major league player. Fortunately, the metaphor ended with baseball as he lived to the ripe old age of 89. He died in 1958 and was buried near his birthplace in Spencer.

George "Dodo" Armstrong

Ditto to Dodo Armstrong for not embracing the nickname. Apparently, Armstrong had a sister with a very "dumb" bird. [6] How the name traveled between the siblings is unclear.

Armstrong was born in Orange, New Jersey, in 1924. He served as a backup catcher for about two months with the Philadelphia A's in 1946. He doubled once in six plate appearances and dropped back into the minor leagues from whence he came. He posted a .272 average in nine minor league seasons.

Emil "Hill Billy" Bildilli

Check out a current map of Diamond, Indiana, the birthplace of Emil Bildilli, and the most glaring feature will be the lack of anything surrounding Diamond. There are no nearby towns and no major highways in the vicinity. In 1912, when Bildilli was born, it was even more rural and isolated. Take a kid from this environment and bring him to a large population center to play baseball and an appropriate nickname will ensue. Had his last name been anything else he might have been crowned a Hick or a Farmer.

When this hayseed kid arrived with the name Bildilli, the somewhat inappropriate label of hillbilly was too much of a temptation of resist. Typically, a hillbilly is an uneducated resident of a backwoods, mountainous area living in squalid conditions. But the new moniker was funny and rolled easily off the tongue. Bildilli wisely chose to go into the archives as simply Emil Bildilli.

The left-handed pitcher reached the major leagues in 1937 with the St. Louis Browns and made a poor impression by getting blasted by the Washington Senators in his first appearance. He completed his rookie year with a 10.13 ERA and a 0-1 record in four games.

He stayed on the St. Louis roster until the spring of 1941 when he wore out his welcome by imploding in his first two games. He was sold to the Toledo Mud Hens where he finished out the season with a 5-9 slate.

Returning to Indiana, Bildilli played on various semi-pro teams until his death in 1946. After competing in a game in Ft. Wayne, he fell asleep at the wheel near Hartford City and suffered a crushed skull. He died the following day, his 34th birthday. His tombstone makes no reference to the nickname Hill Billy. [7]

Nick "Tomato Face" Cullop

Henry Nicholas Cullop entered the world in 1900 and grew up with a ruddy complexion. Perhaps a kinder sobriquet might have been attached to this St. Louis native. He could have been cited for his physical build at 6' tall and 200 pounds. He could have been nicknamed for his play in the outfield or his batting prowess. But no, poor Nick had to been called out for his red-splotched face and garner the discourteous name of Tomato Face. Unlike Boob Fowler, Crazy Schmit and many others, Cullop did what he had to do to escape the name.

After spending six years in the minors, the hunky outfielder arrived in the majors with the 1926 Yankees. He batted twice and stroked one single for a .500 batting average. During the off-season he was traded to the Washington Senators and missed the opportunity to participate in the great awakening of the Yankees dynasty.

He was traded again during the 1927 season, this time ending up in Cleveland. His combined .231 batting average condemned him to the minor leagues for the 1928 season.

Back in the major leagues in 1929 with the Brooklyn Robins, he struggled mightily and spent most of the summer with the Atlanta Crackers in the Southern Association. The 1930 season was very similar, an anemic batting average with the Cincinnati Reds resulting in a ticket to the Minneapolis Millers in the American Association. His .359 average there earned him a slot on the 1931 Reds where he enjoyed his best big league season, batting .263 in 104 games. Unfortunately, that was not good enough to keep his job in Cincinnati. He spent the next 13 years in the minor leagues and could not climb back to the majors.

During his five seasons in the major leagues, he appeared in just 173 games. He batted .249 and hit 11 home runs.

Cullop walloped 420 home runs in the minor leagues, currently fourth best in minor league history. (Mike Hessman currently holds the top spot with 433 dingers). Cullop sits at number one in RBIs in the minors with 1,857.

In 1945 a young baseball executive named Bill Veeck Jr. hired Cullop to manage the Milwaukee Brewers in the American Association. Replacing Casey Stengel, Cullop guided the Brewers to the league championship during his rookie year as a manager. He remained at the helm of the Brewers through the 1949 season, recording a winning record every year but one.

Cullop died in 1978 and was buried in Gahanna, Ohio. He was 78 years old.

Billy "Bald Billy" Barnie

A photo of Mr. Barnie confirms the basis for his nickname. Despite the fact that the nickname had a very lyrical bent, Barnie did not embrace the name. Perhaps he had a vision that someday he would meet a traveling snake oil peddler and purchase an elixir that returned the hair to his head. Allowing himself to become Bald Billy Barnie would create confusion when he walked onto the field with the breeze rustling his curly dark mane.

Barnie was born in 1853 in New York City and played on some of the earliest professional teams such as the 1874 Hartford Dark Blues in the National Association. While he played in the outfield and behind the plate, he is better known for his stint as manager of the Baltimore Orioles from 1883 until 1891. He managed such Oriole stars as John McGraw and Wilbert Robinson. He also helmed the Washington Senators (two games), Louisville Colonels and Brooklyn Bridegrooms. During his 14 years as manager, the highest his team ever finished was the third place finish of the 1887 Orioles.

How did a mediocre player (.171 batting average) and manager survive so long in professional baseball? Barnie was a consummate promoter and entrepreneur. He knew how to put together new teams and new events, and more importantly, how to get himself hired as manager.

Following his acrimonious departure from the Brooklyn Bridegrooms in 1898, he attempted to form a new major league that he named the Union League. When that venture failed to materialize, he bought the Hartford franchise in the Eastern League and named himself manager. He tried to revitalize the club with ballpark upgrades and hiring the former Cleveland Indian Louis "Chief "Sockalexis. Barnie renamed the team the Indians in honor of his new player. The 27-year old former star had destroyed his body with alcohol and could no longer perform like a star, but he did bring fans to the games. [8] The Chief and his .198 average were gone after 24 games.

Midway through the 1900 season, Barnie died suddenly at the age of 47. Asthmatic bronchitis finally removed him from his manager's perch in the dugout.

Clarence "Climax" Blethen

The source of the nickname Climax has not been discovered but Clarence Waldo Blethen had the good sense to turn his back on the new name. Perhaps he was involved in one climactic play that ended an important ballgame. Certainly, he would never want his mother to look in the newspaper and see her son called such an indelicate name.

Blethen pitched for the Boston Red Sox in 1923 and then disappeared from the big leagues until surfacing with the Brooklyn Robins in 1929. His career record is 0-0 with an ERA of 7.32.

Despite the short stint, Blethen did leave his mark on the game. Blethen may be the only player in baseball history to be bitten by his own teeth. In 1923, the right-hander was pitching for the Boston Red Sox and routinely placed his dentures in his back pocket when playing. One fateful day, he slid into second base and his teeth tore into his posterior leaving behind a biting reminder to leave them in the locker room in the future. [9]

He died in 1973 in Frederick, Maryland. At age 79 he probably lived long enough to live down the "bite in the butt" incident.

Mark "Fido" Baldwin

Marcus Elmore Baldwin was born in Pittsburgh, Pennsylvania, in 1863 and attended Penn State University. He was the second Nittany Lion to find his way into the major leagues behind Monte Ward.

Baldwin debuted with the Chicago White Stockings of the National League in 1887. Cap Anson managed the White Stockings, who would later become known as the Cubs. During his two year stay in Chicago, Baldwin ran afoul of Anson so often that teammates called him Fido because he was always in manager's "doghouse." [10]

In 1889, Baldwin slipped his collar and fled to the Columbus Solons in the rival American Association. The nickname of Fido followed him. Ever the workhorse, he led the AA in games played (63), games started (59), innings pitched (513.2), and strikeouts (368). On the other side of the coin, he was also number one in losses (27-34), walks (274) and wild pitches (83).

The following season he jumped to the new Players League and returned to the Windy City with the Chicago Pirates. Baldwin served as a recruiter for the new league, encouraging players from the National League and American Association to jump ship. He was arrested for his proselytizing and jailed in St. Louis but the case was dismissed. Browns owner William Von der Ahe had the charges refilled and Baldwin was thrown into jail again. After surviving jailhouse cockroaches and bedbugs, Baldwin sued and won a $2,500 judgment. [11]

On the field he continued to be productive with the Chicago Pirates as he rang up 33 victories against 24 losses in 56 starts, 53 of them complete games. After one season, the Pirates walked the plank along with the rest of the Players League. Baldwin must have favored the Pirate image. In 1891, he signed with the Pittsburgh Pirates of the National League. He won 47 games in two seasons with the Pirates, a very credible performance on a lousy team.

He moved to the New York Giants in 1893 where he ended his career playing for manager Monte Ward, a fellow alumnus of Penn State. His seven-season record was 154-165, an impressive average of 22 wins per year.

Ironically, the Fido name seemed to be a good fit, for he was continually in someone's doghouse. In 1896, Baldwin, with a group of former players, formed a new semi-pro team in Auburn, New York. Baldwin named himself manager and starting pitcher. Having been raised in the city of Pittsburgh and played in Chicago, he underestimated one aspect of small town life. Auburn had blue laws on their books. Blue laws in Auburn, as in many American towns, were enacted to enforce religious tenets such as observance of the Sabbath. [12]

The Auburn team hosted a Sunday contest and all of the players were arrested for violation of blue laws. The arrest led to a conviction and $5 fine. Unfortunately, the $5 did not buy him a ticket out of Auburn's doghouse. The townsmen, led by local clergy, took up torches and pitchforks (figuratively as far as we know), and drove the team out of business by boycotting the rest of the scheduled games.

Baldwin gave up his interest in the Auburn team and relocated to Pittsburgh. While it may be hard to prove a negative, no records exist to show Mark Baldwin spent time in anyone's doghouse upon his return to his hometown. He died there in 1929 at the age of 66.

Dominic "Dim Dom" Dallessandro

Nicholas Dominic Dallessandro was born in Reading, Pennsylvania, in 1913. He grew to a height of 5' 5". He had short powerful legs sitting atop two very tiny feet. He weighed only 165 pounds.

Dallessandro played professional baseball from 1931 until 1947. From time to time he was called "Short Drawers", "Little Dynamite" and "Spark Plug", but none of these nicknames stuck. [13] In 1944, Charlie Grimm took over as manager of the Chicago Cubs. Grimm must have had an exceptionally good vocabulary for a baseball man. He observed that his veteran outfielder was quite diminutive and named him Diminutive Dominic, which quickly morphed into the beautifully alliterative Dim Dom. [14]

Since many baseball players and fans were not educated enough to understand the etymology of the name, they incorrectly interpreted the nickname as a description of Dallessandro's intelligence. The best measure of Dallessandro's IQ was his decision to disallow the name from following him throughout the remainder of career and into retirement.

Dallessandro labored in the minors from 1931 to 1936 before the Boston Red Sox bought his contract from their AA affiliate in Syracuse in 1937. He hit just .231 in 68 games with the Sox and subsequently could not retain a spot on the 1938 roster.

After two more years in the minor leagues, the Chicago Cubs purchased his contract from the San Diego Padres in the PCL. Serving as the fourth outfielder in 1940, he performed well enough to claim a starting position with the '41 Cubs.

Dallessandro experienced his best season in 1944 when he hit .304 with 74 RBIs playing for the Cubs. The following year he was inducted into the military and missed the first Cubs pennant since 1938. His main job in the Army was playing baseball for the Fort Lewis (Washington) Warriors with fellow major leaguers Danny Litwhiler, Tony York, Ron Northey, Ray Mueller and Bill Fleming. The U.S. won the war and Fort Lewis dominated military baseball in the Northwest. [15]

He returned to the Cubs as a backup after the war, but could not win back his starting job. He spent 1946 and 1947 with the Cubs. He continued playing in the minor leagues through the 1952 season. He retired to the Indianapolis area and worked in the printing business as a pressman. [16]

Dallessandro died in 1988 at the age of 74.

Fred "Whale" Walters

Walters was one of many long-time minor leaguers who finally seized the opportunity to reach the major leagues during World War II. By 1945, big league rosters had been severely depleted causing the quality of play to be watered down.

The Boston Red Sox elevated former backup Roy Partee to starting catcher in 1943. Following the 1944 season, Partee was finally called into the military. Bob Garback became the starting catcher by default. The Red Sox turned to their Class AA team in Louisville and promoted the 6'1" 210 pound catcher Fred Walters, nicknamed "Whale" because of his physique. While Walters was not the largest mammal in baseball, the alliterative combination of names was too much temptation for the unknown author of this nickname.

Walters shared the catching duties with Garback and Billy Holm, allowing him to appear in 40 big league games. He batted .172 with only five RBIs. He played his last game on August 9th and returned to Louisville. He spent 1946 through 1948 in the minors. During the 1947 season he was named player/manager of the New Orleans Pelicans, a position he held for two seasons. In October of 1948 he signed a contract to return to the Louisville Colonels as their manager. His catching services were no longer required. He was drummed out of the Colonels two months into the season. According to the Milwaukee Journal, Louisville ownership was fond of Walters and helped him secure a position in the Boston Red Sox scouting department. [17]

Before the 1949 season had ended, Walters found employment as manager of the New Orleans Pelicans. After the 1950 season, Walters was dismissed again.

All post-retirement newspaper articles referred to him as Fred Walters. The "Whale" was lost at sea for half a century before interest in baseball nicknames called it back to the surface. Walters died in 1980 in his home town of Laurel, Mississippi, little expecting that his baseball nickname would someday come back to claim him.

Walters' biggest claim to fame came on the football field, not the baseball diamond. The 1935 edition of the Mississippi State Bulldogs faced the powerful Army team. Walters was a substitute pass receiver who entered the game with the Bulldogs trailing the Cadets 7-6 and the ball on their own 20-yard-line. Mississippi State quarterback Charles Armstrong found Walters for a 16-yard gain. Armstrong went to Walters again, this time connecting at the Army 35-yard line. Walters raced into the end zone for the winning touchdown. [18]

Bob "Fats" Fothergill

Unlike Fred Walters, Robert Roy Fothergill completely earned and deserved the nickname that spotlighted his girth. Fothergill was able to shed the name "Fats", but not the surplus weight that he carried into left field each time he entered a game. Generally listed at 230 pounds, he steadily gained weight during his 12-year career, approaching 300 pounds at the end. [19]

Fothergill was born in Massillon, Ohio, in 1897. He signed with the Bloomington Bloomers in the Three-I League in 1920. Hitting for average and power, he moved up quickly to the Rochester Tribe and then the Detroit Tigers in 1922. He hit American League pitching at the same clip that he did in the minors, finishing his rookie year with a .322 batting average.

During his first eight seasons with Detroit, he never hit below .301, four times batting over .350. When he reached the mid-point of the 1930 season with a .259 average, the Tigers put him on waivers. When asked about the diet that Tigers ownership demanded, Fothergill explained, "Detroit pays me to hit. I can't hit if I ain't got the power and I ain't got the power if I don't eat. And, when I eat what I like I get fat. When I diet, I don't hit. So what in blazes am I going to do?" [20]

The Chicago White Sox signed him primarily as a pinch hitter and he rewarded them with a .296 average for the remainder of the season. He remained with the ChiSox until being traded to the Boston Red Sox prior to the 1933 season. Despite his .344 average, the Bosox used him sparingly until releasing him in July of 1933.

After a dozen years in the big leagues, he retired with a lifetime batting average of .325. His best year was 1926 when he hit .367, third behind Babe Ruth's .372 and Tiger teammate Heinie Manush's league leading .378.

After finishing the 1933 season in the American Association with the Minneapolis Millers, he returned to Detroit and went to work for Ford Motor Company until his early death at the age of 40 in 1938.

Four More Wise Men

Frankie "Blimp" Hayes ballooned to almost 300 pounds during his 14-year career as a catcher (1933-1947), mostly with the Philadelphia A's. John "Pork Chop" Hoffman (1944 New York Giants) was said to have a compact body. Ted "Porky" Pawelek (1946 Cubs) weighed 210 pounds. Bruce "Fatso" Sloan (1964-1965 Colt 45's) was not especially heavy but carried his weight on a 5' 9" frame. They represent four more wise men who rejected their nicknames.

Unlike Chubby Dean, Hippo Vaughn, Jumbo Brown, Skinny Graham and others, Fred Walters, Bob Fothergill and these four players did not have to carry an unflattering name into their second career and beyond. Many players saddled with an unflattering name found it very difficult to shed the name following their active careers.

What was the trait that allowed them to retain their given names as they fought for a place in the major leagues? Was it a sense of high self-esteem that whispered to them that they were more than a body image? On the other hand, could it have been a touch of insecurity that prevented them from identifying with the nickname chosen for them? The inner dialogue that guided their decisions, one way or another, can never be known.

Above: left – Bob "Fats" Fothergill   right – Bill "Little Eva" Lange
Below: left – Mark "Fido" Baldwin   right – Nick "Tomato Face" Cullop

Chapter Ten - The Negro League Nicknames

The Negro Leagues have always been rife with humorous and quirky nicknames. Cool Papa Bell, Satchel Paige, and Double Duty Radcliffe jump to mind. A more detailed examination of these nicknames produces an interesting observation; the unflattering nicknames are very uncommon. By far, most of the Negro League sobriquets tend to glorify the player rather than making him the victim of a fraternity-type hazing.

Former baseball commissioner Fay Vincent observed, "The Negro League nicknames, it seemed, got to the essence of the player." [1]

The effort to fit players into the format established early in this work does not produce a long list. The first category, **Physical Characteristics**, follows the same pattern as the major leagues, a recognition of the players of large and small stature:

- Frank "Pee Wee" Austin.
- Otha "Little Catch" Bailey
- Dave "Impo" Barnhill
- Tom "Pee Wee" Butts
- George "Tank" Carr
- Ray "Hooks" Dandridge (bowlegged)
- Juan "Pancho" Herrera (pancho means paunch or belly in colloquial Spanish)
- Jesse "Mountain" Hubbard
- Clarence "Fats" Jenkins
- James "Pee Wee" Jenkins
- Josh "Brute" Johnson
- Oscar "Heavy" Johnson (weighed over 250 pounds)
- Wilson "Frog" Redus
- Mamie "Peanut" Johnson (Female)
- Al "Fuzzy" Smith
- Edsall "Big" Walker
- Willie "Curly" Williams
- John "Needle Nose" Wright

The second category, **Personality Traits**, yields a much smaller group of players:

- Harry "Mooch" Barnes
- James "Cool Papa" Bell (originally nicknamed "Cool") [2]
- Raleigh "Biz" Mackey (prankster gave teammates the "biz") [3]
- Dave "Gentleman" Malarcher
- Oliver "Ghost" Marcelle
- Burnis "Wild Bill" Wright

Dave Malarcher was every inch the gentleman. He did not smoke, drink or curse. In the major leagues his behavior would have earned him a derisive name such as Tilly, Lady, etc.

Oliver Marcelle existed on the other end of the spectrum from Marlarcher. The nickname Ghost derived from the way he disappeared after every game and reappeared at game time. An ugly off-field incident shed some light on his whereabouts. One night he engaged in a barroom fight and left without the tip of his nose. His opponent took a large bite out of his proboscis. Whenever he took the field, opposing fans jeered and ridiculed him to the point he withdrew from baseball.

The vast majority of nicknames with a known explanation fall into the category of **Skill Sets**. Unlike the major leagues that had a well-established product to sell, the Negro Leagues needed every promotional edge they could find. Hence, most nicknames held the promise of an exciting day at the ballpark. Come out today and see Fireball, Cannonball, Superman or Bullet Joe.

Conversely, very few of these names mocked the player that lacked a particular skill. One of the exceptions belonged to Norman "Turkey" Stearnes. When he ran the base paths he reminded teammates of a panicked gobbler with a load of buckshot in close pursuit. The remaining players in this category:

- Jim "Fireball" Bolden
- Bib "The Rope" Boyd (line drive hitter)
- James "Fireball" Cohen
- Elwood "Bingo" DeMoss (a relentless singles hitter)
- William "Plunk" Drake (would not hesitate to hit a batter)
- Erwin "Flash" Ford
- Grant "Homerun" Johnson
- John "Mule" Miles (hits harder than a mule kicks)
- Art "Superman" Pennington

- Ted "Double Duty" Radcliffe (would pitch one end of a doubleheader and the catch the other)
- Dick "Cannonball" Redding
- Joe "Bullet" Rogan
- Louis "Big Bertha" Santop (named for German WWI long-range cannon)
- Alfred "Slick" Surratt
- George "Mule" Suttles (used a 50 ounce bat)
- Cristobal "Cuban Strongboy" Torriente (called the Babe Ruth of Cuba)
- Clint "Hawk" Thomas (sharp batting eye)
- Willie "El Diablo" Wells (bedeviled hitters with his defense)
- "Smokey Joe" Williams (some consider him the greatest Negro League pitcher)
- Johnny "Steel Arm" Taylor (outstanding and durable pitcher-brother of "Candy Jim" Taylor)
- Jim "Seabiscuit" Wilkes
- Jud "Boojum" Wilson

Teammates tried to invent a word that would describe the sound of Jud Wilson's powerful line drives striking the outfield fences. The word they came up with was "boojum" and a unique name was born.

Three more names on the Skill Set list need to be handled separately because they appear to fall into another category:

- Ross "Satchel" Davis
- Andrew "Rube" Foster
- William "Judy" Johnson

Davis did not carry baggage for a railroad a la Satchel Paige. He was accorded a nickname of honor, for his great pitching skills, which reminded teammates of Paige.

Rube Foster was not called a "country rube" by his teammates. He bested the great Rube Waddell during an exhibition game in 1902 and benefited from the comparison. Foster is considered the founding father of Negro League baseball.

William Johnson did not eschew the manly characteristics of the early rough-hewn baseball players, thus earning the feminine name Judy. He reminded older players of Jude Gans, a star outfielder for the early Chicago American Giants. He was respectfully renamed Judy.

Manuel "Cocaina" Garcia had a fastball that caused hitters to appear as though they were in a cocaine stupor. How did they know what a cocaine stupor looked like? Hmmm. [4]

The major leagues produced many nicknames that belong in the **Racial/Ethnic and Geographical** category. Not surprisingly, Negro League players seldom dipped into this pool for a nickname. The closest example of an ethnic reference is that of John "Hymie" Leftwich. His last name sounded Jewish and the common ethnic slur of "Hymie" was bestowed upon him. The term is now quite offensive to Jews. Hall of Fame player Reggie Jackson learned this fact the hard way in 1984 when he referred to New York City as Hymietown. A media firestorm ensued forcing Jackson to apologize for the comment.

Despite the many politically incorrect nicknames assigned over the years, no major league player has ever been given the nickname Hymie.

Frank "Wahoo" Pearson was a submarine pitcher who was as hard to catch, as he was to hit. His teammates felt that he looked like a Native American Indian and began calling him Wahoo, a reference to the Cleveland Indians' mascot named Chief Wahoo. [5]

Perhaps because the majority of early Negro Leaguers came from rural surroundings, there are very few nicknames making reference to this. There are no players named Hick or Farmer. The only Rube (Foster) refers to Rube Waddell, not to the player's bucolic background. A short list of players with names relating to their place of origin results:

- Earnest "Gator" Barnwell (born in Florida)
- Lorenzo "Piper" Davis (from Piper, Alabama)
- Herbert "Rap" Dixon (Rappahannock, Virginia)
- Hubert "Country" Glenn
- Paul "Country Jake" Stephens

Negro League players seldom invented the lyrical nicknames seen frequently in the major leagues. Some of the player names were "no brainers," however. If a player brought the name Cain into the locker room, he probably walked out with the name "Sugar" Cain.

Prominent examples of nicknames resulting from **Word Play**:

- Marion "Sugar" Cain

- Bill "Ready" Cash
- William "Dizzy" Dismukes (not a reference to his personality)
- Joe Gentry "Jeep" Jessup
- Richard "King Tut" King
- Orestes "Minnie" Minoso
- Jose "Potato" Piloto
- Andy "Pullman" Porter

The last category is **Miscellaneous and Unknown**. The most famous nickname in the Negro Leagues belongs to Leroy Paige. As a youth, he was employed by the railroad as a porter. He soon learned that carrying several suitcases and satchels simultaneously earned him more tips. He cleverly improvised a pole to fasten multiple bags. His fellow employees began to call him "Satchel Pole" which evolved into "Satchel." Most casual fans would be hard-pressed to identify his real first name.

As a teenager, Arthur Henderson was the victim of a cruel prank. One day he opened his lunch pail to discover a rat. From that day on he was known as Rats Henderson.

Louis "Sea Boy" Gillis graduated from high school in 1943 and was soon drafted into the U.S. Marines. He served in the Pacific Theater as a captain on an anti-aircraft unit. [6]

Charlie "Goulash" Johnson earned his nickname because of his fondness for a local smorgasbord that featured goulash for just a quarter of a dollar. Goulash is a stew made of beef, vegetables, paprika, and other miscellaneous ingredients. [7]

Harry Leon Simpson enjoyed a 17-year career in the Negro Leagues, minor leagues, and major leagues. During his playing days he played for no less than 17 different professional balllclubs. By the time he reached the midpoint in his career, he had acquired a new moniker, "Suitcase" Simpson.

Al "Apples" Wilmore acquired his nickname as a child. On those happy occasions when his mother could spare a few pennies, he and his siblings would run to the store to spend their "largesse." Unlike the other kids who always bought candy, Wilmore uniformly purchased apples. His love of apples was so profound that he ate everything but the stem. [8]

Many of the most interesting nicknames have an unknown, or unclear, origin:

- Matthew "Lick" Carlisle
- James "Bus" Clarkson (also called "Knocky" because of his knock knees)
- Lloyd "Ducky" Davenport (was only 5" 5" tall)
- Leroy "Toots" Ferrell
- Floyd "Jelly" Gardner (jelly and jelly roll were sexual terms in black slang)
- Harold "Bee Bop" Gordon (the term bebop probably came from scat singing)
- Bob "Schoolboy" Griffith
- Acie "Skeet" Griggs
- Wiley Lee "Diamond Jim" Griggs
- Jim "Pig" Harris
- James "Sap" Ivory
- Norman "Jellylegs" Jackson
- Robert "Fox" Jones
- Everett "Ziggy" Marcell (son of "Ghost" Marcelle he dropped the 'e' from his father's name)
- Jose "Smo" Santiago (Puerto Rican pitcher who was signed by the Cleveland in 1948)
- James "Candy Jim" Taylor (teammate of Rube Foster and later a successful manager)
- Harold "Hooks" Tinker (not named for his curve ball-discovered Josh Gibson)
- Maurice "Doolittle" Young

Unless otherwise specified, Negro League nickname sources are from three major sources:
1. The Negro League Baseball Players Association website – nlbp.com.
2. *Baseball Nicknames: A Dictionary of Origins and Meanings* by James F. Skipper
3. *Abba Dabba to Zorro: the World of Baseball Nicknames* by Don Zminda and STATS, Inc.

Three comments about this chapter:

1. Quotation marks are used for all Negro League nicknames. For major leaguers in the previous chapters, quotations around the nickname are used when the player chose not to be known officially by

that name. All prominent sources of individual major league archives clearly and consistently indicate how the player is known. Yogi Berra, for example, is always listed as Yogi Berra, not Lawrence or Larry Berra. Bill Skowron, on the other hand, is listed as Bill Skowron, even though he was commonly called "Moose" Skowron.

Negro League records are inconsistent in the handling of nicknames; hence, quotation marks are used in all cases.

2. Unlike the earlier chapters that focused on unflattering names, this chapter covers names that are positive, negative and neutral in tone. One cannot be sure how committed the Negro League players were to these nicknames.

3. Major leaguers received short biographies in the earlier sections; Negro Leaguers in this chapter do not. This disparity should not be interpreted as a slight. This chapter was included as a "tip of the hat" to the greatness of these men and women. Yes, women were rare in the Negro leagues but not disqualified as they were, and still are, in the major leagues.

Bonus Chapter: The History of "Red"

The number one nickname in all of baseball history is Red. There have been 96 of them. Once again, please note that we are excluding the players who were called Red but didn't officially identify themselves as such. Another 52 were informally or intermittently called Red but chose to play under their given name.

The overwhelming source of this name was hair color, with perhaps facial complexion playing a small part. That said, we could then add the 13 players named Rusty, most of whom also had red hair. I doubt if any of them picked up their name because of rusty baseball skills.

Who was the first Red? Red (James) Woodhead appeared in one game for Baltimore in the National Association in 1873. The next time he surfaced was in 1879 for the Syracuse Stars in the nascent National League. Woodhead, a third baseman, failed to distinguish himself in 131 at-bats, finishing the season with a .160 average. Sadly, Red drove in only two runs and scored only four times. Red Woodhead never experienced the thrill of hitting a big league homer. Not much to show for 34 games.

Cry not for James, the father of all Reds. He most likely returned to his native Boston area and played for a series of town, or industrial teams.

One last thought about Red Woodhead, although he probably brought his nickname from childhood, he must have been smart enough to know that Red was a much finer nickname than many of the possibilities that Woodhead could have produced.

One honorable mention in the history of Red; Joseph McNamara was born in Ireland in 1866. By 1885, he had become known as Reddy Mack, second sacker for Louisville in the American Association. In six years with Louisville and Baltimore, he batted .254. Reddy Foster and Reddy Gray followed. No one named Reddy has played in the big leagues since 1903.

The name Red didn't catch on until after 1900. Only nine pre-1900 players were known as Red. By 1963, the only Red playing in the majors was Red Schoendienst; and barely playing, at that. He appeared in six games with the Cardinals and came to the plate officially five times, getting no hits. In 1962, he struck the last home run by a Red.

The last two active Reds pitching were Red Murff and Red Swanson. Red Murff pitched for the Milwaukee Braves in 1956 and 1957. He appeared in 26 games, starting two of them. He finished his career with a 2-2 record and a 4.65 E.R.A.

Red Swanson was also a pitcher. He appeared briefly for the Pirates in 1955 and 1956. During the 1957 season, Red Swanson went 3-3 with a 4.90 E.R.A. When the 1957 season came to a close, the last pitchers named Red slid into history.

The last Red to play in the American League was Red Wilson, a veteran catcher who enjoyed a ten-year career with the White Sox, Tigers and, finally, the Indians. Red Wilson's career ended in 1960.

The period from 1900-1929 was the heyday for the name Red. A total of 56 players named Red appeared in major league games. Two interesting names stand out from this period, Red Barron and Red Bird. Both of these characters may have become Red without benefit of red hair.

David Irenus Barron most likely got his nickname from Manfred von Richthofen, known in Germany as the Red Battle-Flyer, but known worldwide as the Red Baron. This World War I flyer has always been considered the Ace of Aces. Did Red Barron live up to his glorious nickname? Sorry, but no, he did not. Red Barron patrolled the outfield for the Boston Braves in 1929. He came to the plate officially 21 times and mostly got shot out of the sky by opposing pitchers. He batted .190 with no home runs. His career lasted exactly 27 days. Hopefully, this Red Barron had a soft landing when the Braves shot down his career. He had a degree from Georgia Tech to fall back on. He was named to the Georgia Tech Athletic Hall of Fame, in 1959 for his football exploits, not baseball.

Red (James Edward) Bird may have had red hair, but probably not. He could have been Blue Bird, Black Bird, or maybe even Big Bird (he was 5'11" and weighed 170 pounds). Red Bird was a pitcher with the Washington Nationals, for one day. He completed five innings, giving up three runs. He didn't get a decision, either way. If he had a blazing fastball, he could have been called Humming Bird. It looks like he didn't.

From 1930 to 1959 there were 32 Reds who made the big league, mostly in the 1930's and 1940's. A notable Red from this period is Red (Charles Henry) Barrett. Barrett pitched from 1937 to 1948. He started the 1945 season with the Boston Braves and was 2-3 when he was traded to the St. Louis Cardinals. He proceeded to go 21-9 with the Redbirds for a league leading 23 victories. He was named to the all-star team but was replaced because of injury. The Braves reacquired him prior to the 1947 season and he never had another winning season.

The three most successful Reds have to be Red Ruffing, Red Faber and Red Schoendienst, all of whom are enshrined in the Hall of Fame. Red Ruffing started life as Charles Herbert Ruffing on May 3, 1905, in Granville, Illinois. This right-handed pitcher won 273 games pitching for the Boston Red Sox, New York Yankees, and Chicago White Sox. Ruffing spent six-plus lackluster years in Boston (39 wins and 96 losses) before being traded to the Yankees one month into the 1930 season. His record with the Yankees was a sparkling 231-124. His Hall of Fame plaque reads:

"Winner of 273 games. Won 20 or more games in each of four consecutive seasons. Led in complete games 1928. Tied in shutouts 1938-1939. Won 7 out of 9 World Series decisions. Selected for All Star Teams 1937-1938-1939."

Red Faber was born as Urban Clarence Faber in 1888 in Cascade, Iowa. He pitched for 20 years in the major leagues, all for the White Sox. He was a member of the 1919 Black Sox.

"Faber's Hall of Fame plaque reads: *Durable righthander who won 255, lost 211, ERA 3.13 games in two decades with (the) White Sox. Victor in 3 games of 1917 World Series Against (the) Giants. Won 20 or more games in (a) season four times, three in succession."*

Red Schoendienst was born as Albert Fred Schoendienst on February 2, 1923 in Germantown, Illinois. Had he not sported red hair, he may have been Fritz, Heinie, or Dutch Schoendienst. Schoendienst spent 19 seasons in the majors where he played over 1800 games at second base. A switch-hitter, he had his best year in 1953 when he batted .342 in 564 at-bats and belted a career-high 15 home runs. His Hall of Fame plaque reads:

"Roommate Stan Musial credited him with the "greatest pair of hands I've ever seen". Sleek, far-ranging second baseman for 18 seasons. Led the N.L. in fielding and hit .300 or better seven times. When elected in 1989 had worn major league uniform 45 consecutive seasons as player, coach, and manager, piloting Redbirds to World Series in 1967 and 1968. 14th inning homer won 1950 All-Star game for N.L."

[Author's Note: Update] In 2014, a young man named John William "Red" Patterson pitched in one game for the Los Angeles Dodgers, going 4.2 innings before returning to the Triple A Albuquerque Isotopes. He became the 97th major league player with the name Red. He also dethroned Red Wilson as the most recent player with that name, and Red Murff and Red Swanson as the last Red pitchers

Notes

Chapter One

[1] Baseball Nicknames: A Dictionary of Origins and Meanings - James K. Skipper

[2] NY Times Obits Dec 21, 1970

[3] An elephant's Tale by Susan Wilson in Tuft's Online Magazine

[4] An Elephant Ear on Rye Bread –the story of Jumbo by Bruce Ricketts – The Mysteries of Canada web site

[5] Baseball-Reference.com

[6] Hickok Sports.com – Sports Biographies

[7] Skipper

[8] Baseball Library.com

[9] Baseball-reference.com

[10] Tales From the Cubs Dugout by Pete Cava page 239

[11] Hippo Vaughn by Jan Finkel – the Baseball Biography Project BioProjSABR.org

[12] Tales From the Cubs Dugout by Pete Cava

[13] My greatest day in baseball; forty-seven dramatic stories by forty-seven stars by John P. Carmichael and Jerome Holtzman

[14] Hippo Vaughn by Jan Finkel – the Baseball Biography Project BioProjSABR.org

[15] Ibid.

[16] Tiny Bonham by Warren Corbett in the Baseball biography Project on SABR.com

[17] Baseball-Almanac.com

[18] Who, You Ask, is Tiny Bonham? By Mike Lynch – Seamheads.com

[19] Baseball-Reference.com

[20] Baseball-Almanac.com

[21] Tiny Bonham by Warren Corbett in the Baseball biography Project on SABR.com

[22] Baseball Reference.com

[23] Leather Helmet illustrated – Chicago Maroons in the Hall of Fame

[24] Pro-Football-Refernece.com

[25] Paul Des Jardien – Wikipedia

[26] Baseball Nicknames: A Dictionary of Origins and Meanings – James K. Skipper

[27] CollegeFootball.org

[28] Baseball Nicknames: A Dictionary of Origins and Meanings – James K. Skipper

[29] Your Father's Red Sox: Skeeter Newsome no byline, BostonPastime.com

[30] The Big Book of Baseball Brainteasers by Dom Forker, Rob Obojski and Wayne Stewart

[31] Baseball Nicknames: A Dictionary of Origins and Meanings – James K. Skipper

[32] Ibid.

[33] Ibid.

[34] Walter Johnson pays tribute to George Washington posted by Mark Hornbaker on February 22, 2010 at NationalsPride.com

[35] Skinny Graham Tosses Dollar Over 300 Feet – no byline –The Reading Eagle February 25, 1936

[36] Baseball Nicknames: A Dictionary of Origins and Meanings – James K. Skipper

[37] High and Inside by Joseph McBride

[38] Baseball to Showbiz: Mott's widow keeps memories alive - Herald Tribune July 23, 2006

[38a] Ibid.

[39] Florida's First Big League Ballplayers: A Narrative Story by Wes Singletary page 106

[40] Major-Smolinski.com – the Baseball Names

[41] Baseball to Showbiz: Mott's widow keeps memories alive - Herald Tribune July 23, 2006

[42] The Colonel: the extraordinary story of Colonel Tom Parker and Elvis Presley by Alanna Nash p 29

[43] Cornell Alumni News – June 19, 1912

[44] Official Publications of Cornell University 1913-14

[45] Because I'm Bob Costas, and…well, you know the rest by now – by Mike Freeman CBS Sports.com August 10, 2007

[46] Stub Smith Found by Bill Carle SABR.org –researchers Peter Morris, Richard Malatzky, Reed Howard and Dave Lambert

[47] Ibid.

[48] HistoricBaseball.com

[49] Baseball Nicknames: A Dictionary of Origins and Meanings – James K. Skipper

[50] "Pug" Cavet Sets a Hitting Record – June 29, 1916 Atlanta Constitution

[51] High and Inside: an A-Z guide to the Language of Baseball by Joseph McBride page145

[52] The New Bill James Historical Abstract by Bill James page 500

[53] The Grand Rapids (Mich) Democrat as reported by Jimmy Keenan in SABR's Baseball Biography Project

[54] Cupid Childs by Jimmy Keenan in SABR's Baseball Biography Project

[55] Field of Screams: the Dark Underside of America's National Pastime by Richard Scheinlin page 75

[56] The Cleveland Indian: The Legend of King Saturday by Luke Salisbury page 92

[57] Stealing Signals - Outing Volume 64 1914 page 444

[58] Cupid Childs by Jimmy Keenan in SABR's Baseball Biography Project

Chapter Two

[1] Skipper

[2] The minor league Milwaukee Brewers, 1859-1952 by Brian A. Podol

[3] 'Cuckoo' Christensen Mimics Al Jolson - Milwaukee Sentinel December 17, 1931

[4] Ibid.

[5] Bug Holiday Was a Baseball Clown – The Pittsburgh Press – February 17, 1910

[6] Baseball Rookies Encyclopedia by David Nemac and Dave Zeman

[7] Tainted No-hitters by Allen Lewis Baseball Digest February 2002

[8] Bug Holiday Was a Baseball Clown – The Pittsburgh Press – February 17, 1910

[9] DeadBallEra.com – Too Young to Die

[10] TheDeadballEra.com Beer Drinkers and Hellraisers

[11] Bugs Raymond Dies – New York times September 8, 1912

[12] Ibid.

[13] Ibid.

[14] Ibid.

[15] Ibid.

[16] The Baseball Research Journal 1993 page23

[17] The Baseball Research Journal 1993 page10

[18] Low and Inside by Ira Smith and H. Allen Smith as reported in Rob Neyer's Big Book of Baseball legends page 156

[19] The Baseball Research Journal 1993 page10

[20] Whiz Kid Putsy Caballero by Paul Hagen Philly.com March 25, 2010

[21] Katrina can't keep Caballero down by Joseph Santoliquito - November 16, 2005 MLM.com

[22] Ninety Feet from Fame: Close Calls with Baseball Immortality by Mike Robbins and Michael Robbins

[22a] Ibid.

[23] The pride of Havana: A History of Cuban baseball by Roberto Gonzalez Echevarria

[24] The postal record, volumes 33-34 by National Association of Letter Carriers – 1920 – page 94

[25] FowlerGeneology.com

[26] WorldLingo.com

[27] The Cincinnati Reds by Lee Allen page 162

[28] Tales From the Ballpark: More of the Greatest Stories Ever Told by Mike Shannon page146

[29] Ibid.

[30] Baseball Anecdotes by Daniel Okrent and Steve Wulf page 117

[31] Skipper

[32] Baseball Reference.com, The BR Bullpen

[33] Skipper

[34] Andover marriages – AndoverMaine.com

[35] Random House Dictionary

[36] Six Feet Under; a graveyard guide to Minnesota by Stew Thormley p144

[37] The Baseball Rookies Encyclopedia

[38] Skipper

[39] Short-Term Wonders by Robert L. Burnes – Baseball digest July 1956

[40] Baseball-Refenece.com/bullpen

[41] NIASHF.org

[42] Encyclopedia of ethnicity and sports in the United States by George B. Kirsch, Othello Harris and Claire Elaine Nolte p47

[43] Baseball – an Illustrated History by Geoffrey C. Ward and Ken Burns p 46

[44] Baseball-Reference.com/Bullpen

[45] The Complete Armchair Book of Baseball: an All-Star Lineup By John Thorn page235

[46] A Place for Summer: a Narrative History of Tiger Stadium by Richard Bak page 30

[47] The New bill James Historical Abstract by Bill James page 44

[48] My Life in Baseball: the True Record by Ty Cobb and Al Stump. Page 178

[49] The SABR baseball list & record book; baseball's most fascinating records by Lyle Spatz page 69

[50] Skipper

[51] Baseball Digest April 1956 p10

[52] Early Exits: the premature endings of baseball careers by Brian McKenna p 182

[53] Baseball Digest April 1956 p10

[54] Tilly Shafer Won't Join Feds – New York Times November 26, 1914

[55] McGraw After Tillie Shafer – Los Angeles Times December 6, 1916

[56] State Pro Ball Lacks Color of Oldtime Eastern League by Sam Cohen Bridgeport Herald July 3, 1949

[56a] Eastern League May See Everett Nutter in Action – Hartford Courant April 6, 1925

[57] Swinging Through the Eastern Circuit – Harford Courant September 22, 1923

[58] Gary Bedingfield's Baseball in Wartime – Player biographies

[59] Tri-State News – Spartanburg Herald-Journal Jul7 30, 1950

[60] Skipper

[61] Senators Buy Hurler –The Baltimore Sun September 14, 1949

[62] RetroSheets.com

[63] Behind the Wire - Gary Bedingfield's Baseball in Wartime

[64] The Nickname Game: The 1935 World champion Detroit Tigers by Bruce Markuson

[65] Cobb Would Have Caught It; The Golden Age of Baseball in Detroit by Richard Bak p 242

[66] "Flea" Clifton, Detroit Utility Player, Hailed as Hero by Mates by Earl J. Hilligan Los Angeles times Oct. 6, 1935

[67] Flea Clifton good Milwaukee Journal may 7, 1943

Chapter Three

[1] Baseball Digest may 1972 page 62

[2] The King of Swat: An Analysis of Baseball's Home Run Hitters from the Major, Minor, negro and Japanese Leagues by William McNeil

[3] You Know Baseball? By Harry Simmons – Baseball Digest March 1975 page 78

[4] Henry and Wade Lead Sluggers of Royal Recruits Montreal Gazette March 28, 1929

[5] Henry Signs Contract Montreal Gazette December 10, 1928
[6] Deadball Stars of the National League by Thomas P. Simon page 53

[7] The Pride of Cidertown by Jim Ford – reviewed by Mike Jaquays on UticaOD.com

[8] Connie Mack and the early years of baseball by Norman Lee Macht page 281

[9] The Baseball Rookies Encyclopedia by David Nemec and Dave Zeman page 72

[10] "Snake" Deal Down and Out – The Pittsburgh Press Sept 2, 1906

[11] Baseball Digest May 2001 page 14

[12] Baseball in Mobile by Joe Cuhaj and Tamra Carraway-Hinckle page 20

[13] The Recruit: A Pictorial Naval Magazine (Great Lakes Station) Volume 4 Issue 11 Sept. 1918

[14] BaseballLibrary.com

[15] The Seventh Babe by Jerome Charyn page 30

[16] Danny Litwhiler: Living the Baseball Dream by Danny Litwhiler, James E. Sargent and Stan Musial page 47

[17] The Last Years of the Brooklyn Dodgers: A History, 1950-1957 by Rudy Marzano page 6

[18] Former Pro Baseball Player Forrest Spook Jacobs to Be Inducted into Bridgeton's Sports Hall of Fame by Joe Green in NJ.Com April 9, 2009

[19] Spook Jacobs Steals the Show at the Philadelphia Athletics Historical Society Cuban Celebration – May 6, 2009 – No byline on Baseball.NetHappenings

[20] Ibid.

[21] Boots Poffenberger: Last of Great Baseball Characters by John Steadman -Baseball Digest – December 1992 page 93

[22] Baseball Hall of Shame 3 by Bruce Nash and Allen Zullo page 178

[23] The 10 Spot by Pete McEntegart on SI.com October 19, 2006

[24] Skipper

[25] Trading in Player Market is Lively – Baltimore Sun December 4, 1924

[26] Retrosheets.com

[27] The Cincinnati Reds by Lee Allen page 47

[28] Baseball-Reference.com

[29] Skipper

Chapter Four

[1] Rube Waddell: The Peter Pan of Baseball by John Thorn – Mr. Baseball.com

[2] The Great Shutout Pitchers-20 Profiles of a Vanishing Breed by Joe MacKay page 197

[3] The Pacific Coast league: a Statistical History 1903-1957 by Dennis Snelling page 345

[4] The California Winter League by William McNeil page 24

[4a] Baseball Hall of Shame by Bruce Nash and Allen Zullo page 97

[5] Retrosheet.org/Courtesy.htm

[6] Presentation at SABR Convention 2006 by Richard A. Danko

[7] Ibid.

[8] Tinker, Evers and Chance; a Triple Biography by Gil Bogen page 89

[9] Presentation at SABR Convention 2006 by Richard A. Danko

[10] My Life in Baseball; the True Record by Ty Cobb and Al Stump page 27

[11] Day by Day in New York Yankees History by Mark Gallagher page 19

[12] The California Winter League by William McNeil page 3

[13] Bumpus Jones by Chris Rainey in the Baseball biography Project on SABR.Org

[14] Ibid.

[15] The First Fall Classic: the Red Sox, the Giants and the Cast of Players by Mike Vaccaro page 148

[16] Three I Umpiring Staff is Announced Chicago Daily tribune March 20, 1938

[17] They Pinch Hit for the Greats by Herbert Simons - Baseball Digest February 1962

[18] The Life that Ruth Built by Marshall Smelser page 92

[19] Forrest Cady Dies – the Reading Eagle March 4, 1946

[20] Skipper

[21] Baseball-Reference.com

[22] Morry Steelman's Case – the Hartford Courant August 23, 1901

[23] The Pacific Coast League: a Statistical History1903-1957 by Dennis Snelling page 371

[24] Cubs Journal: Year-by-Year and Day-by-Day with the Chicago Cubs Since 1876 by John Snyder page 86

[25] The Baseball Chronology by James Charlton page 96

[26] A Cycle of Historic Proportions by Tom Singer MLB.com April 16, 2009

[27] Nigger: The Strange Career of a Troublesome Word by Randall Kennedy – The Washington Post January 11, 2001

[28] Neyer/James Guide to Pitching by Bill James and Rob Neyer page 28

[29] Cy Young by Gordon Cobbledick Baseball Digest February 1953

[30] The North American Review Vol. 229 page 601

[31] Baseball the Early years by Harold Seymour page 333

[32] The BaseballPage.com

[33] Reconsidering Japanese Relations by David Strauss in American Literary History – Oxford Journals 1996

[34] Cobb: A Biography by Al Stump page 113

[35] The Pittsburgh Pirates by Fred Lieb page 136

[36] American League Releases; Shay Gets Barbeau and Moran New York Times May 18, 1910

[37] Immigration –The Journey to America on Oracle Think Quest at Library(dot)ThinkQuest(dot)org

[38] Skipper

[39] Bill Lee Baseball Necrology – TheBBNLive.Com

[40] Skipper

[41] Chink Outen by Brian McKenna of The Baseball Biography Project Sabr.org

[42] Jersey City Wins 12-7; Triumphs Over Toronto as Outen Stars With four Hits

[43] Reds Again Trip Angels – Los Angeles Time April 28, 1935

[44] Time Out with Leroy Simerly – Spartanburg Herald March 29, 1939

[45] Flatbush Odyssey A Journey Through the Heart of Brooklyn by Allen J. Abel page 263

[46] SABR Encyclopedia – 1939 Utica Braves sabrpedia.org/wiki/1939_Utica_Braves

[47] Forgotten Heroes: Inspiring leading Portraits from Our leading Historians by Susan Ware page 131

[48] Beating the Breaks: Major League Ballplayers Who Overcame Disabilities by Rick Swaine page 113

[49] Dummy.Hoy.com/overview

[50] Ibid.

[51] Simply Baseball Notebook: Forgotten in Time by David Zingler – May 2004

[52] The Baseball biography Project – Dummy Stephenson by Brian McKenna – Bioproj.Sabr.org/bioproj

[53] The Silent Worker vol. 36 no. 3 December 1923

[54] The Silent Worker vol. 36 no. 7 April 1924

[55] Ibid.

[56] The Baseball biography Project – Dummy Stephenson by Brian McKenna – Bioproj.Sabr.org/bioproj

[57] The Baseball biography Project by David Anderson – Sabr.org

[58] Baseball Hall of Shame 3 by Bruce Nash and Allan Zullo page 162

[59] Deadball Stars of the National League by Thomas P. Simon page 38

[60] The Baseball biography Project by David Anderson – Sabr.org

[61] With the Silent Workers by Alexander Pach The Silent Worker May 1905, Vol. 17 No. 8 page 124

[62] The Cooperstown Symposium on Baseball and American Culture by William M. Simons page 127

[63] Bad Bunch of Champions Chicago Tribune Aug 26, 1902

[64] The Bronx in the Innocent Years. 1890-1925 by Lloyd Ultan page 136

[65] History of the Tarrytowns, West Chester County, New York from Ancient Times to the Present by Jeff Canning and Wally Buxton page 165

[66] Reading Eagle August 26, 1907

[67] Unmanly Professional Athletes: Disability and Masculinity in the United States, 1888-1908 by Robert E. Bionaz Chicago State University - Disability Studies Quarterly – Spring 2005, Vol. 25, No. 2

[68] Ibid.

Chapter Five

[1] Lucky's History of the Yo-Yo by Lucky Meisenheimer – Yo-Yos.Net

[2] Satchel Paige and Company by Leslie A. Heaphy page 127

[3] HeineMeine.Com

[4] Skipper

[5] Baseball in Toledo by John Husman page 45

[6] Forging Genius: the Making of Casey Stengel by Steve Goldman page 93

[7] H.M. Jacob Genealogy web site

[8] Encyclopedia of Baseball Catchers

[9] St. Louis Media Archive

[10] Jawn McGraw Stuck Proper on That Pol Perritt Deal – The Day (New London, Conn.) November 11, 1915

[11] Frank Russo from his Deadball Era.com web site

[12] Just One Bad Century website

[13] Allison-Antrim Museum web site

[14] Baseball Library.com

[15] Skipper

[16] The Pittston Dispatch Oct 12, 2008 The Gentleman First Basemen by Jack Smiles

[17] HistoricBaseball.com

[18] St. Petersburg Times May 18, 1949

[19] CPCTrivia.Blogspot.com

[20] DoraHighSchool.com as appeared in the Daily Mountain Eagle July 2005

[21] Remembering Paul Andrews-a letter by Glenn C. Grant of Dora from the Dora High school webs site

[22] Skipper

[23] TheBaseballPage.com

Chapter Six

[1] Baseball Legends and Lore by Cataneo page 194

[2] Low and Inside by H. Allen Smith and Ira Smith page 238

[3] The New Bill James Historical Baseball Abstract by Bill James page 834

[4] The Dodgers Encyclopedia by William F. McNeil page 30

[5] DMB World Series Replay by Kevin Graham June 29, 2009 –
DMBWorldSeriesReplay.Wordpress.com

[6] Skipper

[7] Dead ball Stars of the National League by Thomas P. Simon page
233

[8] The Cincinnati Reds by Lee Allen page 84

[9] Dead ball Stars of the National League by Thomas P. Simon page
233

[10] The St. Petersburg Evening Independent Oct. 9, 1930

[11] Skipper

[12] The New Georgia Encyclopedia - gerogiaencylcopedia.org

[12] Greasy Neale: Nothing to Prove, Nothing to Ask by Gerald
Holland - Sports Illustrated August 24, 1964

[13] Baseball Digest –September 1986 page 15

[14] Sports Biographies HickokSports.com

[15] The Pro Football Historical Abstract by Sean Lahman page 275

[16] Pro football Hall of Fame Web Site – profootballhof.com

[17] The Mule Who Could Run Like a Deer by Ken Schlager – New
jersey Monthly September 14, 2009 edition

[18] The Mule Who Could run like a deer by Ken Schlager – New
jersey Monthly September 14, 2009 edition

[19] Mules Haas Obituary in Baseball-Reference.com

[20] Mule Haas Obituary New York times July 5, 1974

[21] Goat Anderson Shows He knows How to Field –by George L.
Moreland - Pittsburgh Press March 17, 1907

[22] The Baseball Rookies Encyclopedia by David Nemec and Dave Zeman

[23] Ibid.

[24] Goat Anderson Shows He knows How to Field –by George L. Moreland - Pittsburgh Press March 17, 1907

[25] Low and Inside: A Book of Baseball Anecdotes, Oddities and Curiosities by H. Allen Smith and Ira Smith page 189

[26] Of Kings and Commoners by Robert Smith page 771 from The Complete Armchair Book of Baseball: An All-Star Line Celebrates the National pastime edited by John Thorn

[27] Baseball's Most Wanted by Floyd Conner page 302

[28] Chris von der Ahe and the St. Louis Browns by J. Thomas Hetrick page 102

[29] Chris von der Ahe and the St. Louis Browns by J. Thomas Hetrick page 131

[30] FindAGrave.com

[31] Phillies Reader by Richard Orodenker page 27

[32] Vintage Kewpie Doll History on KewpieDoll.Org

[33] Kewpie a Hold Out – Hartford Courant December 22, 1920

[34] New York Times May 5, 1953 as displayed by TheDeadBallEra.Com

[35] A Fine-looking Lot of Ball-tossers by Richard McBane page 84

Chapter Seven

[1] Online Etymology Dictionary from Dictionary.Com

[2] The Straight Dope Science Advisory Board August 22, 2002

[3] The Truth is Sexauer Didn't Do It by Steve Otto Tampa Tribune September 7, 2006

[4] Tales From the Dugout by Carl Erskine page 48

[5] The Southeast Missourian, October 15, 1948

[6] Gary Bedlingfield's BaseballInWartime.com

[7] Ibid.

Chapter Eight

[1] SABR The Biography Project – Lu Blue by Cort Vitty on bioproj.sabr.org

[2] Lu Blue, Best Fielding First Baseman in Big Loops, Handed Release – The Independent St. Petersburg, FL – February 3, 1933

[3] Dodgers Sign Up Lu Blue - The Youngstown Daily Vindicator April 20, 1933

[4] Lu Blue's Mother Wins Distinction Pittsburgh Post-Gazette September 8, 1928

[5] Orval Overall by Brian Marshall in the SABR's Biography Project bioproj.sabr.org

[6] Ibid.

[7] Obituary - Orval Overall, 66, Once Star Pitcher – New York times July 16, 1947

[8] The California Golden Bears website – Traditions Hall of Fame – calbears.com.

[9] The Baseball Library – baseballlibrary.com

[10] Kluttz Family Crest and Name Origin - TheHouseofNames.com

[11] RetroSheets.Com

[12] BaseballReference.com

[13] Van Mungo is fined $1,000 Lodi News Sentinel May 24, 1937

[14] Baseball-Reference.Com

[15] Orval Overall by Brian Marshall in the SABR's Biography Project bioproj.sabr.org

Chapter Nine

[1] Skipper

[2] Harriet Beecher Stowe; the Story of Her Life by Charles Edward Stowe – 1911 page 203

[3] Cubs Journal: Year by year and Day by Day with the Cubs Since 1876 by John Snyder page 89

[4] Negative Records: The Humbling Side of Baseball by George Vass – Baseball Digest January 2003

[5] Charlie Hickman by John R. Husman in the SABR Baseball Biography Project at bioproj.sabr.org

[6] Skipper

[7] FindAGrave.com

[8] Louis Sockalexis: the First Cleveland Indian by David L. Fleitz page 146

[9] More Tales From the Red Sox Dugout: Yarns From the Sox by Jim Prime and Bill Nowlin pages 7-8

[10] Skipper

[11] Baseball: The Early Years by Harold Seymour page 256

[12] Source Andy Fusco cited on Reference.com

[13] Dom Dallessandro by Bill Nowlin The Baseball Biography Project SABR.com

[14] Skipper

[15] Gary Bedlingfield's BaseballInWartime.com

[16] Dom Dallessandro by Bill Nowlin The Baseball Biography Project SABR.com

[17] Colonels Fire Fred Walters - Milwaukee Journal May 29, 1949

[18] Army defeated by Mississippi State, 13-7 – Sarasota Herald-Tribune November 3, 1935

[19] Skipper

[20] Bob Fothergill Eats Plenty and Gets More Hits - Hartford Courant January 5, 1930

Chapter Ten

[1] The Last Commissioner: A Baseball Valentine by Fay Vincent page 269

[2] Skipper

[3] Ibid.

[4] Baseball's Other Stars by William McNeil page100

[5] The Negro Leagues, 1869 to 1960 by Leslie A. Heaphy page 164

[6] Black barons of Birmingham by Larry Powell page 82

[7] African American Pioneers of Baseball by Lew Freedman p. xiv

[8] The Sportscard Explosion by Mark K. Larson page 149

Index by Surname

www.ingramcontent.com/pod-product-compliance
Lightning Source LLC
LaVergne TN
LVHW051459080426
835509LV00017B/1827